THE ISLAMIC FAITH

THE ISLAMIC FAITH

Edited by

Serhat Şen

Assistant Editors

Semra Demir

Lyndsey Eksili

21 20 19 18   1 2 3 4

Edited by Serhat Şen

Assistant Editors Semra Demir, Lyndsey Eksili

Designed by Sinan Özdemir

Published by Tughra Books
335 Clifton Ave.
Clifton, NJ, 07011, USA
www.tughrabooks.com

ISBN 978-1-59784-939-5

CONTENTS

FAITH

CHAPTER 1

Lesson 1
What is Faith?

Lesson 2
Six Articles of Faith

Faith (*iman*) is the actual reason for human existence

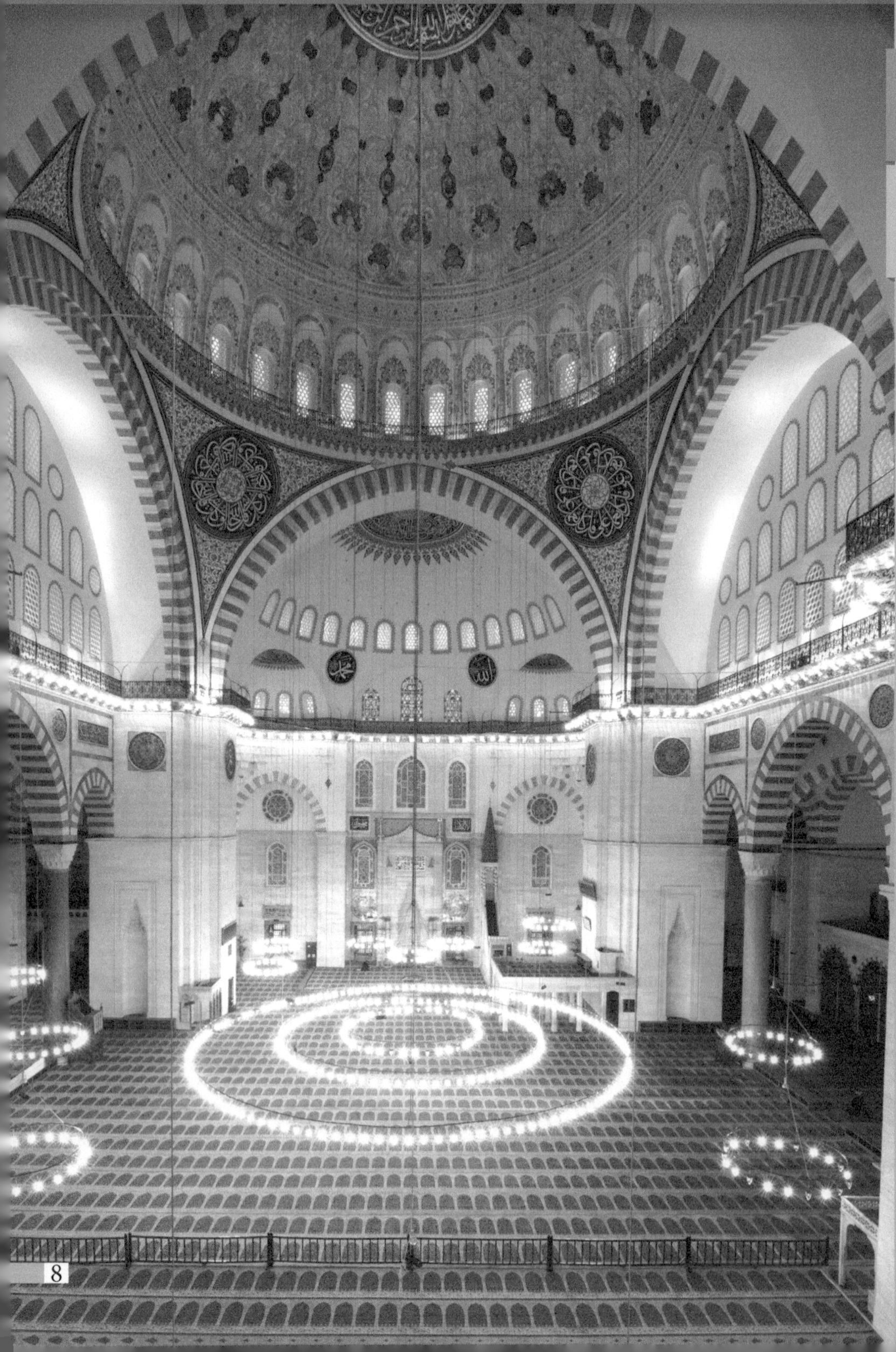

Interior of the Suleymaniye Mosque in Istanbul

Lesson 1
What Is Faith?

FAITH IS THE ACTUAL REASON FOR HUMAN EXISTENCE

Through faith, even death becomes meaningful.

Faith *(iman)* is a seed inserted into the heart of every human being by Almighty Creator. It is up to the individual to nurture it so that it may transform into a spiritual tree, which would eventually produce eternal fruits. Through faith, the human heart reaches its true form which clearly is a shining mirror that reflects the most Beautiful Names of Allah.

Faith is a powerful light that enlightens one's internal and external realms. It is a light that feeds on sincerity and obtains its energy from worship. Without sincerity and worship the light of faith would not glow. This unique metaphysical light is so obvious that it could even be noticed on the face of a believer in the form of a mystical bright glow.

Faith is the actual reason for human existence. Without faith human beings cannot be distinguished from rest of the living beings, even though they may be similar in their physical nature. It is faith that makes human being a human being. Through sincere faith and worship human beings begin an unbreakable connection between themselves and their Creator.

Faith brings hope and meaning to human life. For those who do not have faith, life becomes a battleground where every human being temporarily struggles to survive which eventually ends with death-the inevitable truth. If a person does not have faith, they see death as the absolute end of their existence. Death is a horrible reality that nonbelievers wish to avoid for as long as possible. However, for those who have faith, death is not the end, but the very beginning. It is simply a doorway, which opens to an eternal life, a place of reunion. Thus, the supposed dark face of death can only be brightened with the everlasting light of faith.

"Through faith, even death becomes meaningful."

Key vocabulary

- **Iman:** faith in Arabic.
- **Realm:** the region, sphere, or domain within which anything occurs, prevails,or dominates
- **Metaphysical:** relating to the transcendent or to a reality beyond what is perceptible to the senses.
- **Mystical:** spiritual mystery.

HUMANITY THROUGH FAITH

Since human beings were created for eternity, they can only be satisfied with eternal life.

The purpose of being human can only be understood through faith. Without question, human beings were created in a way that separates them from rest of the creation. Human needs and desires are endless and their fears and doubts are countless. These interesting emotions cannot be satisfied by physical means only. It is nearly impossible to satisfy the carnal desire of human beings.

Human beings were created for eternity. Therefore, the human soul will never be happy with temporary pleasures and wealth. The absolute satisfaction and happiness that the human soul seeks can only be reached through faith.Since human beings were created for eternity, they can only be satisfied with eternal life.

Key vocabulary

- **Carnal desire:** worldly or temporary desires.

WHAT LEADS TO FAITH?

Study of natural sciences is the nourishment of the intellect and study of religious knowledge is the light of the heart.

Faith is the greatest truth in the universe. Thus, human beings have all the necessary tools to investigate and discover this truth. Two of the most important truth-seeking tools given to human beings are the intellect and the heart.

The ultimate truth will only develop with the combination of these two essential studies. Thus, the developing facts will lead to faith. When faith is truly embraced, it will elevate the carrier from a level of a species of mammal to the level of being human. Without faith, a human being will be like any other species of mammal that just lives in order to survive in this world. So, faith is the most important element that separates us from rest of Allah's creation.

Study of natural sciences is the nourishment of the intellect and study of religious knowledge is the light of the heart. A true believer can only observe the nature through the glasses of faith.

Suddenly, everything will take a new meaning and all matter will have a purpose to exist. A true believer will see everything as Allah's servants that exist to perform important duties. The believer will also understand that the universe is a great book published by the Almighty Author. Everything in the universe is a Divine sign and everything created is a word from Him. Reading this great book, along with the holy book (Qur'an) brought down to His beloved Messenger (pbuh) will lead human beings to true faith. Thus, such faith, obtained through reasonable knowledge, will eventually lead to total submission and worship.

In conclusion, faith is the greatest gift given upon humanity. It is more precious than the entire universe and its wealth.

A true believer can only observe the nature through the glasses of faith.

Questions

- **Guiding Question:** how can one satisfy both the intellect and the heart?

TWO TYPES OF FAITH

Once the believer begins to display his faith through worship, he is on the path to fulfilling the purpose of his existence.

Islamic scholars propose that there are two types of faith.

1. Faith through cultural heritage (*al-iman al-taqlidi*)
2. Faith through analytical scrutiny (*al-iman al-tahqiqi*)

Faith through heritage (*al-iman al-taqlidi*) means embracing religion due to an influence from parents, community, society or tradition. Although, this type of faith is still acceptable, it is weak. Unless a person strengthens this faith with knowledge and worship, it can be damaged with the slightest of doubts.

Faith is the essence of religion. Without faith, rituals and worship can only be considered as habitual acts or customs. It is faith that gives meaning to practice. It is faith that helps the good deeds to have a Divine purpose and increase in value. With faith the main intention becomes to please Allah which transforms even the simplest of acts into worship. Once the believer begins to display his faith through worship, he is on the path to fulfilling the purpose of his existence.

Faith through analytical scrutiny (*al-iman al-tahqiqi*), on the other hand, is strong because it is obtained through knowledge, wisdom, logic and experience. This type of faith is embraced by the intellect and the soul. With Allah's aid such faith will be stronger and eternal. Of course, both paths mentioned above are related to human free will thus, they are chosen through the use of intellect, comprehension or sometimes through social influence. However, the reality is obtaining true faith cannot be based on these paths only.

The defined paths can only be considered as ways to obtain faith, because it is Allah Himself who places human beings onto the right path and blesses their hearts with faith. In Islam this is called, hidayah which means guidance towards the path of righteousness. Certainly, Allah puts ***hidayah*** into the hearts of human beings but one must also remember that this has to be earned through intention, sincerity, effort, spirituality and intellect.

It is essential that faith is obtained and strengthened through the study of religious literature, natural sciences and practice. Muslims must recognize the fact that the Almighty Allah has sent two great books which lead to achieving an ideal faith. These two books are: The Holy Qur'an and in a metaphorical sense, "the great book of the universe".

Key vocabulary

- **Analytical scrutiny:** the careful and detailed examination of something by using analysis and logical reasoning in order to get information about it.
- **Hidayah:** guidance towards the path of righteousness.

TESTIMONY OF FAITH

"Ashhadu alla ilaha illa Allah, wa ashhadu anna Muhammadan abduhu wa Rasuluhu".

In order to embrace Islam, a person must first declare that he /she has faith in Islam by reciting the testimony of faith. The testimony of faith is declared by making the following statement:

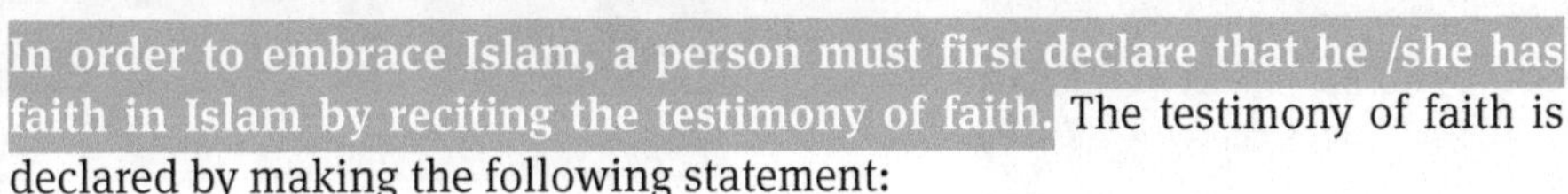

"Ashhadu alla ilaha illa Allah, wa ashhadu anna Muhammadan abduhu wa Rasuluhu".

This is called *Shahadah* and the English translation of *Shahadah* is: "I testify that there is no deity but Allah, and I testify that Muhammad is the servant and Messenger of Allah".

There is one important issue here that needs to be clarified and that is "Why do Muslims use the term Allah instead of God?"

In the Arabic language, *Ilah* is the English version of the word God. It means 'something that is worshipped'. However, just as in the English language, the word god, Ilah can be made plural and it can be defined as male or female. The word "Allah" on the other hand, does not have a plural form and it cannot be associated with gender. Unlike, other personal names in Arabic, Allah is definite and absolute which refers to one Supreme Being only. Although, "Allah" still means God, in Islam it is considered as the personal name of the One and Only God, think of it like a proper noun.

However, there is no harm in using the term God as long as one uses the term with the pure intention of referring to the Almighty Allah. The most obvious difference between the term God and Allah is that the term God is used as an attribute rather than a name. It means, "The creator and the supreme being that is worshipped." However, in Islam, Allah has many Divine Attributes. For example, Rahman means the All-Merciful; Rahim means the All-Compassionate; Karim means the All-Munificent; Hayy means the All-Living; Quddus means the All-Pure and so on.

THINK

Think about a time when you felt your faith to Allah was strengthened by reading or pondering over these two great books mentioned above. For example, think about a knowledge you obtained whether it is scientific or religious and share your thoughts.

Key vocabulary

- **Shahadah:** testimony of faith.
- **Ilah:** english version of the word God in Arabic.
- **Divine Attributes:** quality or characteristics of Allah.

DISCUSS

We have read that "In order to embrace Islam, one must first declare the testimony of faith with his or her tongue and accept it with the heart." Discuss the reason for this with your friends.

Muhammad Rasul Allah

The second component of the testimony of faith is "I testify that Muhammad is the servant and Messenger of Allah". This means that the believer accepts and embraces the Divine truth that Prophet Muhammad, peace and blessings be upon him, is the servant and Messenger of Allah. He is the last Messenger of Allah who comes with Divine revelations to guide humanity onto the right path. This testimony is also an affirmation that the believer accepts the message conveyed by the Prophet and makes the promise to follow and practice his religion.

Servanthood is the very purpose in the creation of human beings and the Prophet holds the highest rank. Therefore, by declaring the testimony of faith, the believer also pledges to take Allah's Messenger as the principal guide to true servanthood.

In order to embrace Islam, one must first declare the testimony of faith with his or her tongue and accept it with the heart.

Following this brief explanation, let us once again clarify the issue of taking the initial step in embracing Islam. In order to embrace Islam, one must first declare the testimony of faith with his or her tongue and accept it with the heart.

In conclusion, the concept of belief in Islam is based on complete faith. Faith cannot be divided or embraced partially. In Islamic terminology, faith is defined as Iman and it consists of six essential principles. The following lesson will discuss the six articles of faith.

Key vocabulary

- **Servanthood:** the role of being a servant.

WHAT DID WE LEARN?

- Faith is a seed implanted into the heart of every human being by the Almighty Creator.
- Faith is the actual reason for human existence.
- Faith brings hope and meaning to human life.
- For those who do not have faith, life becomes a battleground where every human being temporarily struggles to survive which eventually ends with death-the inevitable truth.
- If a person does not have faith, they see death as the absolute end of their existence.
- Human needs and desires are endless and their fears and doubts are countless.
- Since human beings were created for eternity, they can only be satisfied with eternity and eternal life.
- Two of the most important truth-seeking tools given to human beings are the intellect and the heart.
- Study of natural sciences is the nourishment of the intellect and study of religious knowledge is the light of the heart.
- So, faith is the most important element that separates us from the rest of Allah's creation.
- Faith transforms human beings into honorable representatives of Allah's creation.
- There are two types of faith: Faith through cultural heritage & Faith through analytical scrutiny
- Faith through heritage means embracing religion due to an influence from parents, community, society or tradition.
- Faith through analytical scrutiny, on the other hand, is strong because it is obtained through knowledge, wisdom, logic and experience.
- Allah puts hidayah into the hearts of human beings but one must also remember that this has to be earned through intention, sincerity, effort, spirituality and intellect.
- Allah has sent two great books, which lead to achieving an ideal faith. These two books are: the Holy Qur'an and "the great book of the universe".
- In order to embrace Islam, a person must first declare that he /she has faith in Islam by reciting the testimony of faith.
- The most obvious distinction between the term God and Allah is that the term God is used as an attribute rather than a name.
- In order to embrace Islam, one must first declare the testimony of faith with his or her tongue and accept it with the heart.

LESSON REVIEW: INDIVIDUAL ASSESSMENT

1. What is faith? Explain in your own words.
2. What kind of a life do humans live without faith?
3. What are the two tools that lead to faith?
4. Explain the differences between the two types of faith?
5. Define *hidayah*.
6. How are the words God and Allah different?
7. After having complete faith, how do we embrace Islam?

WHAT DID WE LEARN?

ESSAY

What separates human from other species and how? Write a four paragraph informative essay using context details.

LESSON VOCABULARY: DEFINE EACH TERM

- Iman:
- Realms:
- Metaphysical:
- Mystical:
- Carnal:
- Analytical scrutiny
- Hidayah:
- Shahadah:

Lesson 2
Six Articles of Faith

Religion of Islam is based on two sets of imperative articles and pillars:

- 6 Articles of Faith
- 5 Pillars of Islam

There are six articles of faith and a *mu'min* is a believer who wholeheartedly embraces all of these articles. A person becomes a true believer once he/she has complete faith in all the six articles of faith. They are as follows:

1. Belief in Allah
2. Belief in Angels
3. Belief in Divine Books
4. Belief in Prophets
5. Belief in the Day of Judgment
6. Belief in Divine destiny

An individual who rejects any one of these articles will not be regarded as a Muslim even if he/she accepts all of the other five. Therefore, a complete faith can only be obtained by embracing all of the articles of faith and then declaring "There is no deity but Allah, and Muhammad is His servant and Messenger."

Key vocabulary

- **Mu'min:** a believer, a person who has faith in whatever must be believed in and is a righteous and obedient servant of His

INDIVISIBLE SIX ARTICLES OF BELIEF

اٰمَنَ الرَّسُولُ بِمَٓا اُنْزِلَ اِلَيْهِ مِنْ رَبِّه۪ وَالْمُؤْمِنُونَۜ كُلٌّ اٰمَنَ بِاللّٰهِ وَمَلٰٓئِكَتِه۪ وَكُتُبِه۪ وَرُسُلِه۪

> The Messenger believes in what has been sent down to him from his Lord, and so do the believers; each one believes in God, and His angels, and His books, and His Messengers: "We make no distinction between any of His Messengers (in believing in them)..." (2:285)

Belief is a single truth, which is composed of its six articles cannot be divided up. It is a universal that cannot be separated into parts. It is a whole that cannot be broken up. For each of the articles of belief proves the other pillars. They are all extremely powerful proofs of each other. In reality, no one can refuse any one of the articles, or even a single of their truths, and cannot deny them. One might put a veil of non-acceptance by shutting his eyes only and committing an "obstinate belief" to himself. He would then fall into absolute disbelief and lose his humanity.

Belief in Allah proves with its own proofs both the other articles and belief in the hereafter.

The world we live in is ruled by a Divine ruler of the entire universe he created. He is in charge of all his creation. Imagine this world as a country that is being ruled in such order, and directed in such a great organization as if all the creations were soldiers waiting on command and given duties that they act upon. If this Divine ruler can rule this temporary world in such a great way, the ruler can rule it in an eternal world as well.

That means the sovereignty of Almighty Allah's greatness, most of His Names and the proofs of His necessary existence require and leads us to also believe in the hereafter and testify to it. So we must see and understand what powerful support this article of belief has, and we should believe in it as if we are seeing it!

Belief in Allah proves with its own proofs both the other articles and belief in the hereafter.

Think about the same Divine ruler who answers all his creations clearly with act and deed through His infinite gifts. He supplies all of the living being for their natural needs and their desires at the same time. Even if there are no words actual spoken this shows that He can speak to his living creatures by deed and state. So if He speaks with all living beings, by deed and answering their needs, is it possible that He cannot speak with men verbally and send them scriptures, books, and decrees? That is to say, with its certainty and numerous proofs, belief in Allah proves belief in the prophets and sacred scriptures.

Key vocabulary

- **Obstinate belief:** refusing to change your behavior, ideas, or belief.
- **Divine:** addressed, appropriated, or devoted to God or a god; religious; sacred:
- **Sovereignty:** absolute ownership and dominance.

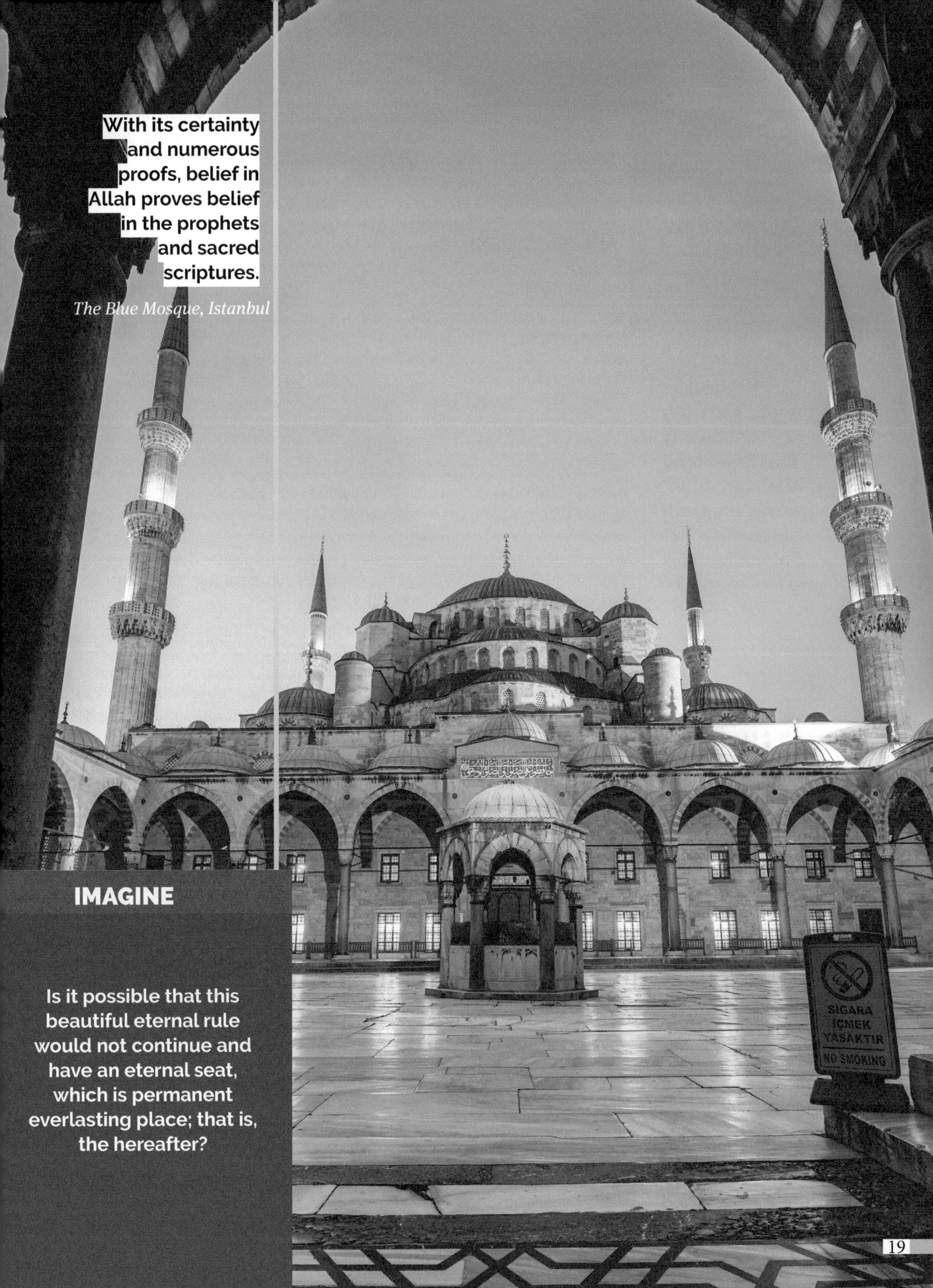

With its certainty and numerous proofs, belief in Allah proves belief in the prophets and sacred scriptures.

The Blue Mosque, Istanbul

IMAGINE

Is it possible that this beautiful eternal rule would not continue and have an eternal seat, which is permanent everlasting place; that is, the hereafter?

DISCUSS

Discuss with your friends the way Allah speaks with you through deed and state.

Think about the same Divine ruler who wanted to make Himself known and loved through all His creatures and seek thanks by deed and state. Is it possible that Allah would not create a man, a messenger who would declare the words of Allah through the books he sent and demonstrate the honor, value, and duties of man along with his miracles as a proof? Allah created our prophet Muhammad (peace and blessings be upon him) to have the whole universe know, love, and praise Him. That is to say, with all its proofs, the truth of "I testify that there is no Allah but Allah" proves the truth of "I testify that Muhammad is the Messenger of Allah."

With all its proofs, the truth of "I testify that there is no Allah but Allah" proves the truth of "I testify that Muhammad is the Messenger of Allah."

Also, think about the same Divine ruler who announces His ruling through the Divine purposes of this universe? Therefore, is it possible that he would not send a book like the Qur'an which will solve its riddles and provide the true answers to the three awesome universally-asked questions: "Where do they come from?", "Where are they going?", and "Why do they follow on caravan after caravan, stop by for a while, then pass on?" That is to say, with all its proofs, belief in Allah proves that the Qur'an is the Word of Allah.

Also, think about the same Divine ruler who continuously fills and empties the earth with living beings and inhabits this world with conscious creatures in order to make Himself known and worshipped and glorified. Is it possible that He would leave the heavens and earth empty, and not create inhabitants suitable to them and settle them in those palaces? He does not leave his permanent and extensive lands empty without servants, functionaries, envoys, and majesty; without lieutenants, supervisors, spectators, worshippers, and subjects?

Think of the same Divine ruler, All-Wise Ruler, the All-Knowing and Compassionate One, Who wrote the universe in the form of a book, who placed the entire life story of a tree in the seeds, and who wrote the duties of each of those seeds and plants. Imagine a ruler who created conscious beings which He sees every action. Imagine a ruler who created Heaven and Hell with supreme scales of justice that will weigh everyone's actions with justice and mercy. Is it possible that he has not written down the acts of men connected with universe, or recorded the deeds so they may be rewarded and punished for their good and bad deeds on the tablets of divine destiny?

With all its proofs, belief in Allah proves that the Qur'an is the Word of Allah.

Key vocabulary

- **Envoys:** a messenger or representative

PRINCIPLES OF ISLAM ARE ALL CONNECTED

With its proofs, the truth of belief in Allah proves the truth of both beliefs in the angels, and belief in Divine Destiny. The articles of belief prove each other as clearly as the sun shows the daylight, and daylight shows the sun.

Principles of Islam are all connected with each other and cannot be separated from one another. What happens if you try to separate an atom's protons, neutrons, and electrons from each other? That is to say, with its proofs, the truth of belief in Allah proves the truth of both beliefs in the angels, and belief in Divine Destiny. The articles of belief prove each other as clearly as the sun shows the daylight, and daylight shows the sun.

Let's repeat the six articles again with their Arabic terms.

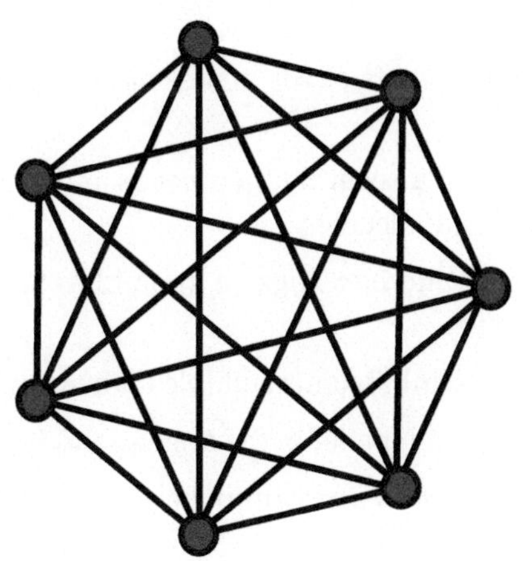

Principles of Islam

6 dots for articles of belief and 1 dot for (5) pillars of Islam = Belief in God x Prophets x Books x Angels x Hereafter x Destiny x 5 Pillars of Islam

Note: This is a multiplication. One zero in it will make the whole equation zero!

THINK

Some of the relations among the articles of belief have been exemplified above. Can you think of some more relations among them?

THE SIX ARTICLES OF FAITH

1. Belief in God (Allah), the One and only One worthy of all worship (tawhid).
2. Belief in the Angels (mala'ika).
3. Belief in the Books (kutub) sent by God (including the Qur'an).
4. Belief in all the Prophets (nabi) and Messengers (rusul) sent by God
5. Belief in the Day of Judgment (qiyama) and in the Resurrection (life after death).
6. Belief in Destiny (Fate) (qadar).

In the following chapters, each article of faith is explained clearly.

WHAT DID WE LEARN?

LESSON SUMMARY

- There are six articles of faith and *mu'min,* a believer is obligated to embrace and have complete faith in all of the six articles.
- An individual who rejects any one of these articles will not be regarded as a Muslim even if he/she accepts all of the other five.
- Belief is a single truth, which is composed of its six articles that cannot be divided up. It is a universal that cannot be separated into parts.
- Allah's greatness, most of His Names and the proofs of His necessary existence require and leads us to also believe in the hereafter and testify to it.
- Allah speaks with all living beings, by deed and answering their needs and also with men (prophets) verbally and through sending them scriptures, books, and decrees.
- Allah created our prophet Muhammad (peace and blessings be upon him) to have the whole universe know, love, and praise Him.
- Allah created the heavens and earth and created inhabitants suitable to them and settled them in those palaces.
- The truth of belief in Allah proves the truth of both belief in the angels, and belief in Divine destiny
- Principles of Islam are all connected with each other and cannot be separated from one another.

LESSON REVIEW: INDIVIDUAL ASSESSMENT

1. What are the six articles of Faith in order?
2. Can a believer only accept couple of these and be considered a muslim? Why or why not?
3. How does belief in Allah prove Belief in prophets and books?
4. Define obstinate-belief in your own words.

ESSAY

Why is all of the six articles indivisible? Write a three-paragraph essay explaining each of them.

WHAT DID WE LEARN?

LESSON VOCABULARY: DEFINE EACH TERM

- Mu'min
- Obstinate-belief
- Divine
- Sovereignty
- Envoys

CHAPTER REVIEW

Answer the following questions in detail:

1. What are the differences between faith through cultural heritage (*al-iman al-taqlidi*) and faith through analytical scrutiny (*al-iman al-tahqiqi*)?
2. What must a person do when they want to embrace Islam?
3. What is the order of the six articles of faith?
4. Can the principles of Islam be separated from one another? Why or why not?

ESSAY

In the first lesson of Chapter one, we learned that faith brings hope and meaning to human life. Write a four-paragraph essay describing how faith (*iman*) has brought hope and meaning to your life using a narrative style of writing.

BELIEF IN GOD

CHAPTER

2

Say, "He is Allah, the One; Allah, the Eternal, Absolute; He begets not, and nor is He begotten; and there is nothing that can be compared to Him."

Interior of the Suleymaniye Mosque in Istanbul

Lesson 1
Understanding God's Existence

The mystery of existence cannot be explained without a creator.

The first and the foremost important article of faith is belief in Allah. The primary purpose in the creation of human beings is that they recognize the Almighty Creator and acknowledge His Might. Furthermore, this recognition must lead to submission and worship. Belief in Allah is the most important requirement of being human. In order to understand this idea one needs to examine the universe and his/her own very existence. The mystery of existence cannot be explained without a creator.

As explained by Gülen, denying the existence of Allah cannot be based on any scientific evidence nor can it be proven. On the other hand, everything in the universe points to a creator. It is evident that physical matter is transitory hence the universe had a beginning. It is also evident that matter cannot create itself. **When we observe the universe and nature around us, we realize that all matter—living and non-living—functions with purpose.** There is design, harmony, beauty, laws and purpose in nature. Accordingly, it is quite logical to affirm that design indicates a designer; art indicates an artist; purpose indicates intelligence; program indicates a programmer and temporary beauty points to eternal beauty. Basically, creation points to a creator.[1]

Inability to see something does not mean it does not exist

We cannot deny the existence of something when we cannot perceive it.

Unfortunately, the argument of "I do not believe in something that I cannot see" has been around for hundreds of years. It is ironic that we still come across people who persist with this argument in spite of the developments achieved by modern science. Assuming that such argument is received, what is a blind person supposed to believe in? In reality, even individuals who possess the gift of vision, observe the world through a very tiny window. Human vision is extremely limited and cannot be used as a tool of denial. This example can be used for all human faculties. Our senses of scent, hearing, touch and taste are also quite limited. Therefore, one cannot deny the existence of something using the argument of "I cannot see, hear, smell, touch or taste it". There are millions of objects in the universe that we cannot see, hear, smell, touch or taste; yet, we detect their existence through scientific knowledge or reason. Denying the existence of Allah by using the argument of "I cannot see or detect Him" is just like denying the existence of a virus inside a human body.

Note / Key vocabulary

- **Transitory:** lasting only for a short time; temporary.

1. Gülen, Fethullah. *Questions and Answers about Islam*, NJ: Tughra Books.

There is perfection, beauty, symmetry, purpose, measurement and precision in all matter.

The existence of Allah is beyond doubt and one should recognize this fact through His art of creation. Talent of the artist is recognized through his art. For example, doesn't the painting of Mona Lisa point to Leonardo Da Vinci? It is quite obvious that art has beauty and purpose. It is presented so that intelligent beings would admire it and in turn acknowledge the talent behind it. When we examine the universe from the perspective of all scientific disciplines and from an artistic point of view, we realize that there is a common factor behind everything. Everything in existence is the product of the very same hand. There is perfection, beauty, symmetry, purpose, measurement and precision in all matter.

Yet everything we observe exists in front of the veil of materialism. Thus, we try to understand nature with our limited perception.

Key vocabulary

- **Materialism:** way of thinking that gives too much importance to material possessions rather than to spiritual things.

Let's explain this argument with an analogy:

Imagine that you are in a theatre, sitting amid a large audience. There is a stage in front of you and on stage there is a canvas, an artist's palette and various colors of paint. You can see a paintbrush jutting from behind the stage curtains. The handle of the brush is behind the curtains so it is not visible to you, but it is in motion. Before your very eyes, it dips into various colors of paint and moves onto the canvas. With every stroke you are viewing a masterpiece of art being created before your very eyes. All the components of this masterpiece are quite visible to you. However, discovering what exists behind the curtains is beyond your physical capability. This is when the ultimate question arises: Is it possible that the handle of the brush is floating in midair?

DISCUSS

How should we, as the audience, interpret this strange phenomenon realizing that we can only analyze what is happening on the stage? Group up with your team and discuss your interpretations.

RANDOM OR ORDER?

Without question, the magnificent art and complexity we observe in nature exceeds by far any human-made art or design. Should we not be thankful to acknowledge the great designer that exists behind the veil of this physical universe? Furthermore, the incredible work done by this mysterious hand is not restricted to design only. It is as if the entire universe was adjusted so that living beings, in particular the human race could exist and maintain its existence. From the requirements of the tiny stomach of an ant to countless needs of human beings, all sustenance is prepared by this merciful hand and serviced to all creatures that cannot otherwise obtain them. The creations work in harmony so that life on earth could be preserved. Any intelligent individual would realize that the millions of events needed for the continuation of life on earth do not take place by means of randomness or chance.

"There is one Commander in Chief who is the cause of all causes."

There is one Commander in Chief who is the cause of all causes.

If we consider all matter in the universe as soldiers that function with certain laws and regulations, then assigning one general to everything would be reasonably logical. Otherwise, we would have quite a difficult task of explaining the perfect order and harmony that exists in nature and throughout the physical universe. Therefore, the design of the universe points to a great Designer and this designer is no other than the Almighty Allah.

Key vocabulary

- **Analogy:** a comparison of two things based on their being alike in some way.
- **Sustenance:** something (such as food) that keeps someone or something alive

This is precisely what the first article of faith requires of believers. Those who have embraced Islam must first recognize the Almighty Allah, the Great Designer, the All-Merciful. He has created the universe and His human servants so that they may recognize and acknowledge Him. He wished to be known hence the primary duty of humans is to acknowledge their Lord and submit to His will. **Thus, one cannot have faith without belief in the One and Only Allah.**

THINK

Is it more logical to assign 100 generals to one soldier or one general to 100 soldiers?

ALLAH IS UNIQUE

The concept of Allah in Islam, however, is quite unique. It is strictly monotheistic. Islam rejects all forms associations with Allah - Allah has no partners. Therefore, in Islam it is forbidden to assign a mother, son, daughter or any partner to Allah. The notion of unity of Allah is described quite unambiguously in the Holy Qur'an in surah Al-Ikhlas:

He does not need anything yet everything needs Him.

قُلْ هُوَ اللّٰهُ اَحَدٌ ۝١ اَللّٰهُ الصَّمَدُ ۝٢ لَمْ يَلِدْ وَلَمْ يُولَدْ ۝٣ وَلَمْ يَكُنْ لَهُ كُفُوًا اَحَدٌ ۝٤

> Say: "He - (He is) God, (Who is) the Unique One of Absolute Oneness. God - (God is He Who is) the Eternally-Besought-of-All (Himself being in need of nothing). He begets not, nor is He begotten. And comparable to Him there is none." (112:1-4)

He is One, but this concept of one is not a mathematical or numerical one. In Arabic, the term is Ahad, a unique one that cannot be compared to other ones. Mathematical concepts of division, multiplication, subtraction and addition do not apply to this form of oneness. The concept of Allah in Islam also teaches us that:

"He does not need anything yet everything needs Him."

This means that He does not depend on anything, including space-time. Before the creation of the entire existence, there was nothing but Him. He is eternal in the past and in the future, therefore, He was not begotten nor does he beget. He is so unique that there is none like unto Him. This means that He cannot be compared with anything physical or metaphysical.

Allah has absolute power over all existence.

Allah has absolute power over all existence

Another most significant issue about the concept of Allah in Islam is His Omnipotence and Sovereignty. Allah has absolute power over all existence. From the motions of atoms to giant galaxies and from a bacterium to a blue whale, everything functions and lives through His power. Everything in nature, including living organisms exist and maintain their existence through His power and inspiration.

Key vocabulary

- **Monotheistic:** the belief that there is only one God
- **Ahad:** Name of Allah, The One and Only
- **Omnipotence:** having complete or unlimited power
- **Sovereignty:** supreme power or authority, unlimited power over something or someone.

CAUSE AND EFFECT

Then what is the logic in producing so many creators when One is capable of creating everything?

One of the most fundamental laws of physics, cause and effect applies only to matter. The laws of physics do not apply to Allah. Therefore, the question put forward by some nonbelievers:

If Allah created everything then who created Allah is not a valid question, because in philosophy one does not enter into a chain reaction. If one were to assume that the creator was created by another being, then the next question would be who created him and so on. The problem won't be solved no matter how far one goes back.

"Then what is the logic in producing so many creators when One is capable of creating everything?"

Therefore, a creation points to a Creator and this Creator cannot be similar to His creation. He is the All-Powerful, All-Knowing and Omnipotent Allah.

IMAGINE

You are sitting on a chair that has two back legs missing. You would obviously fall back. To prevent yourself from falling back, you have placed another chair at the rear-bottom the chair you are sitting on, but this chair also has two back legs missing. So once again you have a third chair supporting the second one at the back, but also with no back legs. No matter how far you go back or how many chairs you place—one after the other, if you are able to sit on the front chair without falling back, this means that at the very end there is a chair with four legs. Evidently, you need a chair that supports all the chairs yet do not need support. Then what use would you have for all the other chairs that cannot even support themselves?

WHAT DID WE LEARN?

LESSON SUMMARY:

- When we observe the universe and nature around us, we realize that all matter—living and non-living—functions with purpose.
- Belief in Allah is the most important requirement of being human.
- Everything in the universe points to a creator
- Existence of Allah can be recognized through his creation.
- Human vision is extremely limited and cannot be used as a tool of denial.
- The magnificent art and complexity we observe in nature exceeds by far any human-made art or design.
- The millions of occurrences needed for the continuation of life on earth do not take place by means of randomness or chance.
- Allah has created the universe and His human servants so that they may recognize and acknowledge Him
- Allah is one, unique, and has no partners.
- Allah has absolute power over all existence.
- The laws of physics do not apply to Allah. One of the most fundamental laws of physics, cause and effect applies only to matter.
- There is no logic in producing so many creators when One is capable of creating everything.
- Therefore, a creation points to a Creator and this Creator cannot be similar to His creation. He is the All-Powerful, All-Knowing and Omnipotent Allah.

LESSON REVIEW: INDIVIDUAL ASSESSMENT

1. Why did Allah create this universe and creations?
2. What does ahad mean? Please explain in detail.
3. Define monotheism.
4. Why is it not credible for one to deny the existence of something using the argument of "I cannot see, hear, smell, touch or taste it"

ESSAY

What is the cause and effect theory, and how does it apply to Allah?

LESSON VOCABULARY

Transitory:	Sustenance:	Beget:
Materialism:	Monotheistic:	Omnipotence:
Analogy:	Ahad:	Sovereignty:

NOTES

1. Gülen, Fethullah. *Questions and Answers about Islam*, Nj: Tughra Books
2. Qur'an: 112:1–4.

Lesson 2
Proofs of God's Existence

God is the most manifest being, but that those lacking insight cannot see Him.

The existence of God is too evident to need any arguments. Some saintly scholars have even stated that

God is the most manifest being, but that those lacking insight cannot see Him.

However, the massive influence of positivism and materialism on science and on all people of recent centuries makes it necessary to discuss such arguments. As this now prevalent "scientific" worldview reduces existence to what can be perceived directly, it blinds itself to the far vaster invisible dimensions of existence. To remove the resulting veil, we will review briefly several traditional demonstrations of God's necessary existence.

No one has ever proven God's non-existence, for to do so is impossible, whereas countless arguments prove His existence.

Before doing so, let us reflect on one simple historical fact: Since the beginning of human life, the overwhelming majority of humanity has believed that God exists. This belief alone is enough to establish God's existence. Unbelievers cannot claim to be smarter than believers. Some of the most innovative scientists, scholars, and researchers have been—and are—believers, as are the field's experts: all Prophets and saints.

"No one has ever proven God's non-existence, for to do so is impossible, whereas countless arguments prove His existence."

IMAGINE

You approach a palace with 1,000 entrances, 999 of which are open and one of which appears to be closed. Would it be reasonable to say this palace is inaccessible?

Key vocabulary

- **Prevalent:** accepted, common or widespread

This power must be infinite, have absolute will and all-comprehensive knowledge. Necessarily, it is God.

Anything can exist anytime and anywhere, in any form, and with any character. Nothing or no one has a role in determining the way, time, and place of its coming into existence, or its character and features. So, there must be a power that chooses between a thing's existence and non-existence, giving it unique characteristics.This power must be infinite, have absolute will and all-comprehensive knowledge. Necessarily, it is God.

Everything changes. Therefore, it is contained in time and space, meaning that it begins and ends. That which has a beginning needs one with no beginning to bring it into existence, for it cannot originate itself, as this would require an infinite regression of originators. As reason cannot accept such a situation, an originator who is infinitely self-existent, self-subsistent, and unchanging is needed. **This original originator is God.**

The original originator is God.

Everything that exists, and the universe as a whole, displays a magnificent harmony. Whatever has been created has a purpose. The existence of one part necessitates the existence of the whole, and the whole requires the existence of all parts for its own existence. For example, a deformed cell may destroy an entire body. Similarly, a pomegranate requires the collaborative and cooperative existence of air, water, soil, and the sun, as well as their mutual and well-balanced cooperation, for its existence. This harmony and cooperation point to a creator of order, who knows the relationships and characteristics of everything, and who can order everything.

DISCUSS

Can something completely devoid of knowledge and consciousness, be responsible for such a miraculous creation?

All living and non-living beings cannot meet almost any of their own needs on their own. For example, the universe can operate and maintain itself only by such universal laws as growth and reproduction, gravitation and repulsion. But these so-called "natural laws" have no actual external, visible, or material existence; they are nominal.

Think about the requirement of absolute power and absolute knowledge, wisdom, choice, and preference.

Plants need air and water, as well as heat and light, to survive. Can they fulfill their own needs? **Humanity's needs are infinite**. Fortunately, all of our essential needs, from our beginning in the womb to death, are met by someone who is able to meet them and chooses to do so. When we enter this world, we find everything prepared to meet all the needs of our senses and intellectual and spiritual faculties. This clearly shows that one who is infinitely merciful and knowledgeable provides for all created beings in the most extraordinary way, and causes all things to collaborate to that end.

Before humanity began to over-pollute the air, water and soil, the natural world was cleansed and purified continually. Even now, it still preserves its original purity in many regions, mostly where modern life has not yet taken hold. Have you ever wondered why nature is so clean? Why are forests so clean, even though many animals die in them every day?

Key vocabulary

- **Regression:** to return to an earlier state.
- **Self-existent:** existing independently of other beings or causes.
- **Self-subsistent:** subsisting independently of anything external to itself
- **Nominal:** existing as something in name only; not actual or real
- **Infinite:** having no limit, endless

This purity points to the All-Holy One, whose attributes include cleanliness and purity.

If all flies born during the summer survived, the earth would be covered completely with layers of dead flies. Nothing is wasted in nature, for each death is the beginning of a new birth. For example, a dead body decomposes and is integrated into the soil. Elements die and are revived in plants; plants die in the stomachs of animals and people and are promoted to a higher rank of life. This cycle of death and revival is one factor that keeps the universe clean and pure. Bacteria and insects, wind and rain, black holes and oxygen in organic bodies all sustain the universe's purity. This purity points to the All-Holy One, whose attributes include cleanliness and purity.

Our conscience is the center of our inclinations toward right and wrong. Everybody feels this conscience occasionally, and most people are inclined to turn to God on certain occasions. For us, this inclination and belief in Him are intrinsic. Even if we consciously deny God, our unconscious belief in Him occasionally shows itself. The Qur'an mentions this in several verses:

The human spirit and conscience are a strong argument for the existence of One God.

> It is He Who enables you to travel on the land and the sea; and when you are in the ship, and the ships run with a favorable wind and they rejoice in it, there comes upon them a strong wind, and waves come on them from every side and they think that they are encompassed. Then they cry unto God, making their faith pure for Him only, (saying): "If you deliver us from this, we truly will be thankful. (10:22)

"The human spirit and conscience are a strong argument for the existence of One God."

THINK

When tens of thousands of Prophets who never lied, hundreds of thousands of saints, and millions of believers, all of whom have adopted truthfulness as a most essential pillar of belief, and then agree on God's existence, is it reasonable to reject their testimony and accept the individual reports of a few liars?

The proofs for the Qur'an's Divine origin are also proofs for God's existence. The Qur'an teaches with great emphasis and focus, as indeed do the Bible's Old and New Testaments, the existence of One God. In addition, tens of thousands of Prophets have been sent to guide humanity to truth. All were justly renowned for their truthfulness and other praiseworthy virtues, and all gave priority to preaching the existence and Oneness of God.

Key vocabulary

- **Conscience:** the part of the mind that makes you aware of your actions as being either morally right or wrong
- **Intrinsic:** occurring as a natural part of something

WHAT DID WE LEARN?

LESSON SUMMARY:

- The existence of God is too evident to need any arguments
- God is the most manifest being, but that those lacking insight cannot see Him.
- Since the beginning of human life, the overwhelming majority of humanity has believed that God exists.
- No one has ever proven God's non-existence
- Whatever has been created has a purpose. The existence of one part necessitates the existence of the whole
- Humanity's needs are infinite
- The human spirit and conscience are a strong argument for the existence of One God.
- The proofs for the Quran's Divine origin are also proofs for God's existence

LESSON REVIEW: INDIVIDUAL ASSESSMENT

1. According to the text, why hasn't anyone been able to prove God's non-existence?
2. What does intrinsic belief in God mean?
3. Using an example given in the text, explain one thing that sustains the universe's purity.
4. Make a list of as many needs as you can think of that you have, but cannot meet on your own. (Example: breathing).

ESSAY

Suppose you have a friend who does not believe in Allah. Using the persuasive essay technique, write a letter to your friend proving Allah's existence siting specific examples from your reading.

LESSON VOCABULARY

Self-Existent:
Self-Subsistent:
Nominal:
Conscience:
Infinite:
Intrinsic:
Prevalent:
Regression:

Lesson 3
The Essence and Attributes of God

IF GOD CREATED EVERYTHING, WHO CREATED GOD?

The Creator must be Self-Subsistent and One, without like or equal. **Only the Creator truly creates and determines possible causes and effects for His creation.** Therefore, we speak of God as the Sustainer, who holds and gives life to all of His Creation. All causes begin in Him, and all effects end in Him.

THINK

How could we make sense of a tree without some prior idea, no matter how vague, of the tree itself? Given such limitations, how can we know or see the Creator of everything?

WHY CAN'T WE SEE GOD?

God is absolutely incomparable to His creation, for the Creator cannot have the same kind of being as His creation. Although this is self-evident, some people still ask why we cannot see God.

As created and finite beings, our potential and capacity are limited. Our Creator, on the other hand, is Infinite. We live and die within His creation, strive for understanding and virtue, and seek our salvation by His Mercy.

We know a great deal about our environment, but all of our knowledge is just a small fragment of the whole. However, our knowledge is guided by understanding. We need some general idea about what we see in order to understand it.

In the Qur'an, we read that: **Vision comprehends Him not, but He comprehends all vision** (6:103). After the Prophet's ascent to the heavens, his Companions asked him if he had seen God. Abu Dharr reported that one time he answered: "What I saw was the Light. How could I see Him?" On another occasion he answered: "I saw a Light." These statements clarify the well-known saying: "The light is the limit or veil of God."

Key vocabulary

- **Finite:** having limits
- **Salvation:** being saved and protected from danger or harm

IMAGINE

You are in a closed room and someone knocks on the door. While you may be able to make some assumptions about who it is based on their attributes, the only thing you know for certain is that someone is knocking. How can you ask this person to make themselves known to you?

Those who ask to see God directly seek to think of or know His Being directly. Just as we cannot see Him, we cannot think of or know His Being, for He is beyond all form, quality, quantity, and human conception or reasoning. In the words of Muslim theologians:

*"Whatever conception of God we form in our minds,
He is other than it."*

This analogy helps us approach the question of how to seek God. Look at creation. Its sheer beauty and harmony make us aware of the Creator's existence. When we see a wide range of fabrics produced from a single material, we know that someone has produced it, we understand that it could not have produced itself. Similarly, we can deduce from what we can see of this creation that someone—the Creator—has made it.

But this is where the similarity ends. While we can find those who made the fabric and persuade them to make themselves known to us, we cannot do so with the Creator.

Key vocabulary

- **Deduce:** to use logic or reason to form an opinion

DISCUSS

It is said, "His Names are known, His Attributes are comprehended, and His Essence exists." What are the differences between His Names, Attributes, and Essence?

Revelation opens this door for us. God's Revelation to the Prophets and their teachings enable us to respond to creation as signs manifesting the Creator's Existence and Attributes.

In the words of Abu Bakr: "To comprehend His Essence means to confess that His Essence cannot be comprehended."

Our duty is to remain committed to our covenant with God, and to beseech Him as follows:

> O You, the only one we worship! We cannot attain to true knowledge of You, yet we believe that You are nearer to us than our jugular veins. We feel Your existence and nearness in the depths of our hearts through the universe, which You created and opened to us like a book, and through the wonderful harmony of form between all parts of Your creation.

WHY DID GOD CREATE THE UNIVERSE?

But why did God create all of this?

When analyzing this issue, some facts must be kept in mind. While we perceive things from a human perspective, God does not. While we act out of necessity or desire, God does not. In other words, we cannot ascribe human attributes and motivations to God.

"But why did God create all of this?"

The Creator wills to introduce Himself to us clearly and thoroughly. He wills to show His Splendor through the variety and beauty of creation; His Will and Might through the universe's magnificent order and harmony; His Mercy, Compassion, and Grace through His bestowal of everything upon us, including our most secret wishes and desires. And He has many more Names and Attributes through which He wills to make Himself known.

Key vocabulary

- **Revelation:** an act of making something known
- **Covenant:** a formal and serious agreement or promise
- **Beseech:** to beg for something
- **Splendor:** great and impressive beauty
- **Bestowal:** to present as a gift

While great artists manifest their talents through works of art; the Owner of the universe created it simply to manifest the Might and Omnipotence of His Creativity.

In other words, He creates and places things in this world to manifest His Might and Will. By passing all things through the view of the intellect and understanding of conscious beings, He arouses their wonder, admiration, and appreciation.

"While great artists manifest their talents through works of art; the Owner of the universe created it simply to manifest the Might and Omnipotence of His Creativity."

WHAT IS THE DIFFERENCE BETWEEN GOD AND ALLAH?

Only Allah is Allah, and only He is worthy of worship.

The Arabic word *ilah* is the counterpart of the English word "god." Both mean the thing or entity being worshipped.

"God," with a capital G, is not an exact equivalent of the term Allah, although we use it for practical reasons throughout this book. Rather, it is closer to the Islamic conception of ilah.

In Arabic, Allah is the specific and personal name of God and comprises all His Beautiful Names (*Asma' al-Husna*). When Allah is said, the One, the Supreme Being, the Creator, the Owner, the Sustainer, the All-Powerful, the All-Knowing, the All-Encompassing, whose Names and Attributes are manifested in creation, comes to mind. This term also refers to His absolute Oneness as well as His having no defect or partner.

As Allah is a proper name peculiar to the One Supreme Being, we say *la ilaha illa Allah* (there is no god but Allah) instead of *la Allah illa Allah.* By saying *la ilaha illa Allah*, we first deny all non-deities and then affirm the One known by the name Allah.

"In other words, only Allah is Allah, and only He is worthy of worship."

Key vocabulary

- **Manifest:** to show something clearly, to reflect.
- **Counterpart:** someone or something that has the same job or purpose as another

WHAT DID WE LEARN?

LESSON SUMMARY:

- Only the Creator truly creates and determines possible causes and effects for His creation.
- Allah is absolutely incomparable to His creation, for the Creator cannot have the same kind of being as His creation.
- "Whatever conception of God we form in our minds, He is other than it."
- Allah's Revelation to the Prophets and their teaching enable us to respond to creation as signs manifesting the Creator's Existence and Attributes.
- While we perceive things from a human perspective, Allah does not.
- Allah creates and places things in this world to manifest His Might and Will.
- There is a difference in meaning of god, God, and Allah
- Only Allah is Allah, and only He is worthy of worship.

LESSON REVIEW: INDIVIDUAL ASSESSMENT

1. What is the difference in meaning of god, God, and Allah? Please explain in detail.
2. According to the text, what was Prophet Muhammad's response when asked if he had seen God?
3. Why did God create and place things in this world? Please support your answer with evidence from the text.
4. According to the text, what does Allah's revelation to the Prophets and their teachings enable us to do?

ESSAY

Earlier in the lesson, you discussed the difference between Allah's Names, Attributes, and Essence. In your own words, summarize what you learned from that discussion.

LESSON VOCABULARY

Deduce
Revelation:
Beseech:
Splendor:
Bestowal:
Finite:
Covenant:
Manifest:
Counterpart:
Salvation:

Lesson 4

God's Essential (al-Sifaat al-Dhatiyyah) & Immutable (Positive) Attributes (al-Sifat al-Thubutiyyah)

God Almighty should be considered from five perspectives.

The first is His "Essence" as Divine Being (*Dhat* in Islamic terminology), which only He can know. A Prophetic Tradition says: "Do not reflect on God's 'Essence'; instead, reflect on His works and acts." The second perspective is His Essential, innate Qualities as God, which are the Attributes' source.

God is absolutely free from any defect and shortcoming.

The third perspective is His Attributes, which are of three kinds: Essential Attributes (e.g., Existence, Having No Beginning, Oneness, Being Unlike the Created); God has no partners, likes or resemblance, as pointed to by the verse: *There is nothing like or compared unto Him* (42:11). Positive Attributes (Life, Knowledge, Power, Speech, Will, Hearing, Seeing, Creating); and "Negative" Attributes, summed up as: God is absolutely free from any defect and shortcoming.

THINK

When you see the reflection of the sun in water, is it conceivable that there is an actual sun in each drop of water? Or, does it make more sense that the sun you see in the drop of water is just a manifestation of the sun's reflection?

Key vocabulary

- **Essential:** extremely important and necessary
- **Innate:** existing as part of the basic nature of something
- **Conceivable:** imaginable or possible

The Attributes are the sources of the Names which is the fourth perspective. Life gives rise to the All-Living (Al-Hayy), Knowledge to the All-Knowing (Al-'Alim), and Power to the All-Powerful (Al-Qadir). The Names are the sources of the acts which is the fifth perspective: giving life has its source in the All-Living, and knowing everything down to the smallest detail or thing originates in the All-Knowing. God is "known" through His Acts, Names, and Attributes.

Whatever exists in the universe is the result of the Names' and Attributes' manifestations: Universal and individual provision points to His Name the All-Providing (Ar-Razzaq). Likewise, the All-Healing (Ash-Shafi) is the source of remedies and recovery for the sick.

The acts, Names, and Attributes are the "links" between Allah and the created, or the "reflectors" with which to have knowledge of Allah.

Although we try to know or recognize God by His acts, Names, and Attributes, we must not think of Him in terms of associating likeness or comparison unto Him, for nothing resembles Him. He is absolutely One, Single, and totally different from all that exists or has the potential to exist.

Just the same way, if everything in the universe is not attributed to One God, the Absolutely All-Powerful One, it will be necessary to accept, in place of One God, as many gods as the particles in the universe.

IMAGINE

A man spends his entire life searching for knowledge. Without proper guidance, think of how many unnecessary, useless, and unimportant facts he would find among his gained knowledge. If you don't seek a way of making scientific and other knowledge useful, and spiritual, your knowledge will be incomplete. What can you do to make sure ALL your knowledge becomes valuable knowledge of Allah?

THE ESSENTIAL ATTRIBUTES (AL-SIFAAT AL-DHATIYYAH)

The Essential Attributes only belong to Allah as they are not seen in any other being except Him. For example, being eternal in the past and future can only be considered with God not with the created.

1. Al-Wujud (Self-Existence): Allah is the Existing One. This essential Attribute of Allah the Almighty denotes that His existence is by Himself. He is the Necessarily Existent One.
2. Al-Qidam (Having No Beginning): Allah is the Eternal in the Past. He existed before everything.
3. Al-Baqah (Having No End): Allah is the Eternal in the Future, He has no end.
4. Al-Mukhalafatun-lil-Hawadith (Being Unlike the Created): Allah is not like the things He created. This Attribute denotes that the All-Majestic, All-Exalted Allah does not resemble, in any way, any of His creatures in His Essence or Attributes.
5. Al-Qiyam-bi-Nafsihi (Self-Subsistence): Allah is the Self-Existing One. He is dependent on nothing else to exist. Allah subsists by Himself in absolute independence of anything else and without needing anything, either in His existence or subsistence, while everything and everyone other than Him owes both their existence and subsistence to Him.
6. Al-Wahdaniyyah (Oneness): Allah is the Unique One. He has no partner; He is not equal to anything. He has no equals nor likes in His Oneness.

Key vocabulary

- **Provision:** the act or process of supplying or providing something
- **Denotes:** to mean something
- **Subsist / Subsistence:** remain in force; maintain / the amount of something needed to stay alive

THE IMMUTABLE (POSITIVE) ATTRIBUTES (AL-SIFAAT AL-THUBUTIYYAH)

DISCUSS

Allah is One, Single and totally different from all that exists. We try to know or recognize Allah by His acts, Names, and Attributes. How can we use the knowledge we gain through this to know Allah without associating likeness or comparison unto Him?

The Immutable Attributes are different than Essential Attributes; other beings like humans, the jinn and angels can have similar attributes, too, but only in a limited capacity and dependent nature. For example Al-Hayat (Life); human being has life too. However, Life as an Immutable Attribute of Allah is not like the one observed in creatures. It is the real life as the source of all lives, it is pre-eternal and post-eternal.

1. Al-Hayat (Life): Allah is alive. He is the Living One. The life in the universe most certainly testifies to the necessary Existence of the Eternally Living One.
2. Al-'Ilm (Knowledge): Allah knows everything. He is the All-Knowing One. Divine Knowledge encompasses everything and nothing is outside this limitless, all-encompassing circle. He is indeed All-Knowing of the states and conditions of all things.
3. Al-Iradah (Will): Allah has an absolute Will. Nothing binds His Divine Will. The book of the Universe and the Divine laws found in nature come from Divine Attributes of Power and Will.
4. Al-Qudrah (Power): Allah is the Almighty and Omnipotent (All-Powerful) One. His absolute Power contains no defect, and dominates everything.
5. As-Sam' (Hearing): Allah hears everything. He is the All-Hearing One. He listens to and hears all sounds and voices.
6. Al-Basar (Sight): Allah sees everything, be it hidden or not. He is the Omniscient (All-Seeing) One.
7. Al-Kalam (Speech): Allah speaks in a unique way. He needs no sounds or letters. The Divine Speech cannot be compared to any kind of speech we are familiar with.
8. At-Takwin (Making Exist): He is the Creator of everything. The Attribute of Making Exist is the Attribute of Glory that is the origin of this creation.

This is pointed to in the verse: "To Allah applies the most sublime Attributes" (an-Nahl 16:60).

SOME OF GOD'S NAMES

Allah: Translated as God, Allah is the proper Name of the Divine Being Who creates and administers His creatures, individually and as a whole, Who provides, brings up, sustains, protects, guides each and all, Who causes to perish and revives each and all, Who rewards or punishes, and so on. All His Attributes are Attributes of absolute perfection, and He is absolutely free from any and all defects. He is Unique and Single, having no like or resemblance and nothing is comparable to Him. He is absolutely beyond any human conception. He is the Unique, Single Being with the exclusive right to be worshipped and to be made the sole aim of life. He is loved in and of Himself.

Key vocabulary

- **Immutable:** unable to be changed
- **Sublime:** very beautiful or good

اَللّٰهُ

اَلرَّحْمٰنُ	اَلرَّحِيمُ	اَلْمَلِكُ	اَلْقُدُّوسُ	اَلسَّلَامُ	اَلْمُؤْمِنُ	اَلْمُهَيْمِنُ	اَلْعَزِيزُ	اَلْجَبَّارُ
اَلْمُتَكَبِّرُ	اَلْخَالِقُ	اَلْبَارِئُ	اَلْمُصَوِّرُ	اَلْغَفَّارُ	اَلْقَهَّارُ	اَلْوَهَّابُ	اَلرَّزَّاقُ	اَلْفَتَّاحُ
اَلْعَلِيمُ	اَلْقَابِضُ	اَلْبَاسِطُ	اَلْخَافِضُ	اَلرَّافِعُ	اَلْمُعِزُّ	اَلْمُذِلُّ	اَلسَّمِيعُ	اَلْبَصِيرُ
اَلْحَكَمُ	اَلْعَدْلُ	اَللَّطِيفُ	اَلْخَبِيرُ	اَلْحَلِيمُ	اَلْعَظِيمُ	اَلْغَفُورُ	اَلشَّكُورُ	اَلْعَلِىُّ
اَلْكَبِيرُ	اَلْحَفِيظُ	اَلْمُقِيتُ	اَلْحَسِيبُ	اَلْجَلِيلُ	اَلْكَرِيمُ	اَلرَّقِيبُ	اَلْمُجِيبُ	اَلْوَاسِعُ
اَلْحَكِيمُ	اَلْوَدُودُ	اَلْمَجِيدُ	اَلْبَاعِثُ	اَلشَّهِيدُ	اَلْحَقُّ	اَلْوَكِيلُ	اَلْقَوِىُّ	اَلْمَتِينُ
اَلْوَلِىُّ	اَلْحَمِيدُ	اَلْمُحْصِى	اَلْمُبْدِئُ	اَلْمُعِيدُ	اَلْمُحْيِى	اَلْمُمِيتُ	اَلْحَيُّ	اَلْقَيُّومُ
اَلْوَاجِدُ	اَلْمَاجِدُ	اَلْوَاحِدُ	اَلْاَحَدُ	اَلصَّمَدُ	اَلْقَادِرُ	اَلْمُقْتَدِرُ	اَلْمُقَدِّمُ	اَلْمُؤَخِّرُ
اَلْاَوَّلُ	اَلْاٰخِرُ	اَلظَّاهِرُ	اَلْبَاطِنُ	اَلْوَالِى	اَلْمُتَعَالُ	اَلْبَرُّ	اَلتَّوَّابُ	اَلْمُنْتَقِمُ
اَلْعَفُوُّ	اَلرَّؤُفُ	مَالِكُ الْمُلْكِ	ذُوالْجَلَالِ وَالْإِكْرَامِ	اَلْمُقْسِطُ	اَلْجَامِعُ	اَلْغَنِىُّ	اَلْمُغْنِى	اَلْمَانِعُ
اَلضَّارُّ	اَلنَّافِعُ	اَلنُّورُ	اَلْهَادِى	اَلْبَدِيعُ	اَلْبَاقِى	اَلْوَارِثُ	اَلرَّشِيدُ	اَلصَّبُورُ

(Al-)'Adl: The All-Just

(Al-)'Afuww: The All-Pardoning (Who overlooks the faults of His servants); The One Who grants remission; The One Who excuses much

(Al-)Ahad: The Unique One (Who is beyond all kinds of human conceptions of Him and absolutely free from having any partners, likes, parents, sons or daughters)

(Al-)Ahir: The Last (Whom there is none that will outlive)

(Al-)'Alim: The All-Knowing

(Al-)'Aliyy: The All-Exalted

(Al-)Amin: The One in Whom Refuge is Sought

(Al-)'Atuf: The All-Affectionate

(Al-)Awwal: The First (Whom there is none that precedes)

(Al-)'Aziz: The All-Glorious with irresistible might (Whom none can prevent from doing what He wills)

(Al-)Baqi: The All-Permanent

(Al-)Bari: The All-Holy Creator (Who is absolutely free from having any partners and Who makes every being perfect and different from others)

(Al-)Basir: The All-Seeing

(Al-)Batin: The All-Inward (Who encompasses the whole existence from within in His Knowledge, and there is none that is more penetrating than Him)

(Ad-)Dayyan: The Supreme Ruler and All-Requiting (of good and evil)

(Al-)Fard: The All-Independent, Single One (free from having any equals or likes in His Essence and Attributes)

(Al-)Fatir: The All-Originating (with a unique individuality)

(Al-)Fattah: The One Who judges between people with truth and separates

(Al-)Ghaniyy: The All-Wealthy and Self-Sufficient

(Al-)Habib: The All-Loving and Loved

(Al-)Hadi: The All-Guiding

(Al-)Hafiz: The All-Preserving and Keeper of records

(Al-)Hakim: The All-Wise (in Whose every act and decree there are many instances of wisdom)

(Al-)Halim: The All-Clement (showing no haste to punish the errors of His servants)

(Al-)Hamid: The All-Praiseworthy (as the Lord Who creates, provides, and rears)

(Al-)Hannan: The All-Kind and Caring

(Al-)Haqq: The Ultimate Truth and Ever-Constant

(Al-)Hayy: The All-Living

(Al-)Jabbar: The All-Compelling of supreme majesty (Who subdues wrong and restores right)

(Al-)Jalil: The All-Majestic

(Al-)Jamil: The All-Gracious and All-Beautiful

(Al-)Jawad: The All-Generous

(Al-)Kabir: The All-Great

(Al-)Kafi: The All-Sufficing

(Al-)Karim: The All-Munificent

(Al-)Khabir: The All-Aware

(Al-)Khaliq: The Creator (Who determines measure for everything and brings it into existence out of nothing)

(Al-)Latif: The All-Subtle (penetrating into the most minute dimensions of all things); the All-Favoring

(Al-)Mahmud: The All-Praised

(Al-)Malik: The Sovereign

(Al-)Mannan: The All-Bounteous and Favoring

(Al-)Ma'ruf: The One Known (with His works); the All-Recognized

(Al)Mubin: The One from Whom nothing is hidden and Who makes all truth manifest

(Al-)Mughni: The All-Enriching

(Al-)Muhaymin: The All-Watchful Guardian

(Al-)Muhit: The All-Encompassing

(Al-)Muhsin: The All-Benevolent

(Al-)Muhyi: The One Who revives, Who gives life to the dead

(Al-)Mu'in: The All-Helping and Supplying

(Al-)Mu'izz: The All-Exalting and Honoring

(Al-)Mujib: The All-Answering (of prayers) and Meeting (of needs)

(Al-)Mu'min: The Supreme Author of safety and security Who bestows faith and removes all doubt

(Al-)Mumit: The One Causing to Die; the All-Dealer of death

(Al-)Mundhir: The All-Informing and Warning

(Al-)Murid: The All-Willing

(Al-)Musawwir: The All-Fashioning

(Al-)Mutakabbir: The One Who has exclusive right to all greatness (Al-)Mu'ti: The All-Granting

(An-)Nur: The All-Light

(Al-)Qaim: The All-Observing and Controlling

(Al-)Qadir: The All-Powerful

(Al-)Qahhar: The All-Overwhelming (with absolute sway over all that exists)

(Al-)Qarib: The All-Near

(Al-)Qawiyy: The All-Strong

(Al-)Qayyum: The Self-Subsisting (by Whom all subsist)

(Al-)Quddus: the All-Holy and All-Pure (Who is absolutely free of any defect and keeps the universe clean)

(Ar-)Rabb: The Lord (God as the Creator, Provider, Trainer, Upbringer, and Director of all creatures)

WHAT DID WE LEARN?

LESSON SUMMARY:

- The Essential Attributes (al-Sifat al-Dhatiyyah)

1. Al-Wujud
2. Al-Qidam
3. Al-Baqah
4. Al-Mukhalafatun-lil-Hawadith
5. Al-Qiyam-bi-Nafsihi
6. Al-Wahdaniyyah

- The Immutable (Positive) Attributes (as-Sifat al-Thubutiyyah)

1. Al-Hayat
2. Al-'Ilm
3. Al-Iradah
4. Al-Qudrah
5. As-Sam'
6. Al-Basar
7. Al-Kalam
8. At-Takwin

- Allah is known through His acts, Names, and Attributes.
- Whatever exists in the universe is the result of the Names' and Attributes' manifestations
- The acts, Names, and Attributes are the "links" between Allah and the created, or the "reflectors" with which to have knowledge of Allah.

LESSON REVIEW: INDIVIDUAL ASSESSMENT

1. According to the text, what are the "links" between Allah and the created, or the "reflectors" with which to have knowledge of Allah?
2. Prophet Muhammad asks us to focus on what instead of Allah's Essence?
3. Which Attribute of Allah is defined as "Allah hears everything. He is the All-Hearing One. He listens to and hears all sounds and voices."
4. In your own words, define Al-Qiyam-bi-Nafsihi.

ESSAY

Choose an Attribute of Allah and write in detail how that Attribute is seen in your life on a daily basis. Use specific details and examples from your own experiences.

LESSON VOCABULARY

Provision
Essential
Denote
Subsists/Subsistence
Immutable
Sublime
Innate
Bonus Word: Requiting

Lesson 5
Tawhid (God's Oneness)

THINK

Tawhid, Divine Unity and/or Oneness, is clearly observed throughout the universe. What examples can you see when you look at yourself and the environment?

The same Creator Who created the particles created the universe.

All religions revealed to the Prophets have the same essence. Over time, however, the original message was misinterpreted, mixed with superstition, and degenerated into magical practices and meaningless rituals. The concept of God, the very core of religion, was debased by anthropomorphism, treating angels as gods, associating others with God, considering Prophets or godly people as incarnations of God, and personifying His Attributes through separate deities.

Prophet Muhammad, upon him be peace and blessings, rejected such trends and restored the concept of God as the only Creator, Sustainer, and Master of all creation to its original purity.

For example, our bodily parts cooperate with each other. Each cell is so connected with the whole body that the One Who created the cell must be He Who created the body. Likewise, each element constituting the universe is in harmony with every other element and the universe as a whole.

Given this, the only logical conclusion is **that the same Creator Who created the particles created the universe.**

EVERYTHING ORIGINATES FROM "ONE" AND RETURNS TO "ONE"

God originates creation and then reproduces it, and He will bring it forth anew (in another world) (10:34)

Key vocabulary

- **Superstition:** belief that certain events or things will bring good or bad luck
- **Degenerated:** to become worse, weaker, less useful, etc.
- **Debased:** to lower the value or reputation of (someone or something)
- **Anthropomorphism:** described or thought of as being like human beings in appearance, behavior, etc.
- **Deity:** a god or goddess

DISCUSS

A tree grows out of a seed or a stone and finally results in a seed or a stone. How does the trees strict obedience to the One Who established this order explain why the universe is so orderly and harmonious? How does it point to the Creator, One, All-Omnipotent and All-Knowing that operates it directly?

As the Qur'an reminds us: E*ach god would have taken off what he created, and some of them would have risen up over others. Had there been gods in the earth and the heaven other than Allah, they both would have been in disorder.* (21:22)

Tawhid is the highest concept that God revealed to us through His Prophets, among them being Moses, Jesus, and Muhammad, upon them be peace. Over time, people began to stray from the pure teachings after their Prophets died. Turning to polytheism or idolatry, they relied upon their own faulty reasoning, false perceptions, and biased interpretations to satisfy their own desires. Such a course is impossible with a tawhid-based system, for this requires that they obey only the One Supreme God's commandments.

'Ali ibn Abi Talib is reported to have said:

> "The foremost in religion is God's knowledge, the perfection of His knowledge is to testify to Him, the perfection of testifying to Him is to believe in His Oneness, the perfection of believing in His Oneness is to regard Him as pure, and the perfection of His purity is to deny all kinds of negative attributes about Him."

HE IS INFINITE AND ETERNAL, SELF-EXISTENT AND SELF-SUFFICIENT

IMAGINE

Reflect on your own inability to keep yourself alive or protect your own power. Imagine it has been suddenly taken away. Doesn't this reality make it clear that all divine powers and attributes must exist in only that one particular Being (Allah)?

As stated in the Qur'an:

> He, God, the Unique One, needy of nothing and Everlasting Refuge; He begets not, nor is He begotten; and there is none like unto Him (112:1–4). There is nothing like or compared unto Him (42:11). Vision perceives Him not, and He perceives all vision; and He (alone) is the All-Hearing and All-Seeing (6:103).

In the words of 'Ali:

> "He is Being but not through the phenomenon of coming into being. He exists but not from non-existence. He is with everything but not by physical nearness. He is different from everything but not by physical separation. He acts but without the accompaniment of movements and instruments. He is the One, only such that there is none with whom He keeps company or whom He misses in his absence."

Key vocabulary

- **Beget:** to become the father of (someone)
- **Phenomenon:** something (such as an interesting fact or event) that can be observed and studied and that typically is unusual or difficult to understand or explain fully?

Literally, tawhid means "unification" (making something one) or "asserting oneness."

Literally, tawhid means "unification" (making something one) or "asserting oneness." It comes from the Arabic verb wahhada (to unite, unify, or consolidate). However, when used in reference to God, it means realizing and maintaining God's Unity in all of our actions that directly or indirectly relate to Him. It is the belief that God is One, without partner in His dominion and His actions, without similitude in His Essence and Attributes, and without rival in His Divinity and in worship.

In the name of God, the Merciful, the Compassionate.

God is the Creator of all things and He is guardian and watcher over everything. To Him belong the keys of the heavens and earth. (39:62-3)

Glory be to Him in Whose hand is the kingdom and inner dimensions of all things. (36:83)

There is not a thing but the stores (for its life and sustenance) are with Us (15:21)

No living creature is there but He holds it by its forelock and keeps it under His complete control. (11:56)

BELIEF IN GOD'S UNITY HAS TWO DEGREES

The first is believing superficially that God has no partners and the universe can belong to none other than Him. It is possible that one who has this degree of belief may be susceptible to certain deviations and obscurities in his understanding.

The other degree is being firmly convinced that God is One and that everything belongs to Him exclusively, and that only He gives existence without any partners whatever and without needing any means to do so. The one with such degree of conviction sees His seal and observes His stamp on all things, and free from any doubts, feels himself always and everywhere in His Presence. Neither deviations nor doubts can find a way to dilute this degree of conviction.

POINTS OBTAINED FROM QUR'AN ABOUT GOD'S UNITY

Making one thing from many things only possible with the Creator of all.

Making one thing from many things only possible with the Creator of all.

God Almighty has set a special seal on each of the things He has made, which shows that He is the Creator of all things. He has set a special stamp on each of His creatures demonstrating that He is the Maker of all things.

For example, among His innumerable seals, look at the one He has put on life.

Key vocabulary

- **Superficially:** not thorough or complete
- **Deviation:** an action, behavior, or condition that is different from what is usual or expected
- **Obscurity:** the state of being unknown or forgotten
- **Innumerable:** too many to be counted

DISCUSS

Consider how, through life, a single this is made into many things, and many things into one thing. For example, the water we drink becomes means for the organs in our systems. Though a single entity, it becomes "many" by God's command. How does this lead to a deeper understanding of God's Divine Unity?

Among His innumerable seals, look at the one He has put on life. Consider how, through life, a single thing is made into many things, and many things into one thing. For example, water that we drink becomes, by God's leave, a means for the formation of innumerable animal organs and systems. Though a single entity, it becomes "many" by God's command. Conversely many varieties of foods become, by God's leave, a particular body or skin or a whole system or sub-system. Thus "many" things become, by God's command, a single entity. So, whoever has intellect, consciousness and heart must conclude that making a single, simple entity from many things and using a single entity in making things of great diversity is a seal special to the Creator of all things.

Everything reflects His Names.

Everything reflects His Names

From planets to drops of water and pieces of glass, in each transparent or apparently transparent thing there is a stamp— an image or reflection. Particular to the sun.

So too, the Unique, Eternal Sun has set on each living thing a seal, a stamp, of reviving and bringing to life showing itself through the manifestations of all His Names on that thing. If all material causes—supposing they had power and will—came together to produce the like of that stamp, they would not be able to do so, even if they helped one another (17.88).

THINK

What types of seals, stamps, and reflections of Allah's name do you see around you every day?

Similarly, assume you do not attribute every living thing and life and every act of bringing to life, to the concentrated manifestation of all the Divine Names. Presume you do not accept that life is the focus of the manifestations of the Divine Names, which could be regarded as the rays of the Eternal Sun. Then you would have to admit that each living thing, even if it be a fly or a flower, has an infinite power of creation, an all-encompassing knowledge, and an absolute will. Also, you would have to attribute divinity to each atom, if you ascribe the existence of everything to itself. Likewise, you would have to attribute absolute divinity to each cause, if you ascribe the existence of everything to causes. This would also compel you to accept countless partners in Divinity which, necessarily, requires absolute independence and never accepts partnership.

A letter in a book points to its writer. All things point to their Maker.

A letter in a book points to its writer

Every "created" letter of the book of the universe points to itself only to the extent of being a letter. However, it points to its Maker in many respects both individually and in the words and sentences in which it is included, and manifests the titles of its Maker.

IMAGINE

The universe is a book, and every "created" letter points to itself to the extent of being a letter. However, doesn't it also point to its Maker in many ways?

FEATURED POEM

Want only One; the rest are not worth wanting.
Call One; the others will not come to your assistance.

Seek One; the rest are not worth it.

See One; the others are not seen all the time; they hide themselves behind the veil of ephemerality.

Know One; knowledge other than that which assists knowledge of Him is without benefit.

Say One; words not concerning Him may be considered meaningless.

Key vocabulary

- **Ephemerality:** lasting a very short time

WHAT DID WE LEARN?

LESSON SUMMARY:

- All religions revealed to the Prophets have the same essence.
- The concept of God, the very core of religion was debased by anthropomorphism
- Everything originates from "one" and returns to "one"
- Tawhid is the highest concept of deity that God revealed to us through His Prophets
- Literally, tawhid means "unification" (making something one) or "asserting oneness."
- Belief in God's Unity has two degrees:

  * Superficial belief

  * Firmly convinced belief
- God Almighty has set a special seal on each of the things He has made, which shows that He is the Creator of all things
- From planets to drops of water and pieces of glass, in each transparent or apparently transparent thing there is a stamp— an image or reflection.
- Making one thing from many things is only possible with the Creator of all.
- Everything reflects His Names.
- A letter in a book points to its writer. All things point their Maker

LESSON REVIEW: INDIVIDUAL ASSESSMENT

1. What is the definition of *tawhid*?
2. According to the text, what was the cause of people deviating from the pure teachings after their Prophets died?
3. Please explain the differences between the two types of Belief in God's Unity, in detail.
4. According to the text, what does Allah's seal on all creatures demonstrate in regards to Allah?
5. What do you understand from the words of the featured poem?
6. Write your own poem about your belief in God's Unity. Be creative!

ESSAY

We all see the signs of Allah around us each day. We have focused a lot on this topic during this chapter. Take a moment to reflect on new ways you see the signs or reflections of Allah in your life now, that you did not notice before. Make a list of them and write how your views have changed. Where do you see the signs and reflections of Allah now that you did not before reading this chapter? Your essay must be a minimum of three paragraphs.

LESSON VOCABULARY

Superstition	Deities	deviation
Degenerate	Begets	* obscurities
Debase	Phenomenon	* innumerable
Anthropomorphism	Superficially	* ephemerality

Lesson 6
Shirk & Implications of Tawhid

SHIRK IS TO ASSIGN PARTNERS TO ALLAH

DISCUSS

What are the differences between Shirk Jali and Shirk Khafi?

There are apparent (obvious), *Shirk Jali*, and concealed (secret) *Shirk Khafi* types of *shirk*. The apparent kind is the one we all know. Believing in three gods, accepting idols as intercessors before Allah, etc. are included in this group.

Concealed shirk is separated into two types. The first is to show hypocrisy and act for the sake of people, forgetting the sake of Allah or pay too much attention to the desires of soul. The second is to give more importance to the created as opposed to the Creator.

Islam is a religion of Oneness (*Tawhid*). The Owner and Possessor of this world is unique. Every favor is absolutely in His blessed treasure. Islam teaches to be grateful excessively neither to sun for its light, nor to a farm for its crops, or to riches for their affluence. Each favor is coming from the Sustainer of the heavens and earth.

IMPLICATIONS OF TAWHID

Monotheists, those who maintain *tawhid*, cannot be narrow-minded. Their belief in One God, Creator of the heavens and the earth, Master of the east and the west, and Sustainer of the universe, leads them to view everything as belonging to the same Lord, to Whom they belong as well. Their sympathy, love, and service are not confined to any particular race, color, or group, and they come to understand the Prophetic saying

"O servants of God, be brothers/sisters as God orders you!"

"O servants of God, be brothers/sisters as God orders you!"

Belief in One God produces the highest degree of self-respect and self-esteem in people. Monotheists know that only God has true power, can benefit or harm them, fulfill their needs, cause them to die, or wield authority and influence. This knowledge makes them indifferent to all powers other than those of God. They never bow in homage to any of God's creatures. They are virtuous and altruistic, for their purpose is to gain God's approval by working for His good pleasure.

Key vocabulary

- **Hypocrisy:** the behavior of people who do things that they tell other people not to do
- **Affluence:** having a large amount of money and owning many expensive things
- **Homage:** respect or honor
- **Altruistic:** feelings and behavior that show a desire to help other people and a lack of selfishness

IMAGINE

Imagine a time in your life when you were faced with a really difficult problem. How did Allah and your belief in Allah help you through your problem? Wouldn't life be much harder to handle without the mercy we receive from Allah?

They know that whatever they possess is given by God, and that God can take away as easily as He gives.

"They know that whatever they possess is given by God, and that God can take away as easily as He gives."

Given this belief, they understand that they can succeed only through living right and just actions.

Believing in One God creates an attitude of peace and contentment, purges the mind of jealousy, envy and greed, and prevents one from resorting to unfair means to achieve success. Monotheists understand that God holds their wealth; that He bestows honor, power, reputation, and authority as He wills and subjects them to His Will.

They know that success and failure depend upon His Grace, for no power can block His Will to give or not to give. They also know that they must strive to deserve His Grace. But many of those who do not believe in God consider success and failure to be the result of their own efforts or by the help of earthly powers, and do not take God's Grace and Will into consideration. This leaves them unable to achieve success.

THINK

Through Islam, humankind finally realized their dignity. What sense of pride does being a Muslim give you? How does Islam help you realize your dignity?

Key vocabulary

- **Dignity:** a way of appearing or behaving that suggests seriousness and self-control

WHAT DID WE LEARN?

LESSON SUMMARY:

There are two kinds of *Shirk*

1. *Shirk Jali*

2. *Shirk Khafi*

Monotheists, those who maintain *tawhid*, cannot be narrow-minded

- Whatever we possess is given by God, and that God can take away as easily as He gives.
- Believing in One God creates an attitude of peace and contentment
- Islam made humankind finally find their dignity
- Believing in One God creates an attitude of peace and contentment, purges the mind of jealousy, envy and greed, and prevents one from resorting to unfair means to achieve success

LESSON REVIEW: INDIVIDUAL ASSESSMENT

1. What is *Shirk Jali*? Explain in a complete sentence.
2. What is *Shirk Khafi*? Explain in a complete sentence.
3. What does the text mean when it says, those who believe in One God (monotheists) cannot be narrow-minded? Describe in your own words.
4. According to the text, how can we remove the feelings of jealousy, envy and greed from ourselves?

ESSAY

We learned today that belief in Islam created the highest form of self-esteem and self-respect. Write a 3-paragraph essay, using the narrative style of writing, telling about your own self-esteem and self-respect and how Islam and your belief in One God (monotheism) makes you a happier person.

LESSON VOCABULARY

Hypocrisy
Affluence
Implications
Homage
Altruistic
Dignity

CHAPTER REVIEW

ANSWER THE FOLLOWING QUESTIONS IN DETAIL:

1. What is the literal meaning of *Tawhid*?
2. What was Prophet Muhammad's response when asked if he had seen God?
3. What is the difference in meaning between god, God, and Allah?
4. What are the "links" between Allah and the created, or the "reflectors" with which to have knowledge of Allah?
5. What are the two degrees of belief in God's Unity?
6. Define: *Shirk*

ESSAY

Now that the chapter on Belief in God is complete, you should have a new understanding of what it means to believe in a monotheistic religion. *Tawhid*, avoidance of *Shirk*, and believing in God's Unity are important aspects of our faith. Write an essay summarizing your understanding of this chapter. The essay should be at least four paragraphs using details from the text, as well as examples from your life.

BELIEF IN ANGELS

CHAPTER

3

The Messenger believes in what has been revealed to him from his Lord, and so do the believers. All believe in Allah, His Angels and His Messengers.
(Qur'an 2:285)

Lesson 1
Introduction

Belief in angels is the second article of the six essential principles of faith.

اٰمَنَ الرَّسُولُ بِمَٓا اُنْزِلَ اِلَيْهِ مِنْ رَبِّه۪ وَالْمُؤْمِنُونَۜ كُلٌّ اٰمَنَ بِاللّٰهِ وَمَلٰٓئِكَتِه۪ وَكُتُبِه۪ وَرُسُلِه۪

The Messenger believes in what has been sent down to him from his Lord, and so do the believers; each one believes in God, and His angels, and His books, and His Messengers: "We make no distinction between any of His Messengers (in believing in them)..." (2:285)

THINK

Did you know? Fundamental needs for human beings such as sustenance do not apply to angels. They are nourished through the act of worship and serving Allah.

Belief in angels is the second of the six articles of faith. In proximity, angels are the closest beings to the Almighty Allah. They are created out of Nur. Angels do not have desires of their own, and neither do they eat or drink. Angels are the honored servants of Allah and they never disobey His exalted commands. They are constantly in the service of their eternal Master.

Some angels worship Allah continuously as they stand in upright position, bowing position or prostration position. Some angels have ongoing individual duties, whereas some perform collective duties. There are angels called up on only in certain circumstances and there are those whose duties are limited to one single mission. Angels do not have a gender. They do not have children.

However, angels do possess intelligence and the power of reasoning. This is quite evident in many Qur'anic verses:

Angels do not have a gender. They do not have children.

وَاِذْ قَالَ رَبُّكَ لِلْمَلٰٓئِكَةِ اِنّ۪ي جَاعِلٌ فِي الْاَرْضِ خَل۪يفَةًۜ قَالُٓوا اَتَجْعَلُ ف۪يهَا مَنْ يُفْسِدُ ف۪يهَا

وَيَسْفِكُ الدِّمَٓاءَۚ وَنَحْنُ نُسَبِّحُ بِحَمْدِكَ وَنُقَدِّسُ لَكَۜ قَالَ اِنّ۪ٓي اَعْلَمُ مَا لَا تَعْلَمُونَ ﴿٣٠﴾

Key vocabulary

- **Proximity:** the state of being near
- **Nur:** pure light
- **Prostration:** to cast (oneself) face down on the ground in humility, submission, or adoration.

... When your Lord said to the angels: "I am setting on the earth a vicegerent." The angels asked: "Will you set therein one who will cause disorder and corruption on it and shed blood, while we glorify You with Your praise (proclaiming that You are absolutely above having any defect and that all praise belongs to You exclusively), and declare that You alone are All-Holy and to be worshipped as Allah and Lord?" He said: "Surely I know what you do not know. (2:30)

It is clear from the verse above that angels were wondering about the purpose behind the creation of human beings, hence, they asked their Lord why He would create a being that would cause mischief and shed blood on earth.

DISCUSS

We know now that the angels wondered about our purpose for being created. What is the purpose of our creation? (Hint: This should be a review from the previous chapters)

Following the creation of Adam, peace be upon him, Allah taught him the names of all things. Then He asked His angels to name these things, yet they could not. When Adam, peace be upon him, spoke and told them all the Names, Allah said:

قَالَ يَا اٰدَمُ اَنْبِئْهُمْ بِاَسْمَائِهِمْۚ فَلَمَّا اَنْبَاَهُمْ بِاَسْمَائِهِمْۙ قَالَ اَلَمْ اَقُلْ لَكُمْ اِنّ۪ٓي اَعْلَمُ غَيْبَ السَّمٰوَاتِ
وَالْاَرْضِ وَاَعْلَمُ مَا تُبْدُونَ وَمَا كُنْتُمْ تَكْتُمُونَ ﴿٣٣﴾

Did I not tell you that I know the unseen of the heavens and the earth, and I know all that you reveal and all that you have been concealing? (2:33)

Following the creation of Adam, peace be upon him, Allah taught him the names of all things.

By the commandment of Allah, the angels then bowed and prostrated before Adam, peace be upon him. The only being who refused to bow down was Iblis (Satan). This incident also teaches us that although Allah has given angels the ability to question and comprehend, they do not possess the free will to disobey. Satan, on the other hand, was not an angel. He was a Jinn created out of smokeless fire, therefore, he possessed free will.

Key vocabulary

- **Commandment:** an important rule given by God that tells people how to behave

CAN ANGELS BE SEEN WITH THE NAKED EYE?

The fact that a thing is not seen does not indicate its nonexistence.

Since angels are spiritual beings, ordinary human beings cannot see them in their natural form, unless they take on a visible form. Prophets, on the other hand, are bestowed with a special gift that allows them to observe angels in their natural form. Prophets also possess the special Allah-given ability to have conversations with angels. The fact that a thing is not seen does not indicate its nonexistence

According to a narration by Aisha, may Allah be pleased with her, recorded in Bukhari, the noble Messenger has seen Jibril (Gabriel) twice in his natural form. Furthermore, he has seen the Angel many times in the appearance of a handsome young man who resembled a Companion named Dihya. This is an indication that with the permission of Allah, angels can take a visible physical form. This is also evident in some Qur'anic verses such as the one that mentions the story of Prophet Ibrahim, peace be upon him. He was given the glad tidings of a son by three angels sent by Allah. These angels also travelled to Prophet Lot, peace be upon him, to assist him. There is also a Hadith recorded in Muslim which states that a man came to the noble Prophet and asked questions about Iman (faith) and Ihsan (perfect goodness). This occurred in front of a public audience and the man who visited the Prophet was no other than Jibril (Gabriel) himself, in human form.

IMAGINE

We now learned that there are two angels who record our every deed and action, as assigned by Allah. Reflect on how this knowledge will help you make good choices in regards to behavior, prayers, and how you treat others?

Although, we as ordinary people may never actually see an angel in our lifetime, we constantly interact with them throughout our lives. The Noble Recorders (Kiraman Katibin) for example, are the two angels who stand by our right and left sides at all times to record our every deed and action. There are also many angels who protect and join us during our Prayers and worship.

There are also many angels who protect and join us during our Prayers and worship.

Apart from the countless number of angels who serve Allah at all times, there are four great angels that were distinguished from the rest. They are Jibril, Mikail, Israfil and Azrael. Allah gave all these great Angels unique duties.

Jibril is the most distinguished of all angels. He is entrusted with conveying the Divine revelations to the Messengers of Allah.

Mikail is the angel who is entrusted with the sustenance of all creatures.

Israfil is the angel who will blow the Trumpet (Sur) indicating the time of the Judgment Day and;

Azrael is the angel of death who is entrusted with the duty of collecting the souls of all living creatures in the universe.

Without question, angels are truly astonishing creations of Allah. Those who contemplate and reflect on the angels of Allah will no doubt strengthen their belief in the All-Powerful and Omnipotent, the Almighty Allah.

Key vocabulary

- **Sustenance:** something (such as food) that keeps someone or something alive
- **Contemplate:** to think deeply or carefully about (something)

WHAT DID WE LEARN?

LESSON SUMMARY:

- In proximity, angels are the closest beings to the Almighty Allah.
- They are created out of Nur (pure light).
- Angels do not have desires of their own, and neither do they eat or drink.
- Angels are the honored servants of Allah and they never disobey His exalted commands. They are constantly in the service of their eternal Master.
- Since angels are spiritual beings, ordinary human beings cannot see them in their natural form
- The Noble Recorders (Kiraman Katibin) for example, are the two angels who stand by our right and left sides at all times to record our every deed and action.
- Apart from the countless number of angels who serve Allah at all times, there are four great angels that were distinguished from the rest. They are Jibril, Mikail, Israfil and Azrael.

LESSON REVIEW: INDIVIDUAL ASSESSMENT

1. According to the text what are angels created out of?
2. Why can't we see angels?
3. Do angels have free will? Are the able to disobey Allah?
4. What are the names and duties of the four great angels mentioned in the text?

ESSAY

Compare and contrast your new understanding of angels with your understanding of them before the lesson. What did you already know, what did you learn, and what else do you want to know?

LESSON VOCABULARY

Proximity	Prostration	Commandment
Nur	Sustenance	Contemplate

Lesson 2
Angels, Their Functions & The Invisible Realm of Existence

They make us perceive the inspirational beauty around us by turning our attention to the works of God.

Angels are created from light (*nur*). The Arabic word for angel is malak. According to its root form, malak means messenger, deputy, envoy, superintendent, and a powerful being. The root meaning also implies descent from a high place.

Angels build relations between the macrocosmic world and the material one, convey God's commands of creation and operation of the universe, direct the acts and lives of beings (with God's permission), and represent their worship in their own realms. Having refined or subtle bodies of light, angels move very rapidly and can be found in all realms of existence. They make us perceive the inspirational beauty around us by turning our attention to the works of God.

Some animals, like honeybees, act according to Divine inspiration. Science asserts that all animals are directed by impulses, but cannot explain what an impulse is and how it occurs. Scientists are trying to discover how migrating birds find their way, how young eels hatched in the waters of Europe find their way to their ancestral waters in the Pacific. Even if such information is encoded in their DNA, this information is assuredly from God, Who knows everything, controls the universe, and assigns angels to direct these creatures' lives.

There are different classes of angels. One class is engaged in constant worship; another worships by working. These working angels have functions that resemble human occupations, like shepherds or farmers. An appointed angel oversees all animal species by the command of the All-Majestic Creator.

Lower ranking angels worship and glorify Almighty God by supervising particular plant species. The Archangel Michael, for instance, oversees the angels of the highest rank.

Angels are never promoted for what they do, for each has a fixed, determined rank and receives a particular pleasure from the work itself as well as a radiance from worship. Their reward is found in their service. Just as we are nourished by and derive pleasure from air and water, light and food, angels are nourished by and receive pleasure from the lights of remembrance and glorification, worship and knowledge, and love of God. Since they are created of light, light sustains them. Fragrant scents are enjoyable nourishment for them as they love fragrant smell. Indeed, pure spirits take pleasure in sweet scents.

DISCUSS

Angels perform services through their partial willpower and a kind of worship and adoration. They do not originate or create their acts, for everything bears a stamp particular to the Creator of all things. Only God creates. How does this make angels different from human beings?

Key vocabulary

- **Descent:** the act or process of going from a higher to a lower place or level
- **Macrocosmic:** a large system (such as the entire universe) that contains many smaller systems
- **Archangel:** an angel of the highest rank

Angels do not sin or disobey

Angels do not sin or disobey. They have fixed ranks, and so are neither promoted nor abased. They have no experience with negative qualities as envy, rancor, enmity, and all the lusts and animal appetites found in human beings and jinn. They have no gender, do not eat or drink, and do not feel hunger, thirst, or tiredness. Although they receive no wages for their worship, they derive special pleasure from carrying out God's commands, delight in being near to Him, and receive spiritual pleasure from their worship. Praise, worship, recitation of God's Names, and glorification of Him are their nourishment, as are light and sweet fragrances.

On the other hand, we struggle with our evil-commanding soul and Satan. While angels invite us to true guidance, inspire us with belief, good conduct and virtue, and call us to resist the temptations of Satan and our evil-commanding selves, Satan and our evil-commanding selves try to seduce us. A person's life is the history of his or her continuous struggle between angelic inspiration and satanic temptation. This is why we can be elevated to the highest rank or abased to the lowest rank. Also, this is why the elect of humanity, the Prophets and great saints, are higher in rank than the greatest angels, and why ordinary believers are higher than common angels. Also, although angels have more knowledge of God and His Names and Attributes than we do, we are more comprehensive mirrors of God's Names and Attributes due to our developed human senses, our ability to reflect, and our complex nature.

DISCUSS

Even though angels have more knowledge of God's Names and Attributes than we do, we are more comprehensive mirrors of God's Names and Attributes. Why do you think this is?

There are four Archangels: Jibril (Gabriel), Mikail (Michael), Azrael, Israfil. These are followed by groups of angels known as Mala'-i A'la (the Highest Council), Nadiyy-i A'la (the Highest Assembly), and Rafiq-i A'la (the Highest Company).

Specific angels have been appointed to Paradise and Hell. As we learned in our last lesson, angels who record a person's deeds are called Kiraman Katibun (the Noble Recorders), and, as stated in a hadith, 360 of them are responsible for each believer's life. They guard their charges, especially during infancy and old age, pray for them, and ask God to forgive them. Other angels help believers during times of war and attend assemblies that praise and glorify God, as well as study meetings held for God's sake and to benefit people.

Angels, particularly angels of mercy, refrain from close contact with ritually impure people. They also avoid those with bad breath (derived from eating onions or garlic or from smoking), and do not visit those who sever relations with their parents and relatives. Although God is All-Powerful and can guard everyone by Himself, He may appoint angels to guard His servants. To earn such a guardianship, believers have to do willingly that which is good and establish a close relation with God Almighty. They must have strong belief in God and all other pillars of faith, never abandon regular worship and prayer, lead a disciplined life, and refrain from forbidden things or sinful acts.

Key vocabulary

- **Abased:** to reduce or lower, as in rank.
- **Rancor:** an angry feeling of hatred or dislike
- **Sever:** to end (a relationship, connection, etc.) completely

THE INVISIBLE REALM OF EXISTENCE

Since our sensory powers are limited, it is not wise to deny the existence of realms beyond our senses. Also, what we know about existence is far less than what we do not know about existence.

There are many other worlds than those we commonly think of, such as those of plants, animals, human beings, and of the world of jinn. Our visible, material world addresses itself to our senses. From tiny particles to galaxies, this world is the realm where God Almighty gives life, fashions, renews, changes, and causes things to die. Science concerns itself with these phenomena.

Science is supported by theories and develops through trial-and-error investigations of those theories. Numerous "facts" that were once considered true are now known to be incorrect. We accept unquestionably, and with no scientific basis, the existence of many things. Since the beginning of time, most people have believed in the existence of spirits and angels, jinn and Satan. So, it seems more scientific to allow their existence in theory and then investigate it. Denying their existence is unscientific, just as a judgment or conclusion must be based on concrete proof. But no one can prove and therefore scientifically claim that invisible realms do not exist.

IMAGINE

This spirit–body relationship is similar to the relationship between electrical power and a factory run by electricity. If there is no electricity, the factory is reduced to heap of junk. Likewise, when the spirit leaves the body because of some rupture or disconnection (e.g., illness or death), we become no more than a mass of tissue and bone that decomposes in soil. This shows that our real existence and uniqueness depend on this spirit.

ARGUMENTS FOR THE EXISTENCE OF INVISIBLE BEINGS

Matter serves & depends on life, not the other way around. Science cannot explain life or how organic matter acquires life. Although matter appears to be the basis for or serves as a receiver of life, it is clearly not its originator.

This world is the arena in which God manifests His Will through natural causes. Life is the result of the direct manifestation of His Name the Ever-Living (al-Hayy).

Angels are pure spiritual beings that represent the purely good aspect in existence, while Satan and his minions represent the purely evil aspect. God is One and Infinite, without opposite. All other beings and existents have an opposite. Therefore, angels represent our good aspect while Satan represents our evil aspect. Angels invite us to our purely spiritual or "angelic" aspect, while Satan tempts toward evil. The resulting struggle, both in us and in the universe as a whole, has been ongoing since the beginning of existence.

All Divine Scriptures and all the Prophets report the existence of angels, spirit beings, jinn, and Satan. All saints and religious scholars agree on this invisible realm's existence. The Qur'an explains the meaning of angelic existence so reasonably that anyone can understand it.

Key vocabulary

- **Minion:** someone who is not powerful or important and who obeys the orders of a powerful leader or boss
- **Rupture:** a crack or break in something

THE SPIRIT COMMANDS OUR INNER FACULTIES

According to the Qur'an, God has given a particular nature to each creature: All that is in the heavens and Earth submits to Him, willingly or unwillingly, and they will be returned to Him (3:83); and Glorify the Name of your Lord, the Most High, Who has created (all things) and well proportioned (them); Who has assigned for each a particular form and a particular way to follow and ordained their destinies, and guided (them) (87:1-3).

God has two kinds of laws, one related to the creation of the universe, including each separate being, and to human (biological) life; the other established to govern human individual and social life. The former constitutes the subject matter of sciences (physics, chemistry, astronomy, biology, sociology, psychology, etc). The second kind of laws can be summed up as being Religion. The whole of creation absolutely obeys the first kind of laws as stated in the ayah above "willingly or unwillingly", while obeying the second is optional.

For example, since God orders the Earth to revolve around its own axis as well as the sun, it always does so. A seed says in the tongue of its being or primordial nature: "I will germinate underground in proper conditions and grow into a plant," and it does what it says. Water declares that it freezes at 0°C and vaporizes at 100°C, and does what it declares.

Similarly, the human conscience, as long as it remains sound, does not lie. If it is not deluded by the carnal self or harmful desires, it deeply feels the existence of God and finds peace through believing in and worshiping Him. Thus, the spirit directs or commands our conscience and other faculties. It seeks the world from which it came, and yearns for its Creator. Unless it is stunted and spoiled by sin, it will find the Creator and attain true happiness in Him.

THE SPIRIT MANIFESTS ITSELF MOSTLY ON A PERSON'S FACE

Truly, our face is a window opened by our inner world, for its features disclose our character. Psychologists assert that almost all of our movements, even coughing, reveal our character. The face's ability to reveal one's character, abilities, and personality resulted in physiognomy, the art of judging character from facial features. The spirit determines these features.

Our body's cells are renewed continuously. Every day, millions of cells die and are replaced. Biologists say that all bodily cells are renewed every 6 months. Despite this continuous renewal, the face's main features remain unchanged. We recognize individuals from their unchanging facial features and fingerprints. The cells of a finger change due to such renewal or injury and bruise, but their prints never change. Each individual's unique spirit makes these distinguishing features stable.

Key vocabulary

- **Physiognomy:** the appearance of a person's face

OUR SPIRIT MAKES US UNIQUE

Each body has one spirit that makes it alive and governs it. So, there must be a single Lord, without partner, to create and govern the universe. Otherwise, disaster and confusion is inevitable.

Our body experiences ceaseless change throughout its existence. This change is directed toward physical growth and development until a certain period, gradually becoming stronger and more perfect. When this growth stops at a certain point, decay begins. Unlike our body, we can grow continuously in learning and development, decay spiritually and intellectually, or stop and change direction while developing or decaying. Our moral, spiritual, and intellectual education does not depend on our bodily changes.

Our physical changes engender no parallel changes in our character, morality, or thinking. How can we explain this, other than by admitting that the spirit exists and is the center of thinking and feeling, choosing and deciding, learning and forming opinions and preferences, and is the cause of unique characters?

OUR SPIRIT FEELS AND BELIEVES OR DENIES

Worshipping and following His Commandments causes us to develop morally and spiritually until finally we are perfected.

All people have innumerable, complex feelings: love and hate, happiness and sadness, hope and despair, ambition and the ability to imagine, relief and boredom, and so on. We like and dislike, appreciate and disregard, experience fear and timidity as well as courage and enthusiasm. We repent, become excited, and long for various things. If we look through a dictionary, we find hundreds of words that express human feelings. Moreover, we do not all "feel" the same way. We may reflect on what is going on around us, the beauty of creation, develop ourselves through learning, compare and reason, and thus believe in the Creator of all things.

"Worshipping and following His Commandments causes us to develop morally and spiritually until finally we are perfected."

Key vocabulary

- **Inevitable:** unable to be avoided or escaped; certain; necessary.
- **Timidity:** feeling or showing a lack of courage or confidence
- **Repent:** to feel or show that you are sorry for something bad or wrong that you did and that you want to do what is right

WHAT DID WE LEARN?

LESSON SUMMARY:

- The Arabic word for angel is malak
- There are different classes of angels
- The Archangel Michael, one of the bearers of God's Throne of Sustenance, oversees the angels of the highest rank
- They have fixed ranks, and so are neither promoted nor abased
- There are four Archangels who carry God's Throne. These angels are known as Mala'-i A'la (the Highest Council), Nadiyy-i A'la (the Highest Assembly), and Rafiq-i A'la (the Highest Company).
- Angels, particularly angels of mercy, refrain from close contact with ritually impure people
- Since our sensory powers are limited, it is not wise to deny the existence of realms beyond our senses
- All Divine Scriptures and all the Prophets report the existence of angels, spirit beings, jinn, and Satan
- Truly, our face is a window opened on our inner world, for its features disclose our character

LESSON REVIEW: INDIVIDUAL ASSESSMENT

1. According to the text, what is the root form of the word malak?
2. Are angels ever promoted for what they do? Why or why not?
3. What are the names of the four Archangels who carry God's Throne?
4. What causes us to develop morally and spiritually until finally we are perfected?

ESSAY

As the text stated "unlike our body, we can grow continuously in learning and development, decay spiritually and intellectually, or stop and change direction while developing or decaying." Write a three-paragraph essay, detailing what YOU can do to make sure your spirit grows continuously, even after your body stops.

LESSON VOCABULARY

Descent	Abased	Minion	Repent
Macrocosmic	Physiognomy	Inevitable	
Archangel	Rupture	Timidity	

Lesson 3
What Can You See?

If you wish to see just how true, self-evident, and rational it is to accept the existence of great numbers of angels and spirit beings, and as the Qur'an shows, just how contrary to truth and wisdom, and what a superstition, aberration, delirium and foolishness it is not to accept them, consider the following comparison.

There were two men, one rustic and uncouth, the other civilized and intelligent, who made friends and went to a splendid city. In a distant corner of that civilized and magnificent city they came across a dirty, wretched little building, a factory. They looked and saw that the strange factory was full of miserable, impoverished men working. All around the building were beings with spirits and animate beings, but their means of livelihood and conditions of life were such that some lived only on plants, while others ate nothing but fish.

The two men watched the scene. Then they saw in the distance thousands of adorned palaces and lofty castles. Among the palaces were spacious workshops and broad squares.

Because of either the distance, or the defectiveness of the men's eyesight, or because they had hidden themselves, the inhabitants of the palaces were not visible to the two men. Moreover, the bad conditions in the factory were not to be seen in the palaces.

In consequence of this, the uncouth man, who had never before seen a city, declared: "Those palaces have no inhabitants, they are empty, there are no beings in them."

Key vocabulary

- **Aberration:** something (such as a problem or a type of behavior) that is unusual or unexpected
- **Uncouth:** behaving in a rude way
- **Impoverished:** reduced to poverty
- **Lofty:** rising to a great height

The fact that a thing is not seen does not indicate its nonexistence.

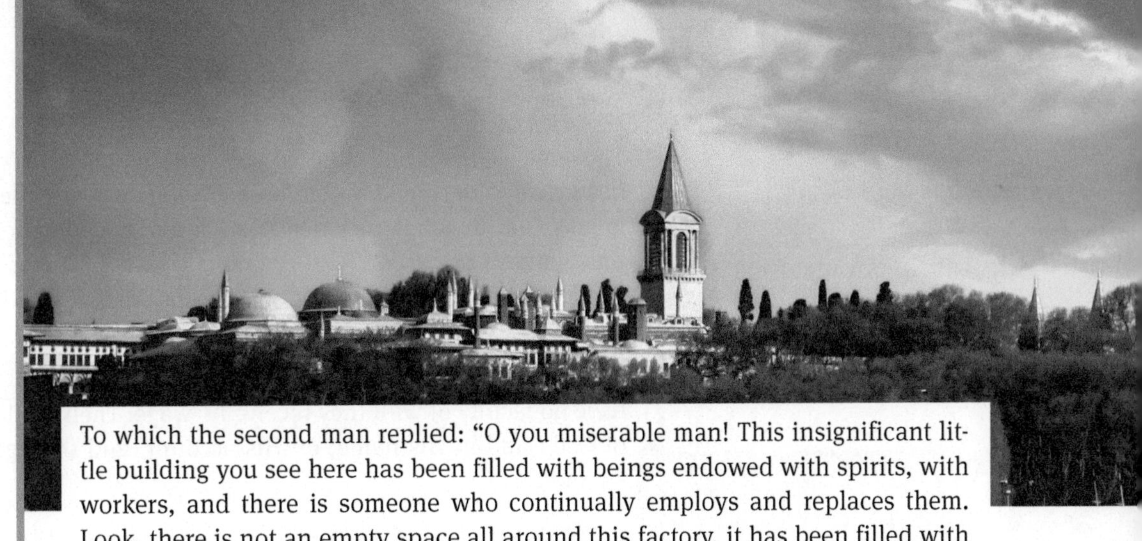

To which the second man replied: "O you miserable man! This insignificant little building you see here has been filled with beings endowed with spirits, with workers, and there is someone who continually employs and replaces them. Look, there is not an empty space all around this factory, it has been filled with animate beings and beings with spirits. Do you think it is at all possible that there would be no high-ranking and suitable inhabitants in that orderly city, in those wisely adorned palaces so full of art, which we can see in the distance? Of course they are occupied, and the different conditions of life there are appropriate for those who live there. They're not being visible to you because of the distance, or your weak eyesight, or their hiding themselves. This at no time points to their not being there." The fact that a thing is not seen does not indicate its nonexistence.

> Do you ever consider that all who are in the heavens and all who are on the earth prostrate themselves to God, and so do the sun, the moon, the stars, the mountains, the trees, and the beasts, and so do many among human beings? (22:18)

THINK

Imagine you are one of the characters described in the comparison above. Reflect and discuss with a partner on which character you relate the most to and why.

We shall point out only a single jewel from the treasure of this extensive and sublime verse: The All-Wise Qur'an states clearly that everything, from the heavens to the earth, from the stars to flies, from angels to fishes, and from planets to particles, prostrates, worships, praises and glorifies Almighty God. But their worship varies according to their capacities and the Divine Names that they manifest; it is all different.

In this realm of causality (this world), we have four types of living workers: Angels, animals, plants and inanimate creatures, and human beings.

The first category of workers is Angels - For the angels there are no endeavor and progress; they all have their fixed station and determined rank, and receive particular pleasure from the work itself and an emanation from their worship. One class of the angels is worshippers, and the worship of another sort is in work. Of the angels of the earth, the class that are workers have a kind of human occupation. If one may say so, one type is like shepherds and another like farmers.

The Second Category of workers in this palace of the universe are animals. Since animals also have an appetitive soul and faculty of will, their work is not 'purely for the sake of God'; to some extent, they take a share for their souls. Therefore, since the Glorious and Munificent Lord of All Dominion is All-Generous, He bestows a wage on them during their work so that their souls receive a share.

Key vocabulary

- **Endow:** to furnish, as with some talent, faculty, or quality
- **Endeavor:** to seriously or continually try to do (something)

The animals, which serve in the palace of the universe, conform with complete obedience to the creational commands and display perfectly in the name of Almighty God the aims included in their natures. The glorification and worship they perform by carrying out the duties related to their lives in this wonderful fashion through the power of God Almighty, are gifts and greetings they present to the Court of the All-Glorious Creator, the Bestower of Life.

The third category of workers are plants and inanimate creatures. Since they have no faculty of will, they receive no wage. Their work is 'purely for the sake of God,' and in His name, on His account, and through His will, power and strength.

IMAGINE

All the species of plants in the field of the face of the earth pray and ask of the All-Wise Creator: "O our Sustainer! Give us strength so that by raising the flag of our species in every part of the earth, we may proclaim the splendor of Your dominicality; and grant us prosperity so that we may worship You in every corner of the mosque of the earth; and bestow on us the power to spread and travel in order to exhibit through our particular tongue the embroideries of Your Most Beautiful Names and Your wonderful, antique arts." Isn't the power of a silent prayer great?

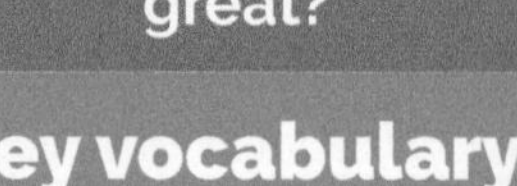

Key vocabulary

- **Obedience:** to comply with or follow the commands, restrictions, wishes, orinstructions

The All-Wise Creator answers their silent prayer and bestows on the seeds of one species tiny wings made of hair: they fly away spreading everywhere. He gives to some species beautiful flesh that is either necessary or pleasant for human beings; he causes man to serve them and plant them everywhere. On some He bestows small claws that grip onto all who touch them; moving on to other places, they raise the flag of the species and exhibit the antique art of the All-Glorious Maker. They work so that numerous tongues will glorify the All-Glorious Creator and recite His Beautiful Names. The All-Wise Creator, Who is All-Powerful and All-Knowing, has created everything beautifully and with perfect order. He has fitted them out beautifully, turned their faces towards beautiful aims, employed them in beautiful duties, caused them to utter beautiful glorifications and to worship beautifully.

The Fourth Category is human nature. Human beings, who are servants of a sort in the palace of the universe, resemble both angels and animals. They resemble angels in universality of worship, extensiveness of supervision, comprehensiveness of knowledge, and in being heralds of Divine Dominicality. However, man is more comprehensive in his worship, but since he has an appetitive soul that is disposed towards evil, contrary to the angels, he is subject to progress and decline, which is of great importance. Also, since in his work, man seeks pleasure for his soul and a share for himself, he resembles an animal. Since this is so, man receives two wages: the first is insignificant, animal, and immediate; the second, angelic, universal, and postponed.

Angels	Animals	Plants and inanimate creatures	Human beings
Created out of light No endeavor and progress Nourished by worship, love of God Representative of inanimate workers' glorification No power of disposal	Appetitive soul and faculty of will Their souls receive a share Some are dominical orators Numerous aims Employed in duties of glorification	No faculty of will, no pain Purely for sake of God Pray through their tongues of disposition for prosperity Given beautiful fleshes Seeds to populate so more can glorify God	Seeks pleasure for his soul Comprehensive in worship Progress and decline
No need for wage or rank Reward within duties Subtle pleasure	A small wage in their duties	No wage Pleasure from their duties of producing seeds and fruits	Two wages: Insignificant/animal/immediate Angelic/universal/postponed

Key vocabulary

- **Appetitive:** large desire
- **Herald:** to be a sign of (something that is beginning to happen or will happen soon)

WHAT DID WE LEARN?

LESSON SUMMARY:

- The fact that a thing is not seen does not indicate its nonexistence
- In this realm of causality (this world), we have four types of living workers:

1. Angels
2. Animals
3. Plants and inanimate creatures
4. Human beings

- Angels

1. Created out of light
2. No endeavor and progress
3. Nourished by worship, love of God
4. Representative of inanimate workers' glorification
5. No power of disposal
6. No need for wage or rank
7. Reward within duties
8. Subtle pleasure

- Animals

1. Appetitive soul and faculty of will
2. Their souls receive a share Some are dominical orators Numerous aims
3. Employed in duties of glorification
4. A small wage in their duties

- Plants

1. No faculty of will, no pain Purely for sake of God
2. Pray through their tongues of disposition for prosperity
3. Given beautiful fleshes
4. Seeds to populate so more can glorify God
5. No wage
6. Pleasure from their duties of producing seeds and fruits

- Human beings

1. Seeks pleasure for his soul
2. Comprehensive in worship
3. Progress and decline

   Two wages:
   1. Insignificant/animal/immediate
   2. Angelic/universal/postponed

LESSON REVIEW: INDIVIDUAL ASSESSMENT

1. List and describe the four categories of living workers
2. What about our appetitive soul makes us different from the angels?
3. Describe your understanding of the wage that is postponed for human beings.
4. Summarize your understanding of this lesson in one paragraph.

ESSAY

The Qur'an describes to us that all that is in the heavens and the earth prostrates to Allah. Using examples from the entire chapter, write 4-5 paragraphs on the different categories of living workers prostrate to Allah in their own ways.

LESSON VOCABULARY

Aberration	Lofty	Emanation	endowed
Uncouth	Defectiveness	obedience	endeavor
Impoverished	Appetitive	herald	

CHAPTER REVIEW

ANSWER THE FOLLOWING QUESTIONS IN DETAIL:

1. What are the names and duties of the four great angels?
2. Describe the root form of the word malak.
3. Why can't we see angels?
4. Describe the duties of Kiraman Katibin.
5. Explain why angels are or are not prompted for what they do.

ESSAY

Summarize your understanding of this chapter, but summarize in a way that you are attempting to convince a friend that you don't need to physically see something to know that it exists. Your summary should be a minimum of four paragraphs.

BELIEF IN DIVINE BOOKS & THE HOLY QUR'AN

CHAPTER 4

Lesson 1
Introduction to the Divine Books

Lesson 2
Did Prophet Muhammac Write the Qur'an?

Lesson 3
The Four Fundamental Aims of the Holy Qur'an

Lesson 4
The Qur'an & Science

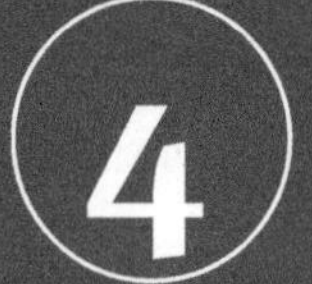

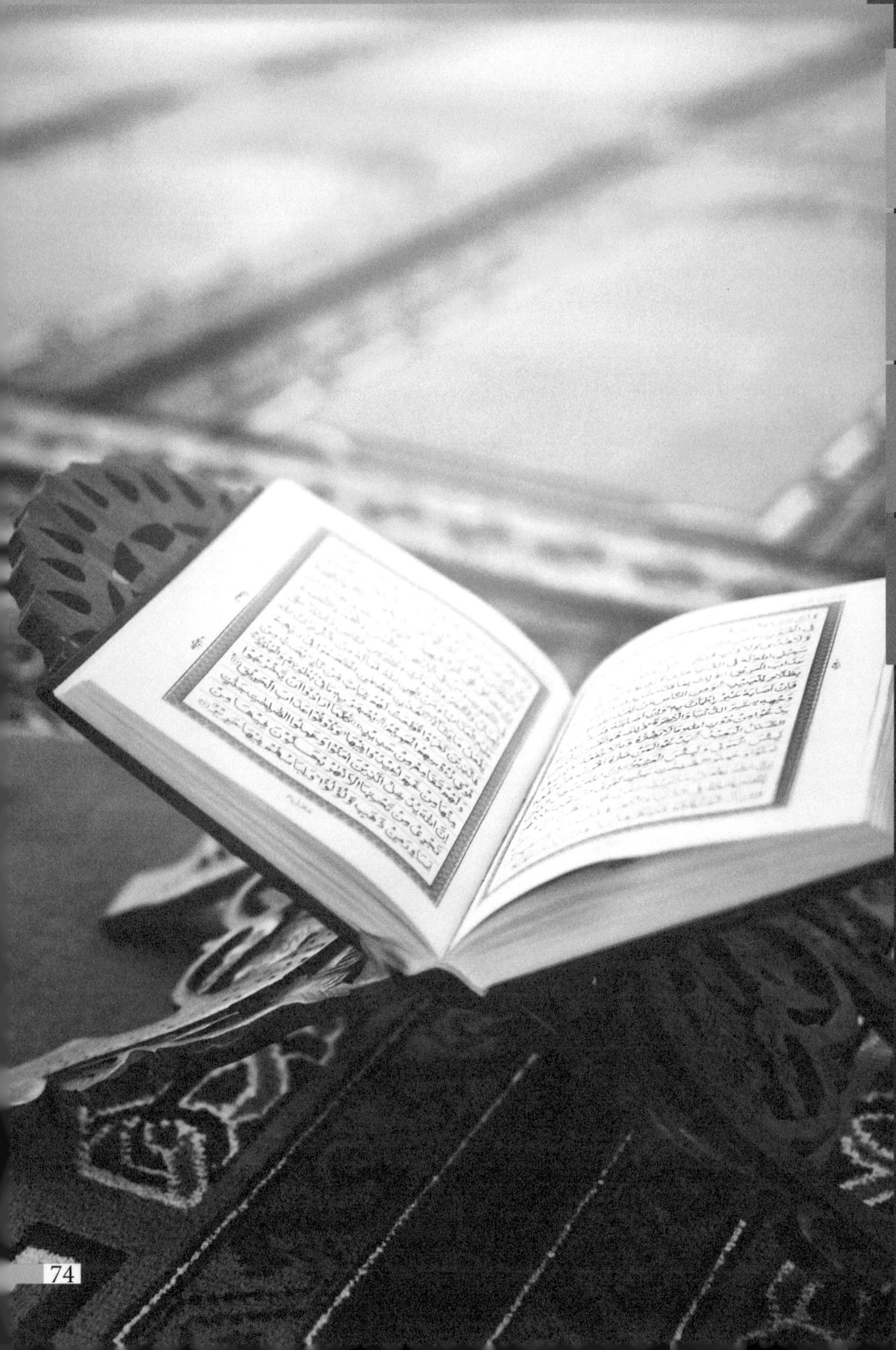

The Qur'an teaches the meaning of existence and humanity, the truth and wisdom, as well as the essence, attributes and the meanings of the Most Beautiful Names of Allah. It is a book that protects the innocent and cautions the tyrant. It is a book of spirituality and worship, as well as a book of social justice, fairness, freedom, equality and human rights.

Qur'an

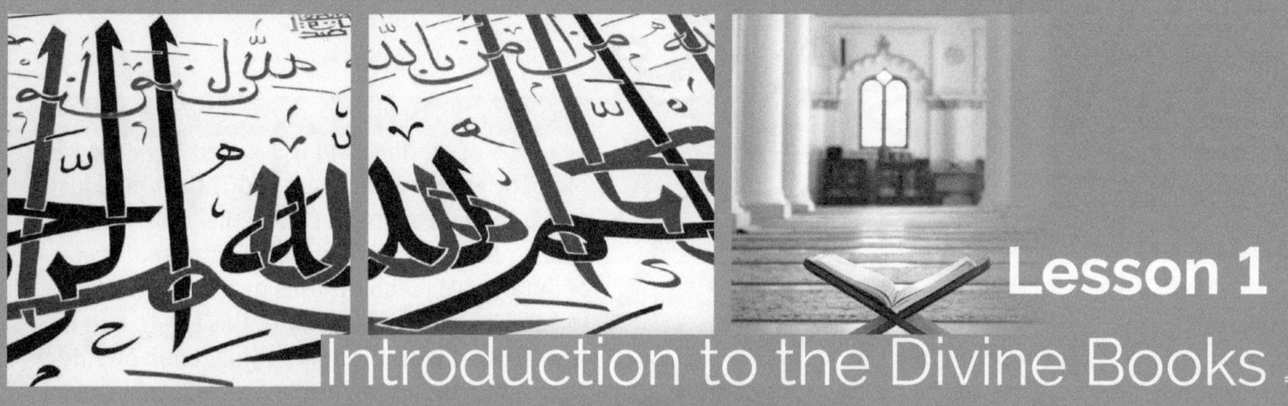

Lesson 1

Introduction to the Divine Books

Belief in Divine Books is the third article of the six principles of faith.

THINK

As the population of the human race grew drastically, they needed more comprehensive books that contained universal principles of guidance for humanity. How does this show Allah's mercy to creation?

"Belief in Divine Books is the third article of the six principles of faith."

Just as the All-Merciful has sent Prophets to guide mankind onto the path of the righteous, He has also blessed some of His Messengers with Divine revelations. The Divine revelations commenced to be revealed with the beginning of the human race. Some Prophets received Divine Books while others received pages (Suhuf). The Suhuf were short revelations sufficient for smaller earlier tribal communities. According to a transmission from a companion, Abu Dharr, may Allah be pleased with him, Adam, peace be upon him, the first Prophet and servant of Allah, received 10 pages; Shite, peace be upon him, received 50 pages; Enoch (Idris), peace be upon him, received 30 pages and Abraham, peace be upon him, received 10 pages. Unfortunately, today, we do not have any copies of these Divine pages in our archives.

As the population of the human race grew drastically, they needed more comprehensive books which contained universal principles of guidance for humanity.

The first of these Divine Books is the Torah, which was revealed to Moses, peace be upon him. It contained a set of Divine laws and principles. No Muslim can deny the original form of the Torah because the Holy Qur'an informs believers that it was brought down as a book that contained Nur (Divine light) and guidance to righteousness. Over the many years, the Torah has lost its originality and could not be preserved as it was revealed.

The second of the holy books was revealed to Dawud (David), peace be upon him. It is called Zabur which means 'The written thing'. In Christian literature, it is called the 'Psalms of David'.

In the fifty-fifth verse of Surah al-Isra, the Almighty states:

وَلَقَدْ فَضَّلْنَا بَعْضَ النَّبِيِّنَ عَلٰى بَعْضٍ وَاٰتَيْنَا دَاوُدَ زَبُوراً ﴿٥٥﴾

Indeed, we have ranked some Prophets above others.
We have bestowed the Zabur upon Dawud.

Key vocabulary

- **Commence:** to begin
- **Suhuf:** pages revealed to some Prophets

The third of the holy books was revealed to Jesus, peace be upon him, and it is called Injil (the Bible). The word Injil means 'Glad Tidings' and just as Torah and Psalms of David, the Bible was too sent to the sons of Israel. The forty-sixth verse of Surah al-Ma'idah informs us that Isa was sent to confirm the authenticity of the Torah, and he was blessed with the Injil, a holy book of guidance and admonition to those who shield themselves from evil.

According to Islamic sources, none of the original contents of the above books were completely preserved. Therefore, it is suggested to Muslims neither to refute nor to confirm the current contents of these books. Muslims accept the people who follow them as "the People of the Book (Ahl al-Kitab)."

"The Holy Qur'an was revealed through a period of twenty-three years."

It has been fourteen centuries since its revelation and the Holy Qur'an has been preserved just as it was revealed to the Prophet. According to Arabic lexicon, the definition of the word Qur'an is, 'to read, to compose or to collect'. The Qur'an is the word of Allah revealed to His Messenger through Angel Gabriel (Jibril) in the form of Wahy (Divine revelation). The Holy Qur'an is also given the title of Kitab Allah (Kitabullah), which means the book of Allah. Even the recitation of the Holy Qur'an is considered a form of worship. Moreover, its verses are also recited during the Prescribed Prayers.

"The Holy Qur'an was revealed through a period of twenty-three years."

"The Holy Qur'an is protected by Allah himself and this is clearly stated in the Qur'an."

It is a book that cannot be altered; even a modification made on a single letter will be noticed immediately by thousands of Islamic scholars and hafiz (people who memorize the entire Qur'an) all over the world.

The Holy Qur'an has descended from the Highest of the most High as a collection of Divine Laws containing the most perfect messages. It is the greatest honor bestowed upon humanity. The Qur'an addresses the mind, spirit, heart and the physical being of humans. As it enters the heart, it illuminates the soul, nourishes the mind and disciplines the physical body.

Key vocabulary

- **Wahy:** Divine revelation
- **Hafiz:** a person who memorized the Holy Qur'an
- **Lexicon:** the vocabulary of a particular language, field, social class, person,etc.

"The Holy Qur'an is protected by Allah himself and this is clearly stated in the Qur'an."

IMAGINE

imagine yourself in the age of ignorance and the desert of savagery where everything was enveloped in veils of lifelessness and nature amid the darkness of ignorance and heedlessness. Then suddenly you hear verses from the Qur'an like: Whatever is in the heavens and earth declares the praises and glory of God, the Sovereign, the Most Holy One, the Mighty, the Wise (62:1) See how those dead or sleeping creatures of the world spring to life at the sound of declares the praises and glory in the minds of those listening, how they awake, spring up, and mention God's Names!

The Qur'an teaches the meaning of existence and humanity, the truth and wisdom, as well as the essence, attributes and the meanings of the Most Beautiful Names of Allah. It is a book that protects the innocent and cautions the tyrant. It is a book of spirituality and worship, as well as a book of social justice, fairness, freedom, equality and human rights.

The Qur'an teaches humanity the secrets of worldly and eternal contentment. It shows the path to happiness and builds a bridge to the realm of eternity. It shows believers how to rise to the highest rank possible for humanity. The Qur'an facilitates a direct conversation with the Almighty Allah, the Creator and the Sustainer of the worlds.

The salvation of humanity is in the Qur'an. It is a book that brings meaning to the universe as it establishes a connection between the physical existence and its Designer. Its literature is unlike any other book or written literature. It was revealed to a person who did not know how to write or read. The scripture in the Holy Qur'an are quite unique. The Qur'an brings solutions to personal, spiritual, social and even scientific issues. Fourteen hundred years after its revelation, scholars and modern academics continue to discover new signs, information and truths in the Holy Qur'an. The Holy Qur'an was the greatest miracle of the Prophet. It is the ultimate miracle bestowed upon humanity and it will continue to guide humanity until the Day of Judgment.

The matchless beauty of the Holy Qur'an is explained by Fethullah Gülen, a contemporary Islamic Scholar, in his book Pearls of Wisdom:

> "In accordance with humanity's worth and value, and considering the human heart, spirit, mind, and physical being, the Qur'an descended from the Highest of the High. Containing the most perfect messages, it is a collection of Divine Laws.
>
> "Followed today by more than one billion people, the Qur'an is a unique book that, with its eternal and unchanging Divine principles, guides everyone to the shortest and most illuminated road to happiness.
>
> "The Qur'an has been a source of light for the most magnificent and enlightened communities that have ruled the world, those that have produced thousands of scholars, philosophers and thinkers. In this sense, no other rule is equal to its rule.
>
> "Since the day it was revealed, the Qur'an has encountered many objections and criticisms. However, the Qur'an has always emerged unscathed and so continues to reflect its victory. The Qur'an crystallizes in the heart, illumines the spirit, and exhibits truths from beginning to end. Only believers who can sense all the beauty of the universe in a single flower and see rainstorms in a drop of water can know and understand its real countenance.

Key vocabulary

- **Salvation:** something that saves someone or something from danger or a difficult situation
- **Tyrant:** any person in a position of authority who exercises power oppressively or despotically
- **Unschathed:** not hurt, harmed, or damaged

DISCUSS

The most orderly life for humanity is that given by the Qur'an. In fact, some of the beautiful things that are today universally commended and applauded are the exact things encouraged by the Qur'an centuries ago. So, whose fault is it if Muslims are in a miserable situation today?

"The Qur'an is a unique book commanding true justice, real freedom, balanced equality, goodness, honor, virtue, and compassion for all creation. It is also the matchless book forbidding oppression, polytheism, injustice, ignorance, bribery, interest, lying, and bearing false witness.

"The Qur'an is the only book that, protecting the orphan, the poor and the innocent, puts the king and the slave, the commander and the private, the plaintiff and the defendant in the same chair and then judges them.

"If only those who criticize the Qur'an and the things it brought could produce something to guarantee the order, harmony, peace and safety of human life even in a short, temporary period...

"The Qur'an enables people to rise to the highest level, namely the station of being addressed by Allah. Those who are conscious of being in this position hear their Lord speak to them through the Qur'an. If they take an oath that they speak with their Lord, they will not be among those who swear falsely.

"Those who have prevented Muslims from understanding the Qur'an and perceiving it in depth have thus removed them from Islam's spirit and essence.

"In the near future, and under humanity's gazes of commendation and amazement, the streams of knowledge, technique, and art flowing toward the Qur'anic Ocean will fall into their essential source and unite with it. At that time, scholars, researchers, and artists will find themselves in that same ocean.

It should not be too hard to see the future as the Age of the Qur'an, for it is the word of One Who sees the past, present, and future at the same moment."

Key vocabulary

- **Plaintiff:** a person who sues or accuses another person of a crime in a court of law (opposed to defendant)
- **Commendation:** the act of praising or approving of someone or something

WHAT DID WE LEARN?

LESSON SUMMARY:

- Belief in Divine Books is the third article of the six principles of faith.
- The Divine revelations commenced to be revealed with the beginning of the human race.
- Some Prophets received Divine Books while others received pages (Suhuf).
- According to Islamic sources, none of the original contents of the above books were completely preserved. Muslims accept the people who follow them as "the People of the Book (ahl al-kitab)."
- The Holy Qur'an was revealed through a period of twenty-three years.
- It has been fourteen centuries since its revelation and the Holy Qur'an has been preserved just as it was revealed to the Prophet

LESSON REVIEW: INDIVIDUAL ASSESSMENT

1. Over how many years was the Holy Qur'an revealed?
2. Which books or pages (Suhuf) were revealed to which prophets? Writing this in a chart may help with ease of view.
3. List the types of wordly problems can be solved by the Qur'an. Find as many as you can from the text. (Hint: they are scattered throughout the text).
4. According to the text, what was the greatest miracle of Prophet Muhammad, peace be upon him?

ESSAY

Saying that "faith is a matter of conscience" means "I affirm, or I have faith in Allah, His Prophets, and the Qur'an" with my tongue and my conscience. How would you explain this to a friend in your own words? Explain what it means to affirm faith in Allah, His Prophets, and the Qur'an in your life through both the words you speak and the way you feel inside. Support your thoughts with details from the text.

LESSON VOCABULARY

- Commenced
- Suhuf
- Wahiy
- Hafiz
- Salvation
- Commendation
- Lexicon
- Tyrant
- Unscathed
- Plaintiff

Lesson 2
Did Prophet Muhammad Write the Qur'an?

Claiming that a person wrote the Qur'an only reflects the failure to understand that all individuals are indebted to God, Who has given us everything. We do not create ourselves, for our lives are given to us, as are our abilities to contemplate, comprehend, and feel compassion. We are given this extraordinarily subtle, varied, and renewable world to exercise these abilities. In addition, the Qur'an is a gift of mercy, for there is no way it could have had a human author.

The first people to make this accusation were the Prophet's own opponents, as we read in the Qur'an: *When Our Revelations, clear as evidence and in meaning are recited (and conveyed) to them, those who disbelieve say of the truth when it reaches them: "This is clearly nothing but sorcery." Or do they say, "He (The Messenger) has fabricated it (the Qur'an)?"* (46:7-8) Their claim that the Qur'an is sorcery is, in fact, an admission that it is not part of ordinary human speech and is something extraordinary. They were desperate to protect their interests against the rising tide of Islam and hoped to spread doubt about the Qur'an's Divine authorship so that Muslims would start doubting its authority as well.

The Qur'an has not been altered, edited, or tampered with since it was revealed.

The Qur'an is unique among Scriptures in two respects, which even its detractors accept. First, the Qur'an exists in Arabic, its original language and one that is still widely spoken today. Second, its text is entirely reliable.

Key vocabulary

- **Detractors:** a person who criticizes something or someone

"The Qur'an has not been altered, edited, or tampered with since it was revealed."

In contrast, Christianity's Gospels have not survived in their original language. In addition, their texts have been shown to be the work of many people over generations, edited and re-edited, altered and interpolated, to promote different interpretations. They have lost their authority as Scriptures, and serve primarily as a national or cultural mythology for groups whose remote ancestors created their particular versions. This is, more or less, the Western scholarly consensus on the status of these once-Divine Books.

Muslims also have a record of the Prophet's teaching in the Sunnah, his implementation of Islam in daily life. Many, but certainly not all, of the Prophet's actions and exact words are preserved in hadith literature. These two sources could not be more dissimilar in quality of expression or content. All Arabs who heard the Prophet speak, regardless of religious affiliation, found his words to be concise, forceful, and persuasive, but nevertheless like their own normal usage. When they heard the Qur'an, however, they were overwhelmed by feelings of rapture, ecstasy, and awe.

In the hadith there is a presence of a man addressing other men, women, and children. A man pondering weighty questions who, when he speaks, does so with an appropriate gravity and in profound awe of the Divine Will. The Qur'an, on the other hand, is perceived immediately as imperative and sublime, having a transcendent, compelling majesty of style and content. It defies sense and reason to suppose that Qur'an and hadith have the same origin.

The Qur'an is absolutely different from any human product in its perspective and viewpoint. Occasionally in a few scattered phrases or passages of other Scriptures, readers or listeners may feel that they are in the presence of the Divine Message addressed to humanity. In the Qur'an, every syllable carries this impression of sublime intensity belonging to a message from One who is All-Knowing and All-Merciful.

Furthermore, the Qur'an cannot be contemplated at a distance, or discussed and debated in the abstract. The Qur'an requires us to understand, act, and amend our lifestyles. It also enables us to do so, for it can touch us in the very depths of our being. It addresses us in our full reality as spiritually and physically competent beings, as creatures of the All-Merciful. The Qur'an also is directed to everyone, regardless of age, gender, race, location, or time. This transcendence and fullness can be felt in every matter that the Qur'an mentions specifically. The Qur'an challenges its detractors to compose a chapter that can equal it. No one has successfully met this challenge. Let's analyze why this is the case.

Some examples of possible answers: Such an achievement is impossible, for only God can assume the Qur'an's all-transcendent and all-compassionate perspective. Our thoughts and aspirations are affected and conditioned by surrounding circumstances.

THINK

The Qur'an challenges its detractors to compose a chapter that can equal it. No one has successfully met this challenge. Analyze why this is the case.

Key vocabulary

- **Interpolated:** to put (something) between other things or parts
- **Rapture:** a state or feeling of great happiness, pleasure, or love
- **Consensus:** a general agreement about something; an idea or opinion that is shared by all the people in a group
- **Defy:** to go against (something); to make (something) very difficult or impossible
- **Transcendence:** far better or greater than what is usual

"Surely, if humankind and the jinn were to come together to produce the like of this Qur'an, they would never be able to produce the like of it, though they backed one another up with help and support." (17:88)

DISCUSS

If someone wrote the Qur'an, how could it be literally true on matters that were completely unknown at the time of its revelation?

Do those who disbelieve ever consider the heavens and the earth were at first one piece, and then We parted them as separate entities? (21:30)

That is why, sooner or later, all human works fail or fade away into obsolescence, and why they are too general to have any real influence or too specific to do much good beyond the specific area they address. Whatever we produce is of limited value for just these reasons. As stated in the Qur'an: Say:

"Surely, if humankind and the jinn were to come together to produce the like of this Qur'an, they would never be able to produce the like of it, though they backed one another up with help and support." (17:88)

The Qur'an is the Word of the All-Knowing and All-Seeing, who knows everything about His creation. It therefore comprehends and tests its audiences as it teaches. For believers, the consciousness of being before the Divine Message can make their skin shiver, in the words of the Qur'an, so suddenly and fully does the atmosphere around and within them change.

The Qur'an's substance also is a compelling argument for its Divine authorship. Those who allege that someone wrote it provide no proof to support their assertion. Other Scriptures have been altered to suit their own understanding, with the result that the progress of science has rendered their understanding making their now-corrupted Scriptures largely irrelevant and obsolete. However, the Qur'an has not been subject to such mistreatment. If someone wrote the Qur'an, how could it be literally true on matters that were completely unknown at the time of its revelation?

Do those who disbelieve ever consider the heavens and the earth were at first one piece, and then We parted them as separate entities? (21:30)

Only in the last few years have we been able to contemplate this verse about the first moment of the universe in its literal meaning.

Yet some people still allege that the Prophet wrote the Qur'an. While asserting that they are on the side of sense and reason, they allege what is humanly impossible.

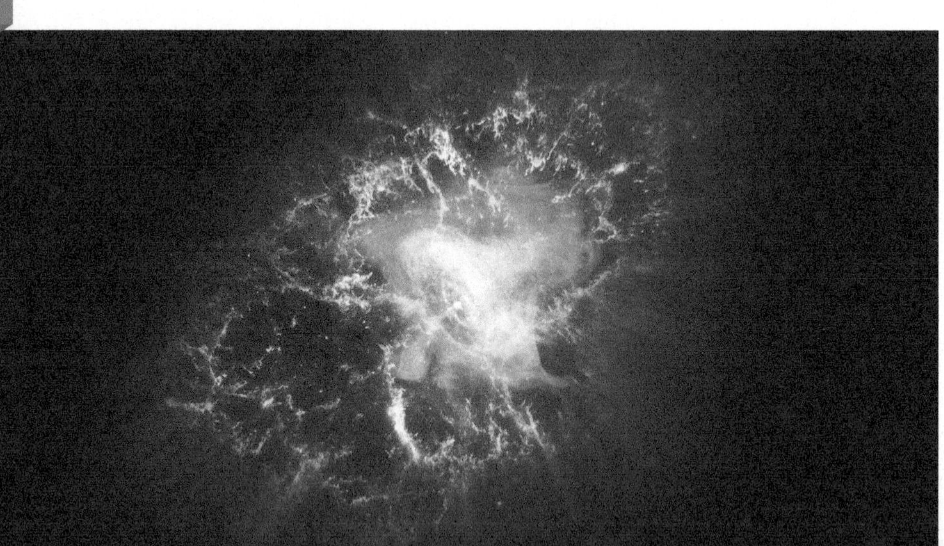

Key vocabulary

- **Asserting:** to state (something) in a strong and definite way
- **Obsolescence:** the condition of no longer being used or useful
- **Allege:** to state without definite proof that someone has done something wrong or illegal

DISCUSS

How could a seventh-century man know things that only recently have been accepted as scientifically established truths? How is that humanly possible?

How could a seventh-century man know things that only recently have been accepted as scientifically established truths? How is it on the side of reason and sense to claim such a thing? How did the Prophet discover, with an anatomical and biological accuracy only recently confirmed, that milk is produced in mammal tissues? How did he discover how rain clouds and hailstones form, or determine a wind's fertilizing quality, or explain how landmasses shift and continents form and re-form? With what giant telescope did he learn of the universe's ongoing physical expansion? By what equivalent of X-ray vision was he able to describe in such great detail the different stages of an embryo's development within the uterus?

Another proof of the Qur'an's Divine origin is that what it predicts eventually comes true. For example:

- The Companions considered the Treaty of Hudaybiya a defeat; the Revelation stated that they would enter the Sacred Mosque in full security and that Islam would prevail over all other religions (48:27-28).

- It also promised that the Romans (Byzantines) would vanquish the Persians several years after their defeat in 615, and that the Muslims would defeat both of these current superpowers (30:2-5), at a time when there were scarcely 40 believers, all of whom were being persecuted by the Meccan chiefs.

Although the Prophet was the ideal man, he was reminded several times in the Qur'an that he could have taken a better choice than the one he acted upon. For example:

- When he exempted certain hypocrites from warfare, he was criticized: *God forgive you! Why did you let them stay behind before it became clear which of them were truthful and which were liars?* (9:43).

- After the Battle of Badr, he was rebuked: *You (the believers) merely seek the gains of the world whereas God desires (for you the good) of the Hereafter. God is All-Mighty, All-Wise. Had there not been a previous decree from God, a stern punishment would have afflicted you for what you have taken...*(8:67-68).

- Once he said he would do something the next day and did not say "if God wills." He was warned: *Nor say of anything, I shall be sure to do so-and-so tomorrow, without adding "if God wills." Call your Lord to mind when you forget, and say: "I hope that my Lord will guide me ever closer than this to the right way"* (18:23-24), and *You feared the people, but God has a better right that you should fear Him* (33:37).

- When he swore that he would never again use honey or drink a honey-based sherbet, he was admonished: *O (most illustrious) Prophet! Why do you forbid (yourself) what God has made lawful to you, seeking to please your wives? And God is All-Forgiving, All-Compassionate.* (66:1)

Key vocabulary

- **Treaty:** a formal agreement between two or more states in reference to peace, alliance, commerce, or other international relations
- **Vanquish:** to defeat (someone) completely in a war, battle, etc.

The Qur'an inspired a genuinely scientific curiosity to study nature and travel in order to study different peoples and cultures.

Many miracles are associated with the Qur'an. One of the clearest is how quickly it established a distinctive and enduring civilization by serving as its constitution and framework. It mandated the administrative, legal, and financial reforms necessary to sustain a vast state of different cultural communities and religions. The Qur'an inspired a genuinely scientific curiosity to study nature and travel in order to study different peoples and cultures. By urging people to lend money for commercial ventures and to abandon interest, it made sure that the community's growing wealth would circulate. It inspired the first-ever public literacy and public hygiene programs, as both were necessary for worship. The Qur'an also commanded the organized redistribution of surplus wealth to the poor and needy, to widows and orphans, for the relief of captives and debtors, the freeing of slaves, and for the support of new Muslims.

One could expand this list considerably, for only the Qur'an has ever achieved what many people have desired. Do we not know of at least one human idea of how to establish or run an ideal society, at least one system or formula for solving equitably social, cultural, or political problems? Have any of them ever worked or lasted?

Some people want Muslims to believe that the Qur'an belongs to the seventh century. They admit, in order to beguile Muslims, that the Qur'an was very advanced for its time. But, scientific progress proves the accuracy of the Qur'an on questions related to the phenomenal world and helps us to better understand the Qur'an, just as improvements in our understanding of human relationships and human psychology will establish its truth in these areas.

Key vocabulary

- **Mandated:** an official order to do something
- **Beguile:** to trick or deceive (someone)

WHAT DID WE LEARN?

LESSON SUMMARY:

- Claiming that a person wrote the Qur'an only reflects the failure to understand that all individuals are indebted to God, Who has given us everything
- The Qur'an is unique among Scriptures in two respects, which even its detractors accept. First, the Qur'an exists in Arabic, its original language and one that is still widely spoken today. Second, its text is entirely reliable.
- The Qur'an has not been altered, edited, or tampered with since it was revealed.
- The Qur'an is absolutely different from any human product in its perspective and viewpoint
- The Qur'an requires us to understand, act, and amend our lifestyles
- The Qur'an's substance also is a compelling argument for its Divine authorship
- Another proof of the Qur'an's Divine origin is that what it predicts eventually comes true
- Many miracles are associated with the Qur'an

LESSON REVIEW: INDIVIDUAL ASSESSMENT

1. According to the text, describe what the Prophet's opponents would say to him regarding the Holy Qur'an and why did they state that?
2. Can the Qur'an be contemplated from a distance? Why or why not?
3. Name a prediction from the Qur'an that came true. Support your choice with evidence from the text.
4. In your own words, explain why the Qur'an is the key to a complete life and why it is a gift from Allah.

ESSAY

Choose any two (2) proofs from the text showing the impossibility for the Holy Qur'an to have been written by a human. Analyze your understanding of those proofs and explain them in your own words through a 3-4 paragraph essay.

LESSON VOCABULARY

- Detractor
- Interpolated
- Asserting
- Mandated
- Beguile
- Rapture
- consensus
- defy
- transcendence
- obsolescence
- allege
- treaty
- vanquish

Lesson 3
The Four Fundamental Aims of the Holy Qur'an

The Qur'an is a revealed Scripture, which comprises in summary of the Books of all the prophets, whose times were all different, and the works of all the purified scholars, whose paths are all different.

The Qur'an is

- the pre-eternal translator of the mighty Book of the universe
- the post-eternal interpreter of the various tongues reciting the verses of creation,
- the commentator of the book of the worlds of the seen and the unseen
- the revealer of the treasures of the Divine Names hidden in the heavens and on the earth,
- the key to the truths concealed beneath the lines of events,
- the clear interpreter of the Divine Essence, Attributes, Names, and functions.
- a book of prayer, and a book of wisdom, and a book of worship, and a book of command, and a book of thought.
- the Qur'an is a revealed Scripture, which comprises in summary of the Books of all the prophets, whose times were all different, and the works of all the purified scholars, whose paths are all different.

The Qur'an has four fundamental aims:

1. Divine Unity
2. The Afterlife
3. Prophethood
4. Integrity (Worship & Justice)

Wisdom of the All Wise Qur'an

يُؤْتِى الْحِكْمَةَ مَنْ يَشَٓاءُۚ وَمَنْ يُؤْتَ الْحِكْمَةَ فَقَدْ اُو۫تِىَ خَيْرًا كَث۪يرًاۜ

وَمَا يَذَّكَّرُ اِلَّٓا اُو۬لُوا الْاَلْبَابِ ﴿٢٦٩﴾

He grants the Wisdom to whomever He wills, and whoever is granted the Wisdom has indeed been granted much good. (2:269)

Key vocabulary

- **Wisdom (Hikmah):** signifies the true nature of and purpose behind the things and events in the universe, including especially human life.

1. The Universe: The mysteries beneath the veil of the decorations vs. the decorations themselves.

Look through the telescope of the following story, which is in the form of a comparison, and see the differences between Qur'anic wisdom and that of philosophy and science: One time, a renowned Ruler who was both religious and a fine craftsman wanted to write the All-Wise Qur'an in a script worthy of the sacredness in its meaning and the miracle of its words, so that its marvel-displaying stature would be arrayed in wondrous apparel. The artist-King therefore wrote the Qur'an in a truly wonderful fashion. He used all his precious jewels in its writing. In order to indicate the great variety of its truths, he wrote some of its embodied letters in diamonds and emeralds, and some in rubies, and other sorts in coral, while others he inscribed with silver and gold. He adorned and decorated it in such a way that everyone, those who knew how to read and those who did not, were full of admiration and astonishment when they beheld it. Especially in the view of the people of truth, since the outer beauty was an indication of the brilliant beauty and striking adornment in its meaning. It became a truly precious antique.

Then the Ruler showed the artistically wrought and bejeweled Qur'an to a European philosopher and to a Muslim scholar. In order to test them and for reward, he commanded them: "Each of you write a work about the wisdom and purposes of this!" First the philosopher, then the scholar composed a book about it. However, the philosopher's book discussed only the decorations of the letters and their relationships and conditions, and the properties of the jewels, and described them. It did not touch on their meaning at all, for the European had no knowledge of the Arabic script. He did not even know that the embellished Qur'an was a book, a written piece, expressing meaning. He rather looked on it as an ornamented antique. He did not know any Arabic, but he was a very good engineer, and he described things very aptly, and he was a skillful chemist, and an ingenious jeweler. So this man wrote his work according to those crafts.

As for the Muslim scholar, when he looked at the Qur'an, he understood that it was the Perspicuous Book, the All-Wise Qur'an. This truth-loving person neither attached importance to the external adornments, nor busied himself with the decorated letters. He became preoccupied with something that was a million times higher, more elevated, subtler, nobler, more beneficial, and more comprehensive than the matters with which the other man had busied himself. For discussing the sacred truths and lights of the mysteries beneath the veil of the decorations, he wrote a truly fine commentary. Then the two of them took their works and presented them to the Illustrious Ruler. The Ruler first took the philosopher's work. He looked at it and saw that the self-centered and nature-worshipping man had worked very hard, but had written nothing of true wisdom. He had understood nothing of its meaning. Indeed, he had confused it and been disrespectful towards it, and ill-mannered even. For supposing the source of truths, the Qur'an, to be meaningless decoration, he had insulted it as being valueless in regard to meaning. So the Wise Ruler hit him over the head with his work and expelled him from his presence.

Key vocabulary

- **Arrayed:** to place (a group of things) in a particular position so that they are in order or so that they look attractive
- **Aptly:** in a manner that is appropriate or suitable in the circumstances
- **Perspicuous:** able to give an account or express and idea clearly

DISCUSS

What have you understood so far from this comparison? Describe your thoughts to your classmate and then share your combined thoughts with the class.

Then he looked at the work of the other, the truth-loving, scrupulous scholar, and saw that it was an extremely fine and beneficial commentary, a wisest composition full of guidance. "Congratulations! May God bless you!", he said. Thus, wisdom is this and they call those who possess it knowledgeable and wise. As for the other man, he was a craftsman who had exceeded his mark. Then in reward for the scholar's work, he commanded that in return for each letter ten gold pieces should be given him from his inexhaustible treasury.

If you have understood the comparison, now look and see the reality:

The ornamented Qur'an is this artistically fashioned universe, and the Ruler is the Pre-Eternal All-Wise One. As for the two men, one —the European— represents philosophy and its philosophers, and the other, the Qur'an and its students.

The All-Wise Qur'an is a most elevated expounder, a most eloquent translator of the Mighty Qur'an of the Universe. It says, "How beautifully they have been made! How exquisitely they point to their Maker's beauty!" showing the universe's true beauty. But natural philosophy or science has plunged into the decorations of the letters of beings and into their relationships, and has become confused when it comes to the way of reality. While the letters of this mighty book should be looked at as bearing the meaning of another, they have not done this. They've looked at beings as signifying themselves.

"That is, they have looked at beings on account of beings, and have discussed them in that way."

Instead of saying, "How beautifully they have been made," they say "How beautiful they are," and have made them ugly. In doing this they have insulted the universe. Indeed, philosophy without religion is a sophistry divorced from reality and an insult to the universe.

Instead of saying, "How beautifully they have been made," they say "How beautiful they are," and have made them ugly.

Key vocabulary

- **Expounder:** one who explains something

2. The Self-sufficient seeker of God's virtue vs. the self-centered seeker of benefit.

A comparison between the moral training the wisdom of the All-Wise Qur'an gives to our personal life and what philosophy and science teach:

The sincere student of philosophy is a pharaoh, but he is a contemptible pharaoh who worships the basest thing for the sake of personal benefit. He recognizes everything from which he can profit from as his 'Lord'. That student is a self-centered seeker of benefit whose aim and endeavor is to gratify his animal appetites; a crafty egotist who seeks his personal interests within certain nationalist interests.

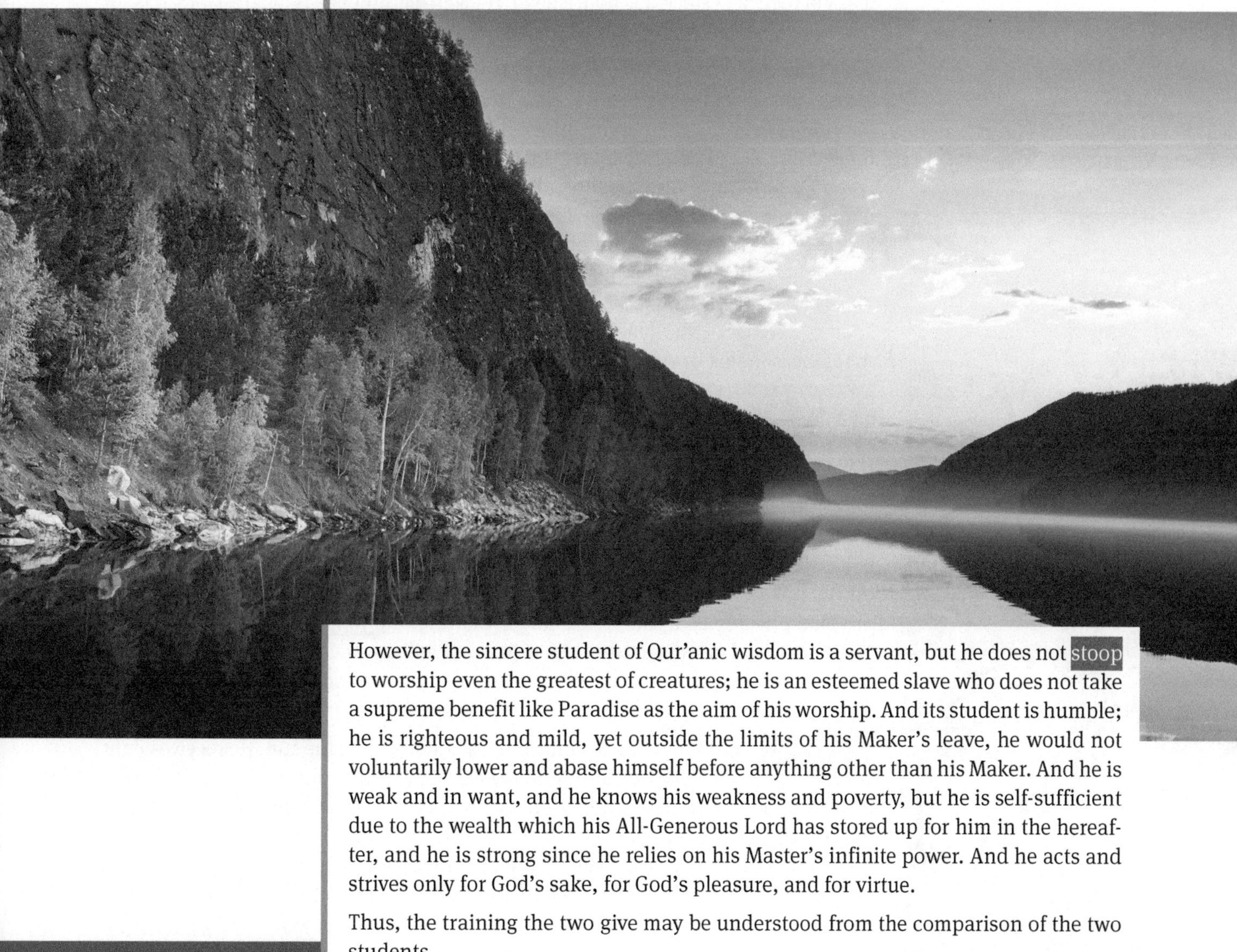

However, the sincere student of Qur'anic wisdom is a servant, but he does not stoop to worship even the greatest of creatures; he is an esteemed slave who does not take a supreme benefit like Paradise as the aim of his worship. And its student is humble; he is righteous and mild, yet outside the limits of his Maker's leave, he would not voluntarily lower and abase himself before anything other than his Maker. And he is weak and in want, and he knows his weakness and poverty, but he is self-sufficient due to the wealth which his All-Generous Lord has stored up for him in the hereafter, and he is strong since he relies on his Master's infinite power. And he acts and strives only for God's sake, for God's pleasure, and for virtue.

Thus, the training the two give may be understood from the comparison of the two students.

Key vocabulary

- **Contemptible:** not worthy of respect or approval
- **Basest:**the very bottom of lowest part of something
- **Stoop:** to bend down or over

3. Social Life: Force/benefits/conflict vs Truth/virtue/assistance

The training philosophy and science and Qur'anic wisdom give to human social life is this:

Philosophy accepts 'force' as its point of support in the life of society. It considers its aim to be 'benefits'. The principle of its life it recognizes to be 'conflict'. It holds the bond between communities to be 'racism and negative nationalism'. Its fruits are 'gratifying the appetites of the soul and increasing human needs'. However, the mark of force is 'aggression'. The mark of benefit —since they are insufficient for every desire— is 'jostling and tussling'. While the mark of conflict is '**strife**'. And the mark of racism — since it is nourished by **devouring** others— is 'aggression'. It is for these reasons that it has negated the happiness of mankind.

As for the Qur'anic wisdom, its point of support is 'truth' instead of force. It takes 'virtue and God's pleasure' as its aims in place of benefits. It takes the principle of 'mutual assistance' as the principle of life in place of the principle of conflict. And it takes 'the ties of religion, class, and country' to be the ties bonding communities. Its aim is to form a barrier against the wants of the soul, urge the spirit to sublime matters, satisfy high emotions, and urging man to human perfection, making him a true human being. And the mark of 'the truth' is **accord**. The mark of virtue is 'solidarity'. The mark of mutual assistance is 'hastening to assist one another'. The mark of religion is 'brotherhood". And the mark of reining in and **tethering** the evil commanding soul and leaving the spirit free and urging it towards perfections is 'happiness in this world and the next'.

THINK

Read these last two paragraphs two more times. Think about the meaning of the bold words. Write down on a piece of paper what you think they mean.

4. Divine Scriptures: Partial manifestation of a particular name vs that of the greatest level of every Name

If you want to understand the Qur'an's superiority among all the Divine scriptures and its supremacy over all speech and writings, then consider the following two comparisons:

The First: A king has two forms of speech, two forms of address. One is to speak on his private telephone with a common subject concerning some minor matter or some private need. The other, under the title of **sublime** sovereignty, supreme vicegerent, and universal rulership, is to speak with an envoy or high official for the purpose of making known and promulgating his commands, to make an utterance through an elevated decree proclaiming his majesty.

The Second: One man holds the mirror he is holding up to the sun. He receives light containing seven colors according to the capacity of the mirror. He becomes connected to the sun through that relation and converses with it, and if he directs the light-filled mirror towards his dark house or his garden covered by a roof, he will benefit, not in relation to the sun's value, but in accordance with the capacity of the mirror. Another man, however, opens up broad windows out of his house or out of the roof over his garden. He opens up ways to the sun in the sky.

Key vocabulary

- **Accord:** a situation or state in which people or things agree
- **Tethering:** limit the range of movement or action within a designated area, length.
- **Strife:** very angry or violent disagreement between two or more people or groups
- **Devour:** to destroy (something) completely, to greatly affect or control (someone)
- **Sublime:** very beautiful, impressing the mind with a sense of grandeur or power; inspiring awe, veneration

THINK

The Qur'an says "If all trees on the land were to become pens and all the seas ink, and if they were to write the words of Almighty God, they would never come to the end of them." How could it be possible that anyone besides Allah Almighty could have possibly written the Holy Qur'an

He converses with the perpetual light of the actual sun and speaks with it, and says in gratitude: "O you beauty of the world who gilds the face of the earth with your light and makes the faces of the flowers smile! O beauty of the skies, fine sun! You have furnished my little house and garden with light and heat the same as you have them." The man with the mirror cannot say that. The reflection and works of the sun under that restriction are limited. Look at the Qur'an through the telescope of these two comparisons and see its miraculousness and understand its sacredness.

Now, the reason the Qur'an has been given the highest rank among the infinite words of God is this:

"The Qur'an has come from the Greatest Divine Name and from the greatest level of every Name."

If you want to understand a little of how the Qur'an comes from the Greatest Name and from the greatest level of every Name, consider the universal, elevated statements of Ayat al-Kursi and the following verses:

- And with Him are the keys of the Unseen (6:59)
- God! Lord of All Dominion (3:26)
- He draws the night as a veil over day, each seeking the other in rapid succession;
- He created the sun, the moon, and the stars, (all) subject to His command. (7:54)
- Earth, swallow up your water! And O Sky, withhold your rain! (11:44)
- The heavens and the earth and all within them extol and glorify Him. (17:44)
- The creation of you all and the resurrection of you all is but like that of a single soul. (31:28)
- We offered the Trust to the heavens and the earth, and the mountains, but they shrank from bearing it, and were afraid of it (fearful of being unable to fulfill its responsibility), but human has undertaken it. (33:72)
- The Day when We will roll up the heaven as written scrolls are rolled up. We will bring the creation back into existence as easily as We originated it in the first instance. (21:104)
- They have no true judgement of God, such as His being God requires, and (such id His Power and Sovereignty that) the whole earth will be in His Grasp on the Day of Resurrection. (39:67)

The Qur'an has come from the Greatest Divine Name and from the greatest level of every Name.

Key vocabulary

- **Gilds:** to cover something with a thin layer of gold

WHAT DID WE LEARN?

LESSON SUMMARY:

The Qur'an has four fundamental aims:

1. Divine Unity
2. The Afterlife
3. Prophethood
4. Integrity (Worship & Justice)

The Qur'an is

- the pre-eternal translator of the mighty Book of the universe
- the post-eternal interpreter of the various tongues reciting the verses of creation,
- the commentator of the book of the worlds of the seen and the unseen,
- the revealer of the treasures of the Divine Names hidden in the heavens and on the earth,
- the key to the truths concealed beneath the lines of events,
- the clear interpreter of the Divine Essence, Attributes, Names, and functions.
- the Qur'an is a revealed Scripture, which comprises in summary of the Books of all the prophets, whose times were all different, and the works of all the purified scholars, whose paths are all different.

LESSON REVIEW: INDIVIDUAL ASSESSMENT

1. List the four fundamental aims of the Qur'an
2. According to the text, the Qur'an is a book of prayer, wisdom, worship, and what two other things?
3. According to the text, why has the Qur'an been given the highest rank among the infinite words of Allah?
4. Briefly describe the differences between the self-sufficient seeker of Allah's virtue, and the self-seeker of Allah's benefit.

ESSAY

Compare and contrast the thoughts and actions of the Muslim scholar and the fine craftsman found under: The Universe: The mysteries beneath the veil of the decorations vs. the decorations themselves.

LESSON VOCABULARY

- Arrayed
- Aptly
- Perscipuous
- Expounder
- Contemptible
- Basest
- Accord
- Tethering
- Gilds
- Stoop
- Strife
- Devour
- Sublime

Lesson 4
The Qur'an & Science

As science cannot be sure about the future, it does not make definite predictions. Doubt is the basis of scientific investigation. However, Prophet Muhammad, peace be upon him, who was taught by the All-Knowing, made many decisive predictions. Most have come true already; the rest are waiting for their time to come true. Many verses in the Qur'an point to recently discovered and established scientific facts.

Does the Qur'an contain everything?

The Qur'an describes humanity and the universe. It declares:

> With Him are the keys of the Unseen. None but He knows them. And He knows what is in the land and the sea. Not a leaf falls but with His Knowledge, not a grain amid the darkness of the earth, nothing of wet or dry but (it is noted) in a Manifest Book. (6:59)

Ibn Mas'ud says that the Qur'an provides information on everything, but that we may not be able to see everything in it. Ibn 'Abbas, the "Interpreter of the Qur'an" and "Scholar of the Ummah," asserts that if he loses his camel's rein, he can find it by means of the Qur'an. Jalal al-Din al-Suyuti, a major scholar who lived in Egypt in the 15th century, explains that all sciences or branches of knowledge can be found in the Qur'an.

Human progress in science and industry has brought about such scientific and technological wonders as airplanes, electricity, motorized transport, and radio and telecommunication, all of which have become basic and essential for our modern, materialistic civilization.

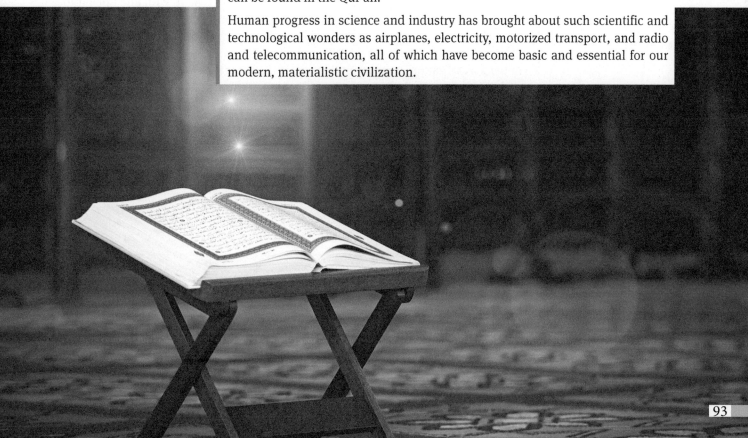

The Qur'an has not ignored them and points to them in two ways:

The first is, as will be explained below, by way of the Prophets' miracles.

The second concerns certain historical events. In other words, the wonders of human civilization only merit a passing reference, an implicit reference, or an allusion in the Qur'an.

For example, if an aircraft told the Qur'an: "Give me the right to speak and a place in your verses," the aircrafts of the sphere of Divine Lordship (the planets, the Earth, the moon) would reply on the Qur'an's behalf: "You may take a place here in proportion to your size." The Qur'an's viewpoint of life and the world is completely different from the modern one. It sees the world as a guesthouse, and people as temporary guests preparing themselves for eternal life by undertaking their most urgent and important duties. As that which is designed and used mostly for worldly purposes only has a tiny share in servanthood to and worship of God, which is founded upon love of truth and otherworldliness, it therefore has a place in the Qur'an according to its merit.

DISCUSS

If it mentioned modern scientific and technological discoveries or everything pertaining to life, nature, history, and humanity, wouldn't creating us in our present form be pointless?

The Qur'an does not explicitly mention everything necessary for our happiness in this world and the next for another reason:

Religion is a divine test to distinguish elevated and base spirits from each other.

Just as raw materials are refined to separate diamonds from coal and gold from soil, religion tests conscious beings to separate precious "ore" in the "mine" of human potential from dross.

Since the Qur'an was sent to perfect us, it only alludes to those future events pertaining to the world, which everyone will see at the appropriate time, and only opens the door to reason to the degree necessary to prove its argument. If everything was explicit, the test would be meaningless, for the truth of the Divine obligations would be readily apparent. Given that we would then be unable to deny or ignore them, the competition behind our testing and trials would be unnecessary, for we would have to confirm their truth. "Coal" spirits would remain with and appear to be no different from "diamond" spirits. As the great majority of people are always "average," the Qur'an uses a style and language that everyone can understand. An ordinary person and a great scientist can benefit from the Qur'an, regardless of his or her specialization. A most suitable way to do this is through symbols, metaphors and allegories, comparisons and parables. Those well-versed in knowledge (3:7) know how to approach and benefit from the Qur'an, and conclude that it is the Word of God.

God Almighty gave us intelligence, and the Qur'an urges us to use it to study ourselves, nature, and surrounding events.

Key vocabulary

- **Dross:** something of low value or quality
- **Metaphor:** an object, activity, or idea that is used as a symbol of something else

Considering science as opposed to religion and scientific study as separate from and independent of the Qur'an is just as mistaken as trying to reduce the Qur'an to a science textbook by showing that every new scientific theory or fact can be found in it.

God created us as the best pattern of creation, and gave us many intellectual faculties. But if everything were clear, we would not need these, for we would already know everything.

Finally, if the Qur'an contained specific references to everything we want to know, it would be so large that its complete recitation would be impossible. We would be unable to benefit from its spiritual enlightenment, and would become really bored while reciting it. Such results contradict the reasons for the Qur'an's revelation and its purposes.

Does the Qur'an Allude to Scientific Developments?

Before answering this question, we should point out one important fact:

"Considering science as opposed to religion and scientific study as separate from and independent of the Qur'an is just as mistaken as trying to reduce the Qur'an to a science textbook by showing that every new scientific theory or fact can be found in it."

For example, some have claimed that dabbat al-ard (a little moving creature) mentioned in Qur'an 27:82 is the virus that causes AIDS. However, this is a hasty conclusion for several reasons: The Qur'an is silent about this particle's nature; if we accept this assertion, we also must accept other venereal disease-causing bacteria or viruses; and, we cannot know whether new and more lethal viral diseases will appear in the future.

Key vocabulary

- **Allude:** to speak of or mention (something or someone) in an indirect way
- **Hasty:** done or made too quickly

Each Qur'anic verse and expression has a universal content. Therefore, any time-specific interpretation can address only one aspect of that universal content.

The context in which dabbat al-ard appears suggests that it will emerge toward the end of this world, when almost no one believes in God. So, we must not show haste in trying to find some type of correspondence between a Qur'anic verse and every new development in science and technology. Scientific theories are usually like clothes, for both are discarded after a while. Trying to show that every new scientific fact or theory can be found in the Qur'an displays an inferiority complex and makes science more important than the Qur'an. Each Qur'anic verse and expression has a universal content. Therefore, any time-specific interpretation can address only one aspect of that universal content.

Every interpreter, scientist, and saint prefers a particular aspect as a result of his or her spiritual discovery or intuition, personal evidence, or natural disposition. Besides, we accept both Newton's physics and Einstein's physics as science and therefore true. Although in absolute terms both may be false, there certainly must be some truth in both.

IMAGINE

Even if a Qur'anic verse appears to point exactly to an established scientific fact, should we restrict its meaning to only that fact? Wouldn't that be leaving out other possible meanings and interpretations as well?

Qur'anic expressions have multiple meanings. For example, consider the verses: He let forth the two seas that meet together, between them a barrier, they do not overpass (55:19-20). These verses indicate all the pairs of "seas" or realms, spiritual and material, figurative and actual, from the realms of Lordship and servanthood to the spheres of necessity and contingency, from this world to the Hereafter (including this visible, corporeal world and all unseen worlds), the Pacific and Atlantic oceans, the Mediterranean and Red seas, salt water and sweet water in the seas and underground, and such large rivers as the Euphrates and Tigris that carry sweet water and salty seas to which they flow. All of these, as well as many others are included in these verses, either literally or figuratively.

The Qur'an is not a science textbook that has to expound upon cosmological or scientific matters; rather, it is the eternal interpretation of the Book of the Universe and the interpreter of all natural and other sciences. It comments upon the visible and invisible worlds, and discloses the spiritual treasures of the Divine Beautiful Names in the heavens and the Earth. The Qur'an is the key leading to an understanding of the hidden realities behind events taking place in nature and human life, and is the tongue of the hidden worlds in the manifest world.

The Qur'an considers creation only for the sake of knowing its Creator; science considers creation only for its own sake. The Qur'an addresses humanity; science addresses only those who specialize in it. Since the Qur'an uses creation as evidence and proof to guide us, its evidence must be easily understandable to all of us non-specialists. Guidance requires that relatively unimportant things should be touched on briefly, while subtle points should be discussed as completely as possible through parables and comparisons. Guidance should not change what is obvious, so that people are not confused.

Key vocabulary

- **Disposition:** to act of think in a particular way
- **Parable:** a short story that teaches a moral or spiritual lesson

THINK

If the Qur'an was not compiled in this way, how could we derive any benefit?

"The Qur'an's primary aims are to make God Almighty known, to open the way to faith and worship, and to organize our individual and social life so that we may attain perfect happiness in both worlds."

To achieve this aim, it refers to things and events, as well as scientific facts, in proportion to their importance. Thus the Qur'an provides detailed explanations of the pillars of faith, the fundamentals of religion, the foundations of human life, and essentials of worship, but only hints at other relatively less significant things.

The Qur'an's primary aims are to make God Almighty known, to open the way to faith and worship, and to organize our individual and social life so that we may attain perfect happiness in both worlds.

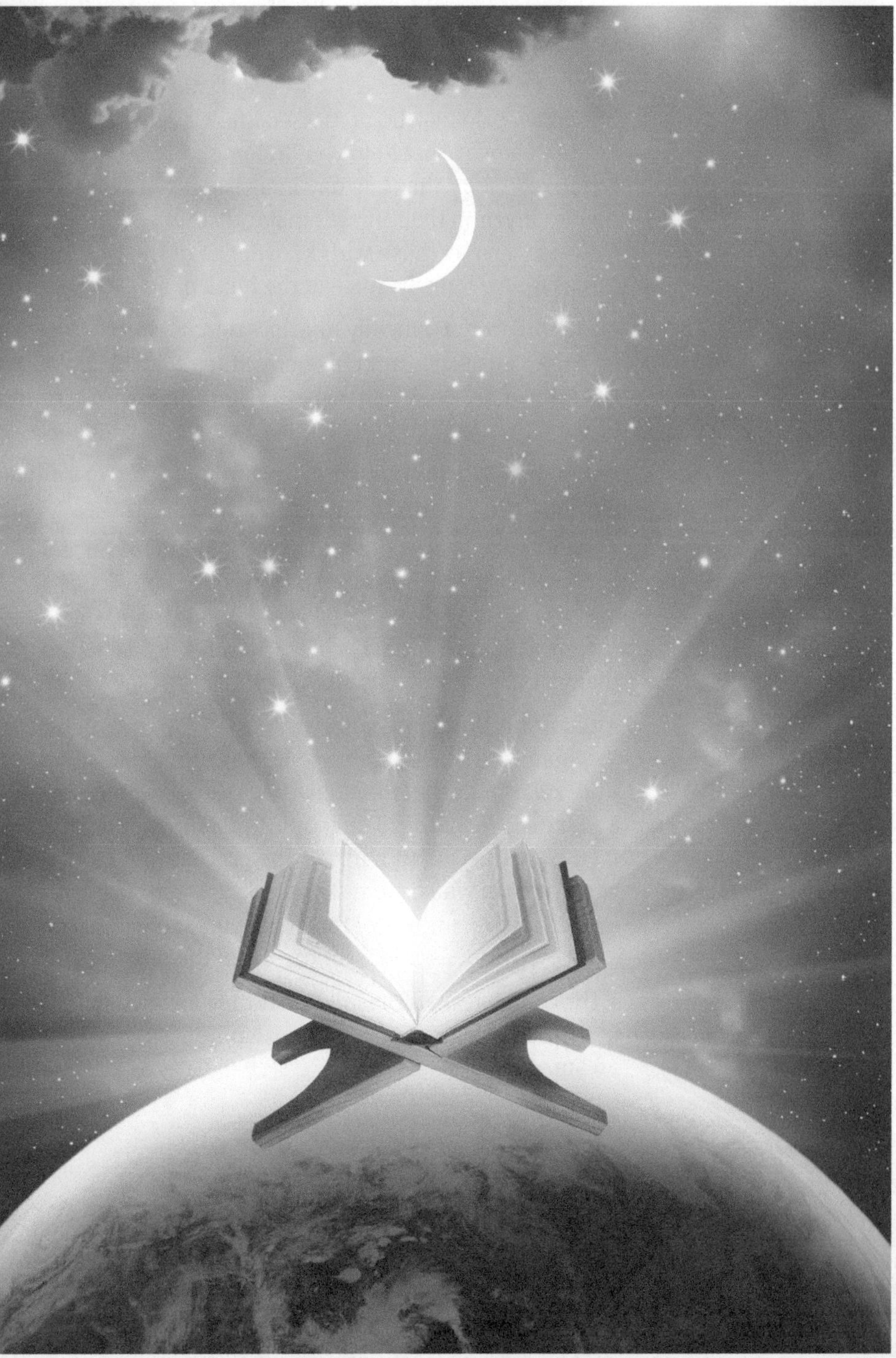

Examples:

• Ways the Qur'an hints of technological advances and marks their final development is by mentioning the miracles of the Prophets.

• It encourages us to fly in the air and alludes implicitly to the fact that one day we will make spaceships and aircraft: And to Solomon (We subjugated) the wind; its morning course was a month's journey, and its evening course was a month's journey (34:12).

• It invites us to learn how to cure every illness: (Jesus said): I also heal the blind and the leper, and bring to life the dead, by the leave of God (3:49), and hints that one day we will be so successful that people will find it hard to believe that they will actually die.

The verse: Said he who possessed knowledge of the Book: "I will bring it (the throne of the Queen of Sheba) to you (Solomon in Jerusalem) in the twinkling of your eye" (27:40), foretells that one day images or even physical items will be transmitted either bodily or in their images instantly through knowledge of the Divine Book of the Universe, just as those with knowledge of the Book of Divine Revelation can bring things from a long distance in the blink of an eye.

• The Qur'an symbolically informs us that it might be possible to identify a murderer by some cells taken from his body at the time of death: A murderer was revealed in the time of Moses, by striking the slain man with part of a cow that God Almighty ordered the Children of Israel to slaughter (2:67-73).

Below are further examples to illustrate the Qur'an's allusions to scientific facts and developments.

• The Creator, Who is not bound by the human concept of time, informs us that, in a general sense, the future will be the age of knowledge and information, as well as an age of faith and belief: Soon We shall show them Our signs in the outer world and in their own souls, until it becomes manifest to them that this is truth. Is it not enough that your Lord witnesses all things? (41:53).

• What the Qur'an says about milk and its production is as brilliant as the drink itself, and our understanding of it has brought us great benefits: And verily in cattle (too) will you find an instructive sign. From what is from their bodies, between waste and blood, We produce, for your drink, milk, pure and agreeable to those who drink it (16:66). The Qur'an narrates the process in remarkable detail: part-digestion and absorption of what is ingested as food, and then a second process and refinement in the glands. Milk is one of the most vital and useful sources of human nourishment, and yet it is not essential for the life of the mother.

• The Qur'an reveals that all things are created in pairs: Glory be to God, who created in pairs all things, of what the earth produces, of themselves, and of which they have no knowledge (36:36).

Key vocabulary

- **Foretell:** to describe (something) before it happens, predict.
- **Slain:** to kill (someone) usually used as (be) slain

WHAT DID WE LEARN?

LESSON SUMMARY:

- As science cannot be sure about the future, it does not make definite predictions. Doubt is the basis of scientific investigation
- The Qur'an does not explicitly mention everything necessary for our happiness in this world and the next
- Qur'anic expressions have multiple meanings.
- Considering science as opposed to religion and scientific study as separate from and independent of the Qur'an is just as mistaken as trying to reduce the Qur'an to a science textbook by showing that every new scientific theory or fact can be found in it.
- The Qur'an alludes to many scientific and technological advances

LESSON REVIEW: INDIVIDUAL ASSESSMENT

1. According to the text, why doesn't the Qur'an specifically address all scientific and worldly issues, only alluding to some?
2. What is the divine test to distinguish elevated and base sprits from each other?
3. Why is it wrong to study religion and science separate and independent from the Qur'an?
4. What is the Qur'an's primary aim, according to the text?

ESSAY

Since Qur'anic verses have multiple meanings, analyze the text and explain in a 2-3 paragraph essay why it is important not to focus on only one meaning of a verse.

LESSON VOCABULARY

- Dross
- Disposition
- Metaphor
- Allude
- Hasty
- Parable
- Foretell
- Slain

CHAPTER REVIEW

Answer the following questions in detail:

1. Why has the Qur'an been given the highest rank among the infinite words of Allah?
2. What are the four fundamental aims of the Qur'an?
3. Over how many years was the Qur'an revealed?
4. Which books or suhuf were given to which prophets?

ESSAY

Now that you have read about the Divine Books, Qur'an and the Qur'ans' direct and indirect relationship with science, write a narrative essay detailing your understanding of the importance of combining science, religion, and the Qur'an together. Support your narrative with specifics and details from the lessons in this chapter.

BELIEF IN THE PROPHETS

CHAPTER

5

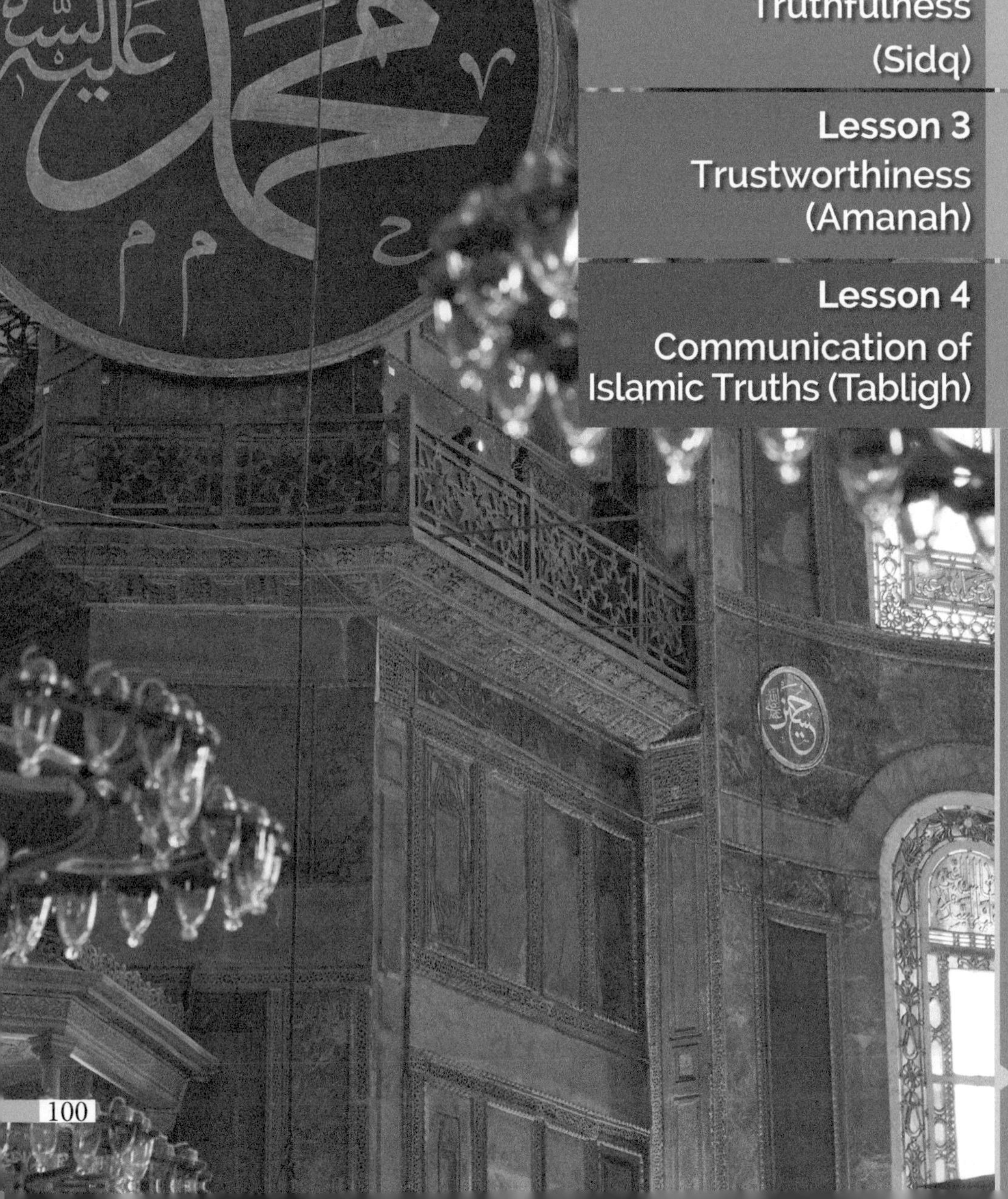

Surely We have sent you as Messenger with the truth, as a bearer of glad tidings,and a warner; and there has never been a community but a warner lived among them. (Qur'an 35:24)

Hagia Sophia, Istanbul, Turkey

BELIEF IN ALLAH'S PROPHETS IS THE FOURTH ARTICLE OF FAITH

THINK

What is our purpose here on earth? Where are we going? Think about the answer and discuss with a partner

Prophethood is the highest rank that any of Allah's servants could ever reach. It is a title that cannot be attained through free will, knowledge or effort. It is a rank granted directly by the Almighty Himself. Prophets are unique individuals whose lives are dedicated to serving the religion of Allah and humanity. They are sent to guide humanity out of the dark abysses of disbelief into the incandescent light of faith. Prophets are the fruits of compassion. Humanity has learned to embrace and implement the most basic essentials of human values and ethics through the exalted teachings of the Prophets.

Prophets arrive with answers to most intricate philosophical and scientific questions generated by the human mind, such as,

"Who am I? Where do I come from? What is my purpose on earth and where am I going?"

Prophets deliver an elixir, which brings hope, tranquility, peace and contentment to the heart. And they bring principles that establish order, harmony, understanding, justice and compassion among human beings. It is through them, we discover the secrets of eternity and immortality.

Without Prophets, the past would be regarded as an immense grave that has swollen every living creature on its path and the future would be considered as the inevitable end that waits impatiently to destroy all forms of life in the universe. Therefore, the luminous torch carried by the Prophets sheds a light into the dark past and onto the unknown future.

"Who am I? Where do I come from? What is my purpose on earth and where am I going?"

Key vocabulary

- **Abyss:** a hole so deep it cannot be measured
- **Elixir:** a magical liquid that can cure sickness
- **Incandescent:** light or glowing
- **Intricate:** complex; complicated; hard to understand

Beginning with Adam, peace be upon him, the All-Compassionate has sent thousands of Prophets who guided humanity onto the right path. It was Noah, peace be upon him, who battled colossal waves to deliver a handful of believers to the safety of Mt. Judi. It was Abraham, peace be upon him, who had to be cast into a blazing inferno in order to deliver his sanctified message. Jonah, peace be upon him, struggled in the belly of a giant fish and Moses, peace be upon him, wandered through the dry desert for many months as he starved and suffered for his noble cause. David, peace be upon him, had to confront Goliath and Jesus, peace be upon him, endured the pain of torture and harassment.

DISCUSS

Would we be able to understand the Qur'an without the help and guidance of our Prophets?

"Throughout history, human tribes and nations have never been deprived of Prophets."

Key vocabulary

- **Colossal:** very large or great
- **Inferno:** a very large and dangerous fire

In the Holy Qur'an, Allah the Almighty informs us that He has sent a Messenger to all human clans and nations:

> Surely We have sent you as Messenger with the truth, as a bearer of glad tidings, and a warner; and there has never been a community but a warner lived among them. (Qur'an 35:24)
>
> And verily, We have sent among every community, nation a Messenger... (Qur'an 16:36)

"It is quite clear that Allah has sent a Messenger to all nations and tribes so that they would be guided onto the right path."

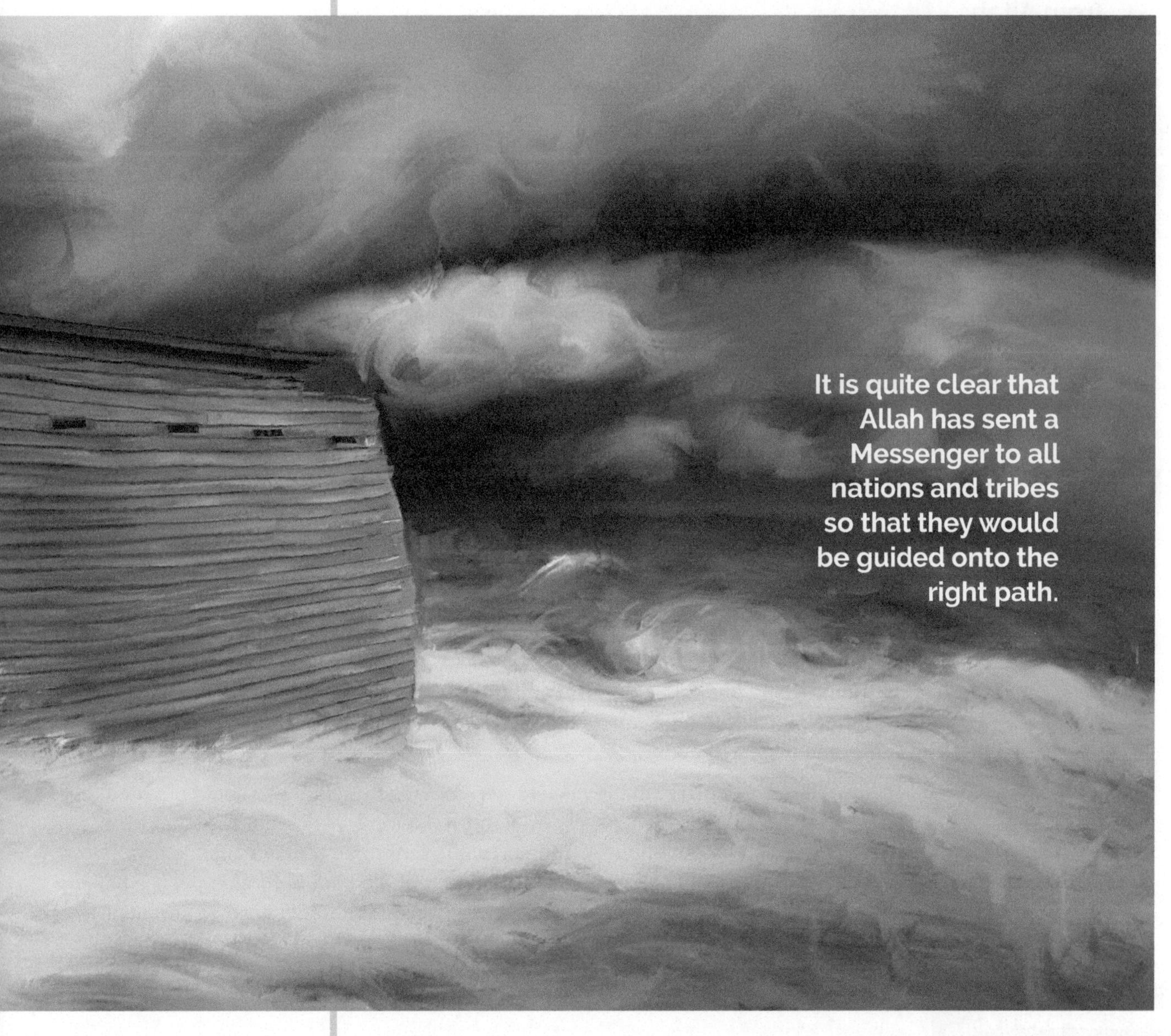
It is quite clear that
Allah has sent a
Messenger to all
nations and tribes
so that they would
be guided onto the
right path.

Historically, whenever mankind inclined towards evil and rebellion, they were blessed with a Prophet who came to them with a sacred message from Allah.

Allah has sent approximately 124,000 Prophets to humanity.

Historically, whenever mankind inclined towards evil and rebellion, they were blessed with a Prophet who came to them with a sacred message from Allah. The Holy Qur'an mentions the names of twenty-five most significant Prophets.

The Prophets mentioned in the Qur'an are listed below:

Adam (Adam)	Musa (Moses)
Idris (Enoch)	Harun (Aaron)
Nuh (Noah)	Dhul-Kifl (Ezekiel)
Hud	Dawud (David)
Saleh	Suleyman (Solomon)
Ibrahim (Abraham)	Ilyas (Elijah)
Lut (Lot)	Al-Yasa (Elisha)
Ismail (Ishmael)	Yunus (Jonah)
Ishaq (Isaac)	Zakariya (Zachariah)
Yaqub (Jacob)	Yahya - John the Baptist
Yusuf (Joseph)	Isa - Jesus
Ayyub (Job)	Muhammad
Shuayb (Jethro)	(peace and blessings be upon them all)

However, according to a hadith, sayings of the Last Prophet, Allah has sent approximately 124,000 Prophets to humanity since the beginning of history.

THE EMERGENCE OF THE LAST PROPHET

Pre-Islamic Arabia was dominated by superstitions, barbaric and violent customs, and degraded moral standards. Feeling disgraced and ashamed, fathers would bury their daughters alive. Children of the poor who could not pay their debts, would be taken away to be enslaved and sold in the slave markets. Tribe members would slay each other over the simplest of issues and the women of this society were classified as second grade human beings. Human life had no value and there was no justice system to protect the innocent. Out of various materials, people would make idols and worship them as gods.

The people of wisdom and righteousness were looking for a light that could brighten their world and liberate their society from this repugnant way of life. The coming of the light of salvation mentioned in the previous scriptures was impatiently awaited by a handful of righteous people who believed in the Lord of Ibrahim, peace be upon him. They also lived amongst this tribal society but denounced all forms of idol worshipping and the wicked ways of the polytheists. They knew that their Lord would soon send a savior. According to previous scriptures the awaited one would be Allah's last Messenger on earth.

Key vocabulary

- **Emergence:** the act of becoming known
- **Repugnant:** causing a strong feeling of dislikes or disgust
- **Savior:** someone who saves something or someone from danger, harm, failure

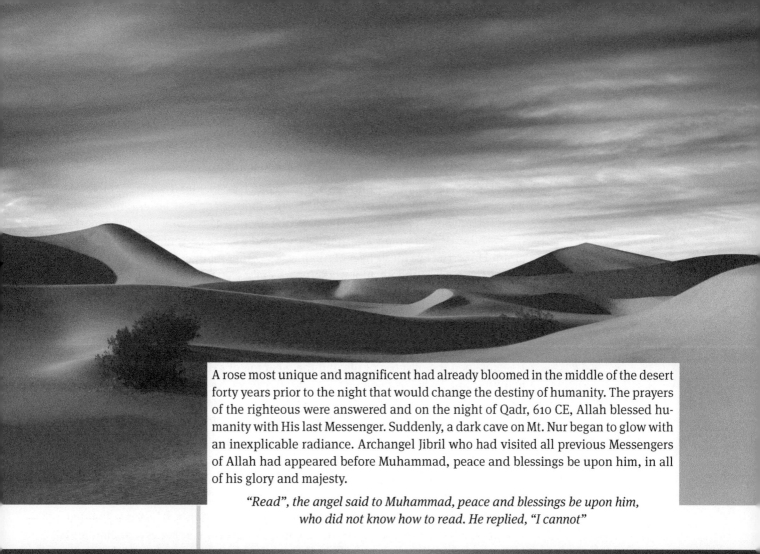

A rose most unique and magnificent had already bloomed in the middle of the desert forty years prior to the night that would change the destiny of humanity. The prayers of the righteous were answered and on the night of Qadr, 610 CE, Allah blessed humanity with His last Messenger. Suddenly, a dark cave on Mt. Nur began to glow with an inexplicable radiance. Archangel Jibril who had visited all previous Messengers of Allah had appeared before Muhammad, peace and blessings be upon him, in all of his glory and majesty.

"Read", the angel said to Muhammad, peace and blessings be upon him, who did not know how to read. He replied, "I cannot"

"Read", the angel said to Muhammad, peace and blessings be upon him, who did not know how to read. He replied, "I cannot"

Read

The angel then repeated, "Read in the name of your Lord". Miraculously, Muhammad, peace and blessings be upon him, began to read. These were the first verses revealed from the Holy Qur'an. An orphan from the tribe of Quraysh was given the noblest of all duties. He was the last Messenger of Allah. Through him, Allah would complete His religion.

IMAGINE

The character of Prophet Muhammad was so concrete that even his enemies know him as trustworthy. Take this moment to reflect on your life. How trustworthy are you? How can you improve? Imagine you were standing face to face with Prophet Muhammad. How would you want him to see you?

The Messenger of Allah was unique in all aspects. The matchless qualities of all the previous Prophets were congregated in him. On the day he was born, he had cried out "my community... my community." Throughout his sanctified life, he uttered the very same words and on the day he passed away, he left in the same manner as he repeated the words, "my community... my community."

The Prophet was so unique that the Almighty had blessed him the title of Habib-Allah which meant the beloved of Allah. Furthermore, people of his era, those who believed him and those who did not, gave him the title of al-Amin, which meant the trustworthy. He was a man who emitted trust and a sense of tranquility to all those around him. The last Messenger of Allah was so different that there were occasions where the most stubborn idol-worshippers embraced his faith by just taking a glimpse of his luminous face. Once he had declared his mission of Prophethood to a tribal chief. Following a brief gaze of the Prophet's noble face, the man replied, "There is no lie on this face".

The noble Messenger came with a key that unlocked the mysteries of the universe. He explained the purpose of life and the meaning of existence. Through him, humanity learned what awaited them beyond the grave. He cleared all forms of ambiguity and haziness from the minds of confused human beings. He brought hope and exuberance into the lives of those in despair and desolation.

"It was the noble Messenger who showed humanity ways to satisfy the heart and the soul."

These were the two entities that could only be satisfied with the love and remembrance of Allah. Following the arrival of the noble Prophet, life began to take on a new meaning. Heads began to bow before the Almighty Allah and hearts submitted to Him with absolute obedience. He taught believers how to believe, submit and how to practice the religion of Allah. He preached love, compassion, understanding, mutual respect, harmony, fairness, charity and empathy for all of Allah's creatures. He practiced whatever he preached with utmost sensitivity and more than anyone ever could.

"It was the noble Messenger who showed humanity ways to satisfy the heart and the soul.

Key vocabulary

- **Emitted:** to send light (or energy) out from a source
- **Stubborn:** refusing to change one's ideas or to stop doing something
- **Haziness:** not clear in thought or meaning

The noble Messenger of Allah turned an ignorant, barbaric, tribal community into a noble society that established the foundations of modern civilization.

It was through him that humanity learned to worship the one and only Allah and to respect their elders and fellow human beings. And it was his teachings that taught people to refrain from stealing, cheating, lying and deceiving each other. He encouraged the wealthy to help the poor, needy, orphan and the widower. He showed believers how to pray, fast, perform the holy pilgrimage and to give charity. He showed people how to live and die like true human beings. And he taught his followers how to please Allah as he guided them to the path that led to eternal paradise. The noble Messenger of Allah turned an ignorant, barbaric, tribal community into a noble society that established the foundations of modern civilization. It had taken him a mere twenty-three years to accomplish such an astonishing change that encompassed spiritual, personal, social and political renewal.

The Qur'an astounded the Arabs of his era and continues to amaze people of sound understanding. Moreover, no book of similar articulateness has ever been produced to this day. The Holy Qur'an has also been read and memorized for over fourteen hundred years by millions of non-Arabs, even those who do not understand or speak Arabic find pleasure in reading it.

THE PROPHET'S DEPARTURE FROM THIS WORLD

The Messenger of Allah lived a life of struggle. From the age of forty to the age of sixty-three, he conveyed the message of Allah to humanity and dedicated his life to serving Allah and establishing the foundations of a pious, righteous, harmonious and just society that would be the benchmark for all future generations. He was the beloved servant of Allah, a man loved passionately by his followers and respected even by his enemies.

Following a short twenty-three years of Prophethood, in which he managed to squeeze accomplishments of a grandeur nature that could only be achieved in a thousand years, the noble Messenger of Allah completed his mission at the age of sixty-three. As his mission had been fulfilled, for him, the worldly life had lost its meaning. There was no reason for him to remain on earth any longer.

The time of departure had arrived. He had come to a stage where prayer was the only thing that attached him to this life. He was sixty-three and calendars were displaying the 8th of June 632 CE. The noble Messenger became so ill that the high fever had rendered him unconscious. Each time he regained consciousness, he uttered the following words with great concern on his face, "The Prayer!" His beloved Companions replied, "The Prayer time has not entered yet, oh noble Messenger of Allah". Many times they had poured buckets of cold water over his noble head. His body temperature was at critical levels. Finally, the time for the Prayer had arrived. They helped him to stand up and two of his Companions supported him with their shoulders as he walked towards the mosque.

- **Astounded:** shocked or greatly surprised
- **Articulate:** able to express ideas clearly and effectively in speech or writing
- **Grandeur:** a great and impressive quality

This would be the last Prayer that the noble Messenger performed. At the conclusion of the Prayer, he returned to his blessed house. He asked his beloved daughter, Fatima, may Allah be pleased with her, to come close. She leaned over and placed her ear next to her father's mouth. The noble Messenger whispered some words into her ear. Fatima began to weep desperately. Once again, the Prophet asked her to approach. This time, upon hearing the words of her father, Fatima began to smile. They asked her why she had behaved this way. She replied, "On the first occasion he said, "Do not worry my daughter, from this day on your father will never feel pain again". This is when I began to weep. And then he said, "You will be the first one from my household to join me." This is when I smiled".

The time of departure had arrived, and angel of death Azrael requested permission from the noble Messenger to enter his house. The permission was granted. The angel said, "O Muhammad! I was sent by your Lord who gives you the option to live for as long as you wish". The noble Messenger replied, "Take me to the Highest Abode." The noble Prophet then departed from this world.

"As followers of the noble Messenger we say: "Oh the noble Prophet of Allah! Do not deprive us of your blessed intercession *on the Day of Judgment!"*

"As followers of the noble Messenger we say: "Oh the noble Prophet of Allah! Do not deprive us of your blessed intercession on the Day of Judgment!"

Key vocabulary

- **Intercession:** to speak in order to help another person

WHAT DID WE LEARN?

LESSON SUMMARY:

- Belief in Allah's Prophets is the fourth article of the six articles of faith.
- Prophethood is the highest rank that any of Allah's servants could ever reach.
- It is a title that cannot be attained through free will, knowledge or effort.
- It is a rank granted directly by the Almighty Himself.
- 25 Prophet's are mentioned by name in the Qur'an
- Prophets are sent to guide humanity. Allah has sent a Messenger to all nations and tribes so that-they would be guided onto the right path.
- The Prophet was so unique that the Almighty had blessed him the title of Habib-Allah.
- Prophet Muhammad was the last messenger of Allah.

LESSON REVIEW: INDIVIDUAL ASSESSMENT

1. We know the 25 Prophets named in the Qur'an, but how many do we know approximately were sent to mankind?
2. What year was Prophet Muhammad (pbuh) born?
3. What was Prophet Muhammad's (pbuh) first response when Jibril told him to "Read"?
4. What did Prophet Muhammad (pbuh) continuously ask about on his deathbed?

ESSAY

Briefly describe your understanding of why Prophets were sent and their mission to humanity. Use examples from the text. You should have 3 paragraphs with an opening, body, and conclusion.

LESSON VOCABULARY

- Abysses
- Elixir
- Incandescent
- Colossal
- Inferno
- Emergence
- Repugnant
- Emitted
- Intercession
- intricate
- glad tidings
- savior
- stubborn
- haziness
- astound
- articulate
- grandeur

Lesson 2

Truthfulness (Sidq)

THE ESSENTIALS OF PROPHETHOOD

They never lie, even just for a joke. They are truthful in all circumstances.

The next few lessons will focus on the Essentials of Prophethood, with one essential highlighted in each lesson.

The prophets are, like us, human beings. They eat, drink, rejoice, and worry... However, they have exceptionally good characters, and they have special attributes, given to them by Allah.

These features are as follows:

1. Sidq (Truthfulness): They never lie, even just for a joke. They are truthful in all circumstances."
2. Amanah (Trustworthiness): The prophets are trustworthy. They are reliable in all circumstances.
3. Tabligh (Communication): They directly communicate divine messages to the people.
4. Fatanah (Intellect): They have the highest degree of understanding, intelligence, and foresight.
5. Ismah (Innocence, infallibility): The prophets are virtuous people. Allah protects them from doing wrong. They do not commit sins.

TRUTHFULNESS

Truthfulness is the cornerstone of Prophethood. No lies or deceit, whether explicit or implicit, were ever heard from them. The Qur'an declares: *Mention Abraham in the Book: Surely he was a most truthful Prophet* (19:41); *Mention Ishmael in the Book; surely, he was a man of his word, and he was a Messenger, a Prophet* (19:54); and *Mention Enoch (Idris) in the Book; surely he was a most truthful Prophet. We elevated him to an exalted place* (19:56–57). We also read in the Qur'an that a fellow prisoner addressed Prophet Joseph: *Joseph, O most truthful one* (12:46).

The Prophets had to be endowed with truthfulness, for God wants everybody to be truthful and extol the truthful: *O you who believe, fear God and be with the company of the truthful!* (9:119), and: *The believers are those who believed in God and His Messenger without ever feeling doubt thereafter, and strove with their souls and possessions in the cause of God; those are the ones who are the truthful* (49:15).

The Qur'an praises believers who, without faltering, carry out their promises:

> Among the believers are the valiants who have kept their promise which they gave to God: Some of them carried out their word (and were martyred) and the others are expecting (their turn); they have never thought of going back on their word. (33:23)

Key vocabulary

- **Extol:** to praise someone or something highly
- **Valiants:** having or showing courage

DISCUSS

The Qur'an states in the above verse (33:23) those martyrs who fulfilled their promise to God through his Messenger, as well as others expecting martyrdom, to show that they were true to their words. Are they the only ones praised here? Or rather, does it include all who fulfill their words and keep their promises?

"O God, forgive my people, for they do not know."

This verse extols the heroes of Uhud, a decisive turning point in Islamic history. After the unbelievers of the Quraysh were defeated at Badr, they had spent a whole year preparing for a deadly retaliatory blow at the Muslims. Meeting at the foot of Mount Uhud, a few miles from Medina, the Muslims at first were victorious and the Quraysh began to flee. At this crucial point, the archers whom God's Messenger had positioned at 'Aynayn pass left their positions, against the Prophet's command, and pursued the enemy. Khalid ibn al-Walid, commander of the enemy's cavalry, took this opportunity to surround the Muslims from behind. As a result, the Muslims experienced a reverse. Such leading figures as Hamza, Mus'ab ibn 'Umayr, 'Abd Allah ibn Jahsh, and Anas ibn Nadr were martyred. Even the Prophet was wounded.

Let us note here that during the battle, God's Messenger, the Prophet of forgiveness and mercy who was sent as a mercy for creation, raised his hands to the heavens with a heart-felt prayer and, while bleeding profusely, asked for the enemy to be forgiven:

"O God, forgive my people, for they do not know."

As mentioned in the last lesson, God's Messenger was known as a truthful person even before Islam. The Meccans, even the unbelievers, called him al-Amin (the Trustworthy One, the Truthful). Even his enemies did not accuse him of lying after he proclaimed his Prophethood. Abu Sufyan, for example, confessed to the Emperor of Byzantium that he never lied. Struck by Abu Sufyan's answers, at that time the bitterest enemy of Islam, the Emperor acknowledged Prophet Muhammad's position: "It is inconceivable for one who has never told a lie during his whole life to invent lies against God." He was right.

Once before his conversion, Yasir asked his son 'Ammar where he was going. 'Ammar said that he was going to the Prophet. Being fully satisfied of his son's safety while with him, he replied: "Muhammad is a trustworthy person. The Meccans recognize him so. If he claims Prophethood he must be telling the truth, for no one has ever heard him tell a lie."

God's Messenger always encouraged truthfulness, as can be seen in his words as recorded in the following Traditions:

Key vocabulary

- **Unanimously:** agreed to by everyone
- **Inconceivable:** impossible to imagine or believe

THINK

Why would a believer who had never told a lie, even jokingly, suddenly begin to lie, especially against God?

"Promise me six things and I will promise you Paradise: Speak the truth, keep your promises, fulfill your trusts, remain chaste, don't look at what is unlawful, and avoid what is forbidden."

"Abandon what arouses your suspicions and follow what is certain. Truthfulness gives satisfaction; lying causes suspicion."

"Seek truthfulness even if it might bring you to ruin."

"Always be truthful, for truthfulness leads to righteousness and righteousness leads to Paradise."

If you are always truthful and seek truthfulness, God records you as such. Never lie, for lying leads to shamefulness and shamefulness leads to Hell. If you insist on lying and seek deceit, God records you as such. Due to his truthfulness, God's Messenger rose to such a high rank that his nearness to God is expressed metaphorically in the Qur'an as follows: *Then he approached and came nearer, till he was (distant) two bows' length, or even nearer* (53:8-9). Truthfulness always brings salvation, even if it causes one's death. We die through truthfulness only once, whereas each lie is a different kind of death.

Always be truthful, for truthfulness leads to righteousness and righteousness leads to Paradise.

One of the most striking examples of this is the case of Ka'b ibn Malik, a famous Ansari poet who swore allegiance to God's Messenger at 'Aqabah. Although he took part in almost all the battles, he missed the campaign of Tabuk without a justifiable excuse.

The Tabuk campaign was very difficult. It took place in mid-summer and, what is more, against the Eastern Roman (Byzantine) Empire. Although God's Messenger always kept the destination of such campaigns secret, this time he disclosed it and wanted every believer to participate. Ka'b completed his preparations but at the last minute, uncharacteristic negligence kept him from joining the army.

When God's Messenger returned from the campaign, he asked those who had not fought why they had stayed at home. The hypocrites lied and made excuses, but Ka'b, being unable to lie, told the truth. God's Messenger told him to leave. Thereafter, Ka'b and two other believers who had done the same thing were boycotted. On the order of God's Messenger, no Muslim met with them or spoke to them. They repented publicly, begging God for forgiveness, for 50 days. After this, the following revelation came:

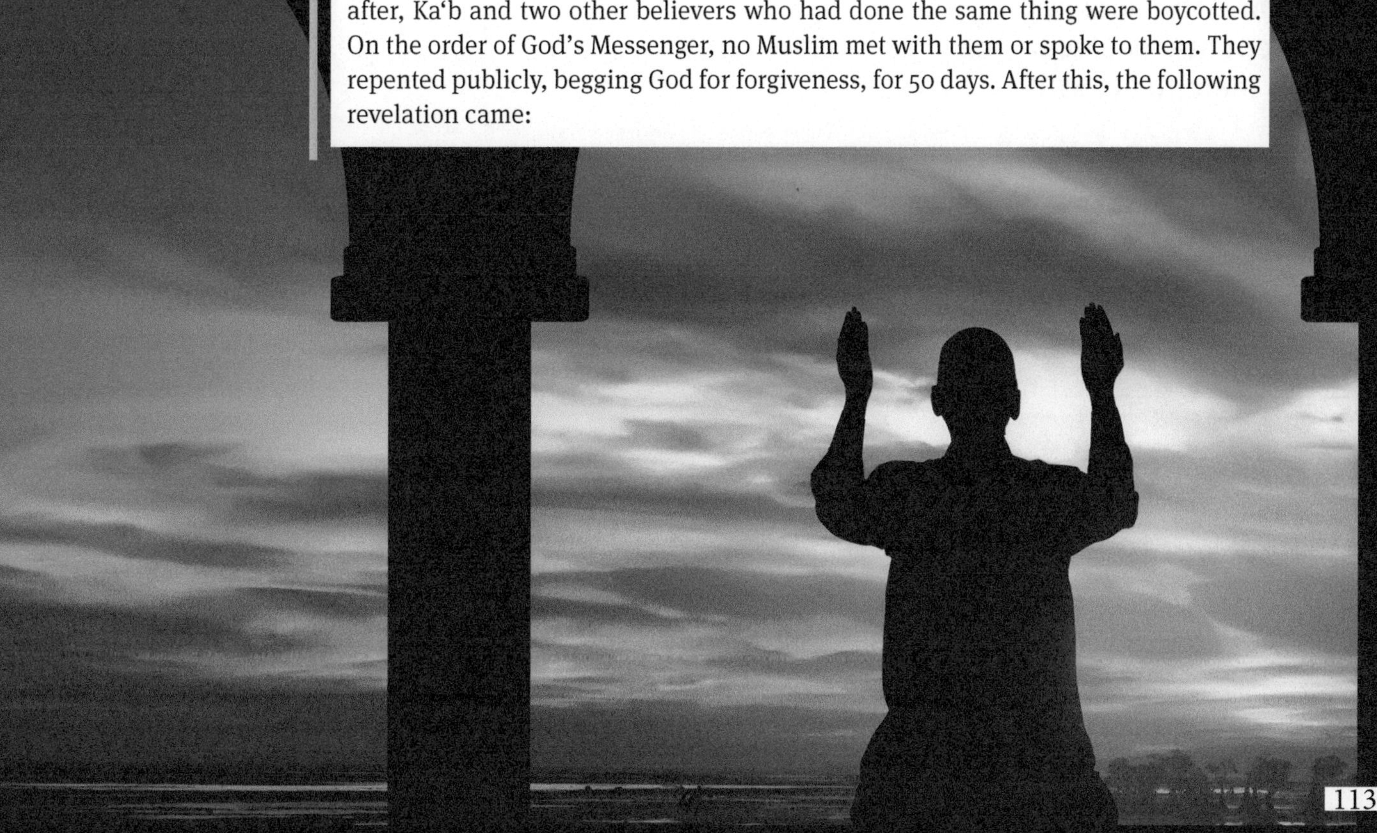

IMAGINE

Imagine it was you who waited for three days because you gave your word. Reflect on how you personally would have acted as well. How can you teach yourself to be more cautious of your truthfulness after reading this lesson?

As for those three, the acceptance of their repentance was delayed until, for them, the Earth, vast as it is, was straitened and their own souls were straitened to them, and they perceived that there is no fleeing from God and no refuge but with Him. Then He accepted their repentance so that they could recover their former state. Verily, God is the One who accepts repentance, Most Merciful. (9:118)

After this revelation, Ka'b ibn Malik told the Messenger, upon him be peace and blessings: "I promise to speak the truth as long as I live."

Truthfulness is the pivot of Prophethood. It could not be otherwise, for if a Prophet were to lie, everything connected with the Divine religion would be upset. All it takes is one lie to call a mission into question. Thus God declares:

> If he (Muhammad) had invented false sayings concerning Us, We would surely have grasped him firmly, and then cut off the artery of his heart, and none of you could have withheld Us from doing this. (69:44–47)

A Companion remembered:

"Before his Prophethood, we made an appointment to meet somewhere. It was, however, 3 days after the appointed time when I remembered it. When I hastened to the appointed place, I found the future Prophet waiting for me. He was neither angry nor offended. His only reaction was to say: 'O young man, you have given me some trouble. I have been waiting here for you for three days.'"

Then He accepted their repentance so that they could recover their former state. Verily, God is the One who accepts repentance, Most Merciful. (9:118)

Key vocabulary

- **Pivot:** a person or a thing that is central or important to someone or something else

WHAT DID WE LEARN?

LESSON SUMMARY:

- Sidq (Truthfulness): They never lie, even just for a joke. They are truthful in all circumstances.
- The prophets are, like us, human beings. They eat, drink, rejoice, and worry... However, they have exceptionally good characters, and they have special attributes, given to them by Allah
- No lies or deceit, whether explicit or implicit, were ever heard from the Prophets
- God's Messenger always encouraged truthfulness
- Always be truthful, for truthfulness leads to righteousness and righteousness leads to Paradise.
- Never lie, for lying leads to shamefulness and shamefulness leads to Hell

LESSON REVIEW: INDIVIDUAL ASSESSMENT

1. What is the cornerstone of Prophethood? Why?
2. The Qur'an praises which kind of believers in 33:23? Explain in detail.
3. Which things was Prophet Muhammad referring to when he said "promise me six things and I will promise you paradise."
4. What was the reason Ka'b Ibn Malik's repentance was accepted after 50 days, and what was his promise afterwards?

ESSAY

"If you are truthful and seek truthfulness, God records you as such...If you insist on lying and deceit, God records you as such" Explain your understanding of this quote. Pay extra attention to the word choices: seek, insist, and deceit. Be sure to reference your text and your essay must have an introduction, body, and conclusion.

LESSON VOCABULARY

- Extol
- Valiant
- Pivot
- Unanimously
- Inconceivable

Lesson 3

Trustworthiness (Amanah)

Prophet Muhammad was completely trustworthy toward all of God's creatures. He was loyal and never cheated anyone.

"Yes, you have conveyed it!" He then would call upon God to witness their words.

"God's Messenger never thought of concealing even a word of the Qur'an."

The second attribute of Prophethood is amanah, an Arabic word meaning trustworthiness and derived from the same root as mu'min (believer). Being a believer implies being a trustworthy person. All Prophets were the best believers and therefore perfect exemplars of trustworthiness. To stress this principle, God summarizes the stories of five Prophets using the same words:

> When their brother Noah asked them: "Will you not fear God and avoid evil? I am a trustworthy Messenger to you." (26:105-7)

Replace the name Noah with those of Hud, Salih, Lut, and Shu'ayb, and you have a summarized version of these five Prophets' trustworthiness (26:122-5, 141-3, 161-4, 177-180).

Trustworthiness is also an essential quality of Archangel Gabriel. The Qur'an describes Gabriel as one obeyed and trustworthy (81:21). We received the Qur'an through two trustworthy Messengers: Gabriel and Prophet Muhammad. The former conveyed it; the latter related it to us.

Prophet Muhammad was completely trustworthy toward all of God's creatures. He was loyal and never cheated anyone.

God chose the Messenger for his trustworthiness so that he would devote himself totally to delivering the Message truthfully. He was so concerned about his duty that he would repeat the verses while Gabriel was reciting them to him. God finally revealed:

> Move not your tongue concerning (the Qur'an) to make haste therewith. It is for Us to collect it, to establish it in your heart and enable you to recite it. (75:16-19)

As the Qur'an was given to him as a trust, he conveyed it to people in the best way possible, aware of his responsibility. In the last year of his life, when he was delivering the Farewell Sermon at Mount 'Arafat, he reiterated the Commandments of God once more. At the end of each sentence, he told the people: "In the near future, they will ask you about me." He then would ask them if he had conveyed the Message to them, to which they responded, each time, with great enthusiasm:

"Yes, you have conveyed it!" He then would call upon God to witness their words.

- **Primitive:** very simple and basic
- **Sociological:** related to the society

THINK

We read in the Qur'an several mild Divine warnings for a few actions of this. If he wrote it, as some mistakenly claim, why would he have included such verses?

"God's Messenger never thought of concealing even a word of the Qur'an."

In fact, we read in the Qur'an several mild Divine warnings for a few actions of his. If he wrote it, as some mistakenly claim, why would he have included such verses?

The Prophet was raised in a primitive society characterized by customs that contradicted reason as well as sociological and scientific facts. For example, as adopted children enjoyed the same legal status as natural children, a man could not legally marry his adopted son's widow or ex-wife. In order to separate a legal fiction from a natural reality, and to establish a new law and custom this practice was abolished through the Messenger's life, for adoption does not create a relationship comparable to that with one's biological parents.

Zayd, an emancipated black slave and servant of God's Messenger, was also his adopted son. At the Prophet's request, Zayd married Zaynab bint Jahsh. Nevertheless, it soon became clear that the marriage would not last long. Admitting that he was spiritually and intellectually inferior to his wife, Zayd thought it would be better for him to divorce her. In the end, the Qur'an commanded the Prophet to marry her. Of course, doing so would violate a strong social taboo. As such, and because the hypocrites would use this to defame him, he delayed announcing the Divine decree. God reminded the Prophet that His command must be fulfilled:

DISCUSS

Think about what Allah is saying in "God will protect you from men. God does not guide the unbelievers." (5:67) How could this help to ease the worries of both Prophet Muhammad and yourself?

> Then you said to him on whom God bestowed grace and unto whom you had shown favor: "Keep your wife to yourself and fear God." But you hid in your heart that which God was about to make manifest because you feared the people (would slander you), whereas God had a better right that you should fear Him. We gave her in marriage to you (33:37).

'A'isha later commented: "If God's Messenger could have concealed any Revelation, he would have concealed that verse." If the Prophet had not been trustworthy, he would have done just that. However, such an act is contrary to his character and mission, and would mean that he had not delivered the Message. Furthermore, God prohibits him from doing this:

> O Messenger, deliver what has been sent down to you from your Lord; for if you do not, you will not have fulfilled your task of His Messengership. God will protect you from men. God does not guide the unbelievers. (5:67)

Key vocabulary

- **Emancipated:** to set someone or something free

HIS RELATIONS WITH OTHERS

He warned his people against lying, breaking their word, and breaching their trust.

God's Messenger was trustworthy and encouraged others to follow his example. Once during the last ten days of Ramadan, his wife Safiyya visited him while he was keeping vigil (i'tikaf) in the mosque. As he was escorting her home, two Companions happened to pass by. The Messenger stopped them and, unveiling his wife's face, said: "This is my wife Safiyya." They said: "God forbid any evil thought about you, O Messenger of God." The Messenger was warning them against having evil thoughts about him, for that could cause them to lose their faith and enter Hell. He gave them and us a lesson, saying: "Satan continuously circulates within people's blood vessels."

"He warned his people against lying, breaking their word, and breaching their trust."

All of these were condemned as "signs of hypocrisy. "He was so meticulous in this matter that when he saw a woman call her child, saying: "Come on, I'll give you something," he asked her if she was telling the truth. She replied that she would give him a date, to which God's Messenger responded: "If you were to give him nothing, you would have lied."

His concern in this matter extended even to animals. Once, annoyed at seeing a Companion trying to deceive his horse, he said: "Stop deceiving animals. Instead, be trustworthy with them."

Another time, while returning from a military campaign, a few Companions took some baby birds from a nest to pet them. The mother bird returned after a short while and, finding her babies gone, began to fly around in distress. When God's Messenger was informed, he was so upset that he ordered the birds to be returned immediately. Such an order was meant to show that representatives of trustworthiness should harm no living creatures.

Each Companion was an embodiment of trustworthiness. By virtue of this and other laudable virtues, cities and states submitted to Islam. During 'Umar's caliphate, Abu 'Ubayda, the embodiment of justice, commanded the Muslim armies in Syria. When the Eastern Roman (Byzantine) Emperor set out to recapture Hims, Abu 'Ubayda decided to evacuate the city, for his forces were vastly outnumbered. He had the non-Muslim population assembled and announced: "We collected the protection tax from you because we had to defend you. Since we can't defend you against the coming Byzantine assault, we are returning the tax we collected." This was done. Pleased with the Muslim administration, Christian priests and Jewish rabbis flocked to the churches and synagogues to pray that God would cause the Muslim army to be successful.

Such was the attitude of Muslim conquerors and administrators in the lands they ruled. They epitomized lofty virtues.

- **I'tikaf:** a practice of staying in a Masjid for a certain amount of time solely to worship Allah and devoting oneself to worship.
- **Meticulous:** very careful about doing something in an extremely accurate and exact way
- **Deceive:** to make (someone) believe something that is not true
- **Lofty:** very high and good; deserving to be admired

Muslim soldiers used to hang coin pouches on branches in return for the fruit they had eaten in the orchards when on their way to war.

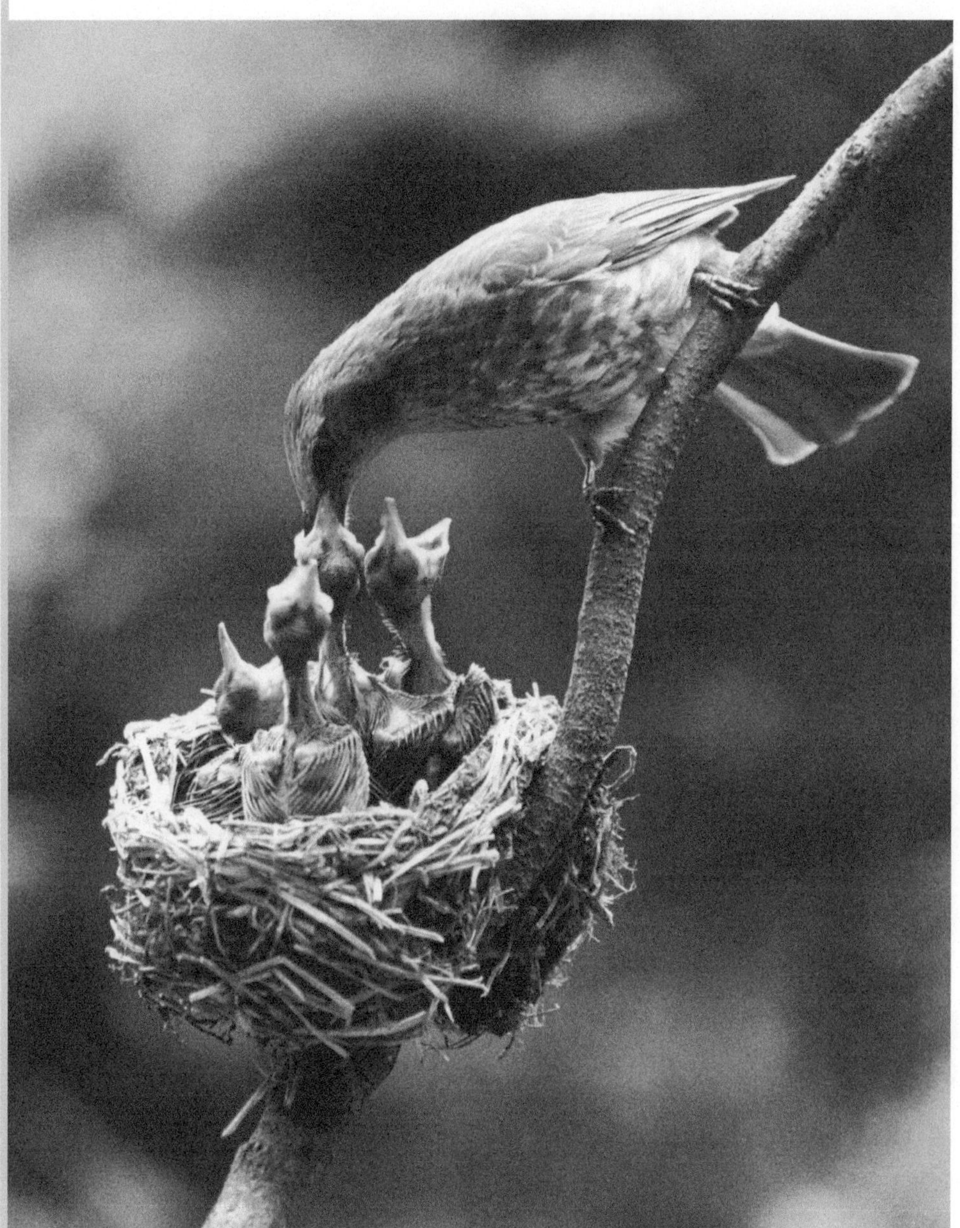

"Muslim soldiers used to hang coin pouches on branches in return for the fruit they had eaten in the orchards when on their way to war."

They conquered the hearts of people. Muslims stayed in Spain for eight centuries, and in the Balkans and some parts of the Central and Eastern Europe for around five centuries. Muslim rulers did not interfere with a conquered people's religion, language, or culture. If they had done so, there would have been no followers of other religions in the lands they had conquered to recapture those lands.

Islam emphasizes trustworthiness and security to such an extent that suspicion and gossip are forbidden

IMAGINE

God's Messenger was so sensitive on this point that once when A'isha commented: "How long her skirt is," he said: "You have gossiped about her and so ate of her flesh!"

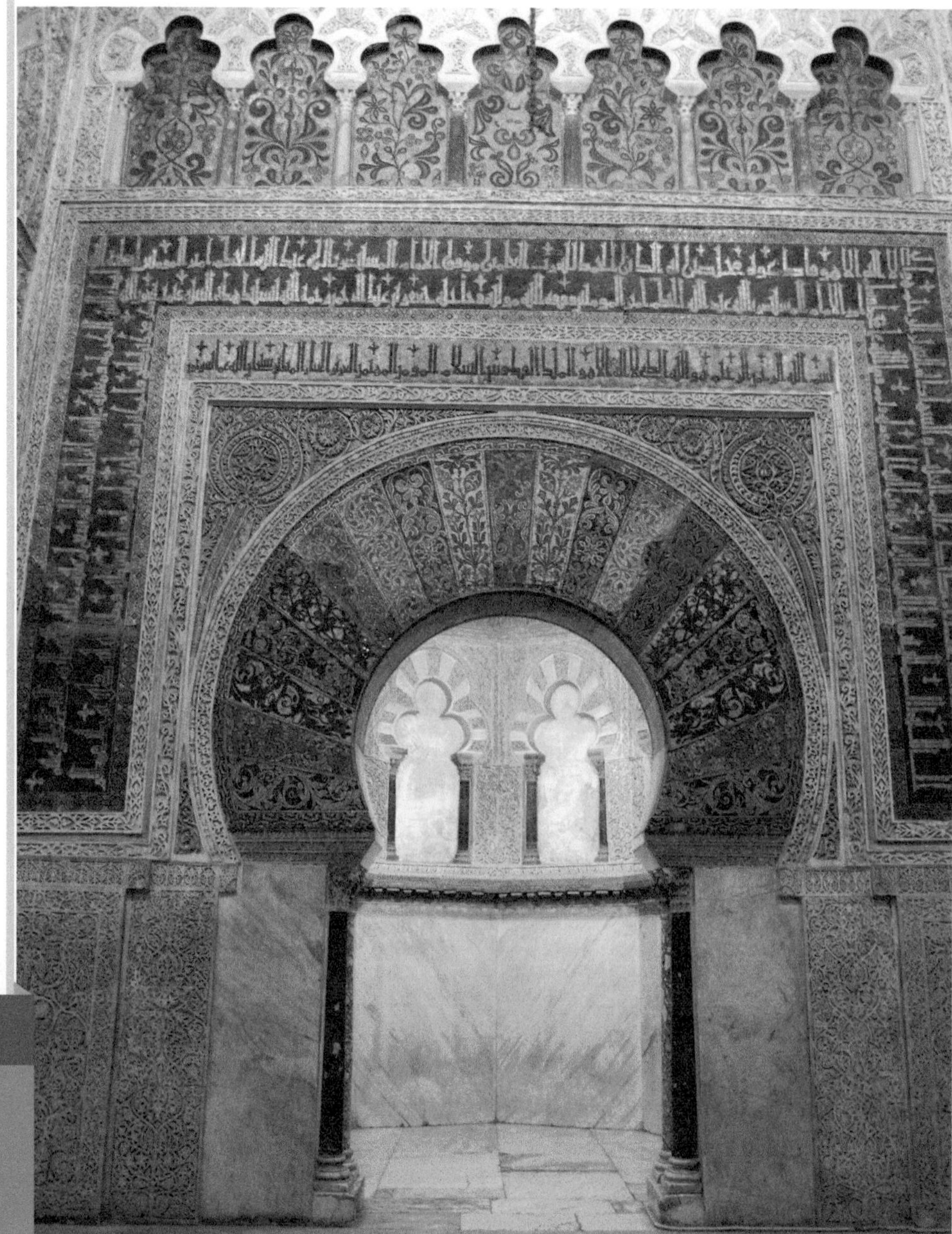

"Islam emphasizes trustworthiness and security to such an extent that suspicion and gossip are forbidden."

O you who believe! Avoid much suspicion, for suspicion in some cases is a grave sin. Do not spy on or gossip about one another. Would one of you like to eat the flesh of his dead brother? You would abhor it. Fear God, for verily God is the Acceptor of repentance, the Most Merciful. (49:12)

- **Abhor:** to dislike (someone or something) very much

He always prayed: "O God, I seek refuge in You from hunger, for how bad a companion it is! I also seek refuge in You from betrayal, for what an evil confidant it is!"

He always prayed: "O God, I seek refuge in You from hunger, for how bad a companion it is! I also seek refuge in You from betrayal, for what an evil confidant it is!"

He also had harsh words for those who betray and are disloyal: "When God gathers together on the Day of Judgment all the people preceding and to come, a banner will be raised on behalf of every disloyal person. It will be announced: 'This is because of the disloyalty of so and so!'" The heart of God's Messenger was closed to all evil, but open to all good. He lived in a climate of security, faithfulness, and trustworthiness. He never cheated, lied, betrayed people, just as he never gossiped about, slandered, or harbored evil suspicion about someone. In return, people relied on him and confided in him. His enemies slandered him, but no one ever accused him of lying and disloyalty. Those who turned their backs on him were deceived and dragged into wrong ways.

God's Messenger was totally reliable. His trustworthiness had two aspects: his relationship with people, and his relationship with God. The former manifested itself as complete reliability; the latter as perfect reliance on God. When combined, these two aspects ensure a peaceful atmosphere of steadfastness and security.

The Qur'an gives several examples concerning the Prophets' confidence in, and perfect reliance on God. To cite only a few:

> Relate to them the exemplary history of Noah when he said to this people: "O my people! If my presence (among you) and my reminding (you) by God's Revelations are offensive to you - well, in God have I put my trust. So, coming together, decide upon your course of action, and (call to your aid) your (so-called) associates of God; then let not your affair be a worry to you, and then carry out against me (whatever you have decided), and give me no respite!" (10:71)
>
> (Hud said to his people:) "I call God to witness and bear you witness that I am free from all that you ascribe as partners in worship to God, beside Him. So, plot against me, all of you, and give me no respite. I put my trust in God, my Lord and your Lord. There's not a moving creature but He has grasp of its forelock. Verily my Lord is on a straight path." (11:54-56) Indeed there has been an excellent example for you in Abraham and those with him, when they said to their people: "Verily we are free from you and from whatever you worship besides God; we have rejected you, and there has arisen between us and you hostility and hatred for ever, until you believe in God alone," except Abraham's saying to his father: "Verily I ask forgiveness (from God) for you, but I have no power to do anything for you before God. Our Lord! In you (alone) we put our trust, and to You (alone) we return in repentance, and to You (alone) is our final return." (60:4)

His enemies slandered him, but no one ever accused him of lying and disloyalty.

"The nature of unbelief is deviation and opposition."

- **Respite:** when something difficult or unpleasant stops or is delayed
- **Enmity:** a feeling or condition of hostility; hatred; ill will
- **Eradicate:** to remove (something) completely

The Messenger's reliance on God made him fearless.

"The nature of unbelief is deviation and opposition." Unbelievers see the world in darkness and feel alone in an alien world; believers see the whole universe as a cradle of brotherhood and sisterhood, and feel connected to everything. By its nature, unbelief severs relations and, as a result, unbelievers feel enmity against everything, especially believers. They cannot bear the believers' existence, so they try their best to eradicate belief. That is why all Prophets encountered severe opposition and, with their followers, suffered pitiless acts of cruelty. But due to their complete confidence in and perfect reliance on God, they never lost heart because of what befell them in God's Way, nor did they weaken (in will) nor were they brought low (3:146).

"The Messenger's reliance on God made him fearless." He appeared in the heartland of a desert inhabited by one of the most uncivilized peoples. Despite their harsh treatment, and the strident hostility of one of his own uncles, he challenged the whole world and, through complete trust in God, carried his mission to victory. He had only a handful of supporters, and his victory came in a very short period—an unparalleled achievement. We can understand his fearless nature, which developed out of his absolute confidence in God, through the following anecdotes.

"Do not be anxious, for God is with us (9:40). What do you think of the two men beside whom God is the third?"

The Quraysh were so eager to kill him that just before his emigration to Medina they selected one man from each clan. These numbered roughly 200. Led by Abu Jahl and Abu Lahab, they besieged his house. God's Messenger told his cousin 'Ali to spend the night in his bed and, throwing some dust at the hostile men while reciting: *We have put a barrier before them and behind them, and thus covered them so that they cannot see* (36:9), he departed without being seen. He left Mecca with his closest friend, Abu Bakr, and reached Thawr cave, which is at the top of a steep mountain. Finding him gone, the Quraysh chiefs sent out search parties. One of these climbed the mountain up to the cave. Abu Bakr became anxious, fearing for the life of God's Messenger. However, the latter comforted him: "Do not be anxious, for God is with us" (9:40), and added: "What do you think of the two men beside whom God is the third?"

As related through various channels, during the military campaigns of Ghatfan and Anmar, a courageous chieftain named Ghowras unexpectedly appeared beside God's Messenger, who was lying under a tree. Unsheathing his sword, he asked him:

Key vocabulary

- **Unparalleled:** not found elsewhere or experienced before
- **Strident:** sounding harsh and unpleasant

"Trustworthiness is a cornerstone of belief"

"Who will save you from me now?' "God," said the Messenger, with no sign of panic, having full trust in God. All of a sudden, Ghowras' blood ran cold and the sword slipped from his hands; he froze in shock. God's Messenger picked it up and asked him: "Now, who will save you from me?" Ghowras began to tremble and pleaded for his life: "You are a noble, forgiving man; only forgiveness is expected of you." God's Messenger forgave him, and when Ghowras returned to his tribe, he said: "I have just come from the best of humanity."

"Trustworthiness is a cornerstone of belief"

> God commands you to deliver the trusts (including public and professional duties of service) to those qualified for them, and when you judge between people, to judge with justice. How excellent is what God exhorts you to do. Surely God is All-Hearing, All-Seeing. (4:58)

According to God's Messenger, breaching a trust is a sign of the end of time: "When the trust is breached, expect the end of time." When his Companions asked how that would be, he answered: "If a job or post is assigned to the unqualified, expect the end of time."

Assigning qualified people to jobs or posts is a social trust and plays a significant role in public administration and social order. Its abuse causes social disorder. There should be order at all social levels, for some are to be given responsibilities by others. God's Messenger declared: "Each of you is a shepherd (manager), and each of you is responsible for your flock. The ruler is a shepherd responsible for his subjects. A husband is a shepherd responsible for his family. A woman is a shepherd responsible for her husband's house. A servant is a shepherd responsible for managing the duties or property his master entrusted to him." If everyone in a society were to carry out their responsibilities, we would be living in a "society of trustworthy ones." Until that time, we can only imagine such utopias.

To live in absolute security is only possible if trustworthy people are in power. If the Muslim world observes the Divine Trust and becomes the representative of trustworthiness and security in the world, a "new world order" based on justice and balance will be possible. Otherwise, humanity will continue to chase after mirages of justice, security, and happiness.

- **Breaching:** failure to do what is required by a law, an agreement, or a duty
- **Utopia:** an imaginary place in which the government, laws, and social conditions are perfect

WHAT DID WE LEARN?

LESSON SUMMARY:

- Trustworthiness is a cornerstone of belief
- Prophet Muhammad was completely trustworthy toward all of God's creatures. He was loyal and never cheated anyone.
- God chose the Messenger for his trustworthiness so that he would devote himself totally to delivering the Message truthfully
- God's Messenger never thought of concealing even a word of the Qur'an.
- The Prophet was raised in a primitive society characterized by customs that contradicted reason as well as sociological and scientific facts
- Islam emphasizes trustworthiness and security to such an extent that suspicion and gossip are forbidden
- The Messenger's reliance on God made him fearless

LESSON REVIEW: INDIVIDUAL ASSESSMENT

1. Describe an example of the primitive customs from society that was challenged and changed through Islam.
2. What is the verse A'isha stated Prophet Muhammad would have left out had he concealed any Revelation?
3. List as many examples as you can find that show the trustworthiness and just treatment shown by the Companions.
4. In order for it to be possible that "new world order" could be established, what must happen first?

ESSAY

"Trustworthiness is the cornerstone of belief." In an explanatory essay, analyze why this is a true statement. Be sure to reference the text. Your essay must be a minimum of 3 paragraphs.

LESSON VOCABULARY

- Emancipated
- Primitive
- Sociological
- Breaching
- Unparalleled ekleyelim
- Meticilous
- Deceive
- Lofty
- Abhor
- Respite
- Enmity
- Eradicate
- Strident
- Utopia

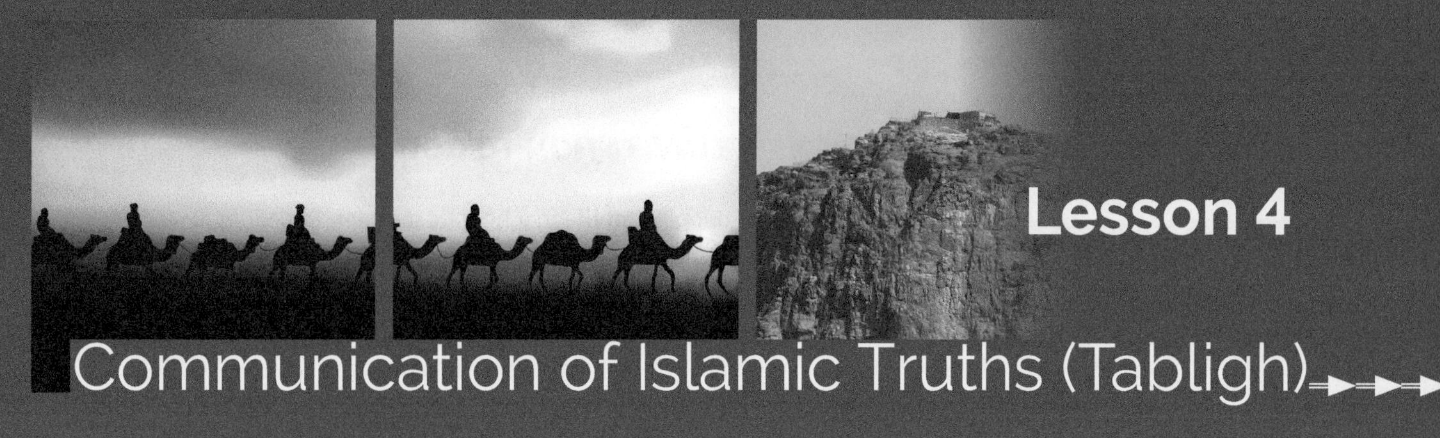

Lesson 4

Communication of Islamic Truths (Tabligh)

The third attribute of Prophethood is communication of Islamic truths, otherwise known as "enjoining good and forbidding evil."

The third attribute of Prophethood is communication of Islamic truths, otherwise known as "enjoining good and forbidding evil (amr bi-l ma'ruf wa-n nahy 'anil munkar)."

We say Islamic truths because every Prophet came with the same Divine Religion based on submission to God, and had as his sole mission the communication of this Message.

Just as God manifests His Mercifulness through the sun's warmth and light, He manifested His Mercy and Compassion for humanity through Prophets. He chose Muhammad, whom He sent as a mercy for all worlds, to establish eternally the Message of compassion and mercy. If he had not been sent to revive and revise the Messages of previous Prophets and then spread that knowledge throughout the world, we would be wandering in a terrifying desert of unbelief, misguidance, and ignorance.

Prophets were sent to convey this Message and to illuminate the path to happiness in this world and the next. Now we will discuss three essential points regarding how a Prophet conveys the Divine Message.

A COMPREHENSIVE INVITATION TO GOD

DISCUSS

Human beings are active. Therefore, shouldn't they be led to those activities that form a real purpose for their lives, as determined by God and communicated by the Prophet?

The Prophets dealt with people and life in a holistic manner, appealing to each person's intellect, reason, spirit, and all outer and inner senses and feelings. They never ignored or neglected any human faculties.

The position of a Prophet in relation to Divine Revelation is similar to that of a corpse in the hands of a mortician: The individual can do nothing of his own volition. God directs and guides a Prophet as necessary so that he can lead his people. Without this Divine direction, he would be unable to guide anyone. If he neglected their intellects, the end result would be a community of poor, docile mystics. If he neglected their hearts or spirits, a crude rationalism devoid of any spiritual dimension would be produced. As each individual is comprised of intellect, spirit, and body, each must be assigned its due part of the Message.

God did not create people only to have them to become passive recluses, activists without reason and spirit, or rationalists without spiritual reflection and activism.

Only when the intellect, spirit, and body are harmonized, and people are motivated to activity in the illuminated way of the Divine Message, can they become complete and attain true humanity. All Prophets sought this goal, and those who seek to follow them should strive for it:

Say (Muhammad): "This is my way: I call (people) to God with wisdom and insight, I and those who follow me" (12:108).

A Prophet is totally dedicated to his mission, and thus is an altruist who lives for the happiness and good of others. His happiness lies in seeing people devote themselves to God in the hope of salvation, not in expecting some great reward for his services. He knows that his reward is with God alone. This indispensable fact is emphasized in the Qur'an: O my people! I ask of you no wealth for it; my reward is from none but God (11:29).

The Prophets were charged with conveying the Divine Message. They did their best, patiently faced many misfortunes and even torment, fulfilled their responsibilities, and then left the result to God. They knew with full certainty that only God brings about the desired result. These three fundamentals set the principles for all those who wish to call others to Islam.

They did their best and then left the result to God. They knew with full certainty that only God brings about the desired result.

Say (Muhammad): "This is my way: I call (people) to God with wisdom and insight, I and those who follow me" (12:108).

Key vocabulary

- **Holistic:** relating to or concerned with complete as a whole rather than with individual parts
- **Mortician:** a person whose job is to prepare dead people for burial and manage funerals
- **Volition:** the power to make your own choices
- **Devoid:** entirely lacking or free from
- **Recluse:** a person who lives alone and avoids other people
- **Altruist:** a person who is devoted to the welfare of others

THE METHOD

"Many Prophets lived with no one accepting their Message."

Constant striving is an essential feature of delivering the Message, as well as an important element of the Prophetic method. A Prophet is, so to speak, obsessed with how to perform his duty. With that goal always uppermost, he considers all circumstances and does everything permitted. As he is not responsible for the results, he leaves them to God. He knows that he cannot cause anyone to accept the Message, for he is only sent to convey it as effectively as possible: You (O Muhammad) cannot guide to truth whomever you like, but God guides whomever He wills. He knows best who are guided (and open to guidance) (28:56).

"Many Prophets lived with no one accepting their Message."

However, they did not lose heart, weaken, or resort to such improper means as violence, terror, or deception even when faced with relentless hardship and torture.

When tormented and accused of false allegations, all Prophets responded in a similar way. Take this story from Noah for example:

> The leaders of Noah's people said: "We see you in clear deviation." He said: "O my people, there is no deviation in me. I am a Messenger from the Lord of the worlds. I convey unto you the messages of my Lord, and give sincere advice to you. And I know from God that which you don't know." (7:60-62)

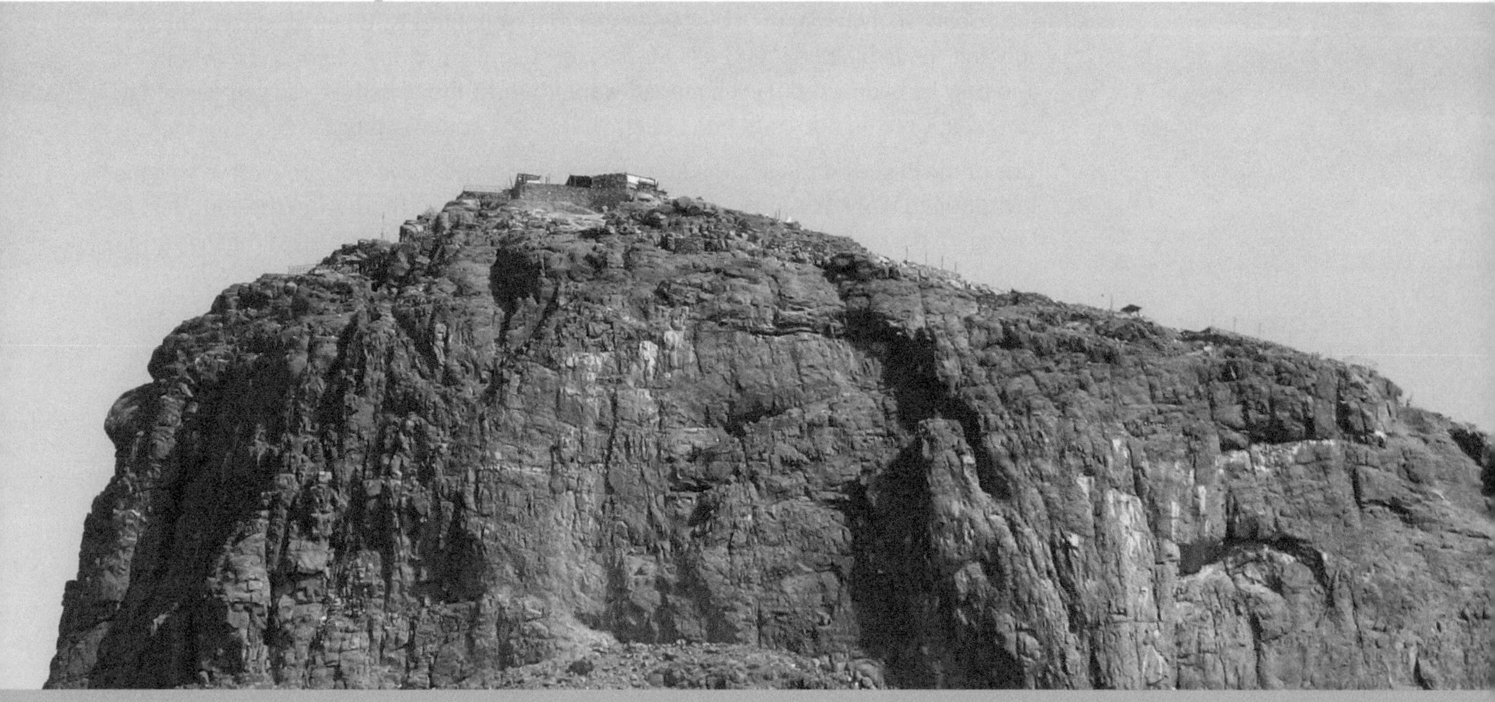

- **Deception:** the act of making someone believe something that is not true

CONSISTENT EFFORT

THINK

We become worried when we are hungry or thirsty or have trouble breathing. Prophet Muhammad was worried if a day passed during which he could not convey the Divine Message to someone.

"Communicating the Divine Message was the most essential characteristic of God's Messenger."

He was so concerned about guidance and so pained by unbelief, that God advised him to take care of his health: *(O Muhammad) it may be that you will kill yourself following after them, with grief that they do not believe in this Message* (18:6).

God's Messenger invited all Meccans, both publicly and privately, to God's path. He called some extremely stubborn people, among them Abu Jahl, at least fifty times. He particularly sought his uncle Abu Talib's conversion, for he had raised him and protected him from the Meccan polytheists. In the eleventh year of his Prophethood, when Abu Talib was dying, God's Messenger again invited him to belief. However, the Meccan chiefs surrounded him to prevent this.

He was so grieved at Abu Talib's unbelief that he said: "I will ask forgiveness from God for you as long as I am not forbidden to." A verse was revealed some time later, forbidding him to do this:

> It is not fitting for the Prophet and those who believe to ask (God) to forgive polytheists, even though they be near of kin (to them), after it has become clear to them that they (died as polytheists and, therefore,) are condemned to the Blazing Flame. (9:113)

Abu Bakr, the Prophet's closest Companion, knew how much God's Messenger desired his uncle to be a believer. He took his aged father, who converted on the day of the Conquest of Mecca, to God's Messenger and wept bitterly. When asked why he was sobbing, he explained: "O God's Messenger, I so wanted my father to be a believer and now he believes. But even more, I wanted Abu Talib to believe, for you desired it. However, God did not grant him belief. That is why I am weeping."

One of the best examples of the Messenger's concern for everyone to believe was his invitation to Wahshi, who had killed his uncle Hamza at Uhud. After the conquest of Mecca, God's Messenger sent for him to accept Islam. Wahshi returned the invitation with a letter, including the following verses:

> Who invoke no other deity along with God, and do not kill any soul—which God has made forbidden—except by right, and do not commit unlawful sexual intercourse. Whoever commits any of these will face a severe penalty. His punishment will be greater on the Day of Resurrection, and he will abide in it in ignominy. (25:68-69)

"Communicating the Divine Message was the most essential characteristic of God's Messenger"

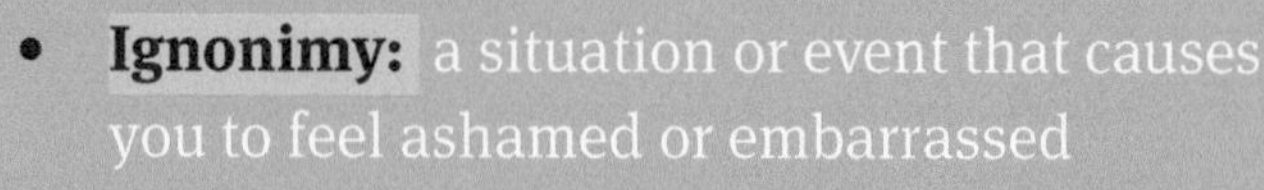

- **Ignonimy:** a situation or event that causes you to feel ashamed or embarrassed

After the verse Wahshi added: "You invite me to accept Islam, but I have committed all the sins mentioned therein. I have lived immersed in unbelief...in addition, killed your uncle, who was most beloved by you. Can such a person really be forgiven and become a Muslim?" God's Messenger sent him a written reply, containing the following verse:

> God forgives not that partners should be associated with Him, but He forgives save that (anything else) to whom He wills. Whoever associates partners with God has invented a tremendous sin. (4:48)

Wahshi returned the letter with the excuse that the forgiveness promised in the verse depended on God's Will. Upon this, God's Messenger sent him a third letter, in which the following verse was included:

> Say: "(God gives you hope): 'O My servants who have been wasteful (of their God-given opportunities and faculties) against (the good of) their own souls! Do not despair of God's Mercy. Surely God forgives all sins. He is indeed the All-Forgiving, the All-Compassionate.'" (39:53)

Through this correspondence, God's Messenger opened Wahshi's heart to belief, and Wahshi could see himself included in the verse mentioned in the last letter. This correspondence enabled Wahshi to repent sincerely and become a Companion. Nevertheless, Hamza's martyrdom had affected God's Messenger so deeply that he whispered to Wahshi: "Try not to present yourself to me too often. I might remember Hamza, and thus be unable to show you the proper affection."

Wahshi did his best to comply with this request. He would stand behind a pole and try to catch a glimpse of God's Messenger in the hope that he might be allowed to present himself. When God's Messenger died soon thereafter, Wahshi set out to find a way of atonement for his act. When the war of Yamama broke out against Musaylima the Liar, he hastened to the front lines with the spear he had used to kill Hamza. At the most critical point, he saw Musaylima trying to flee. Immediately, he threw his spear at the impostor and killed him. After this, Wahshi prostrated before God. With tears flowing from his eyes, he was as if saying: "Will you now allow me to show myself to you, O God's Messenger?" We cannot but to wish that God's Messenger was present in spirit at Yamama and embraced Wahshi to show his pardon and full admission into his noble company.

Another fine example of God's Messenger's concern about people's guidance, is his acceptance of Ikrima as a Companion. Ikrima was one of the staunchest enemies of Islam and the Messenger, and an active participant in all plots to defeat him. He fled to Yemen with his wife on the day Mecca was conquered, and many of his comrades chose conversion. His wife, Umm Hakam, convinced him to go to God's Messenger and ask forgiveness. Despite his previous hostility, Ikrima was welcomed by God's Messenger with the compliment: "Welcome, O emigrant rider!" After the conquest of Mecca, there was no "emigration" in the true sense; God's Messenger was alluding to Ikrima's long journey from Yemen to Medina.

Key vocabulary

- **Emigration:** a person who leaves a country or region to live in another one
- **Alluding:** to speak of or mention (something or someone) in an indirect way

Ikrima was deeply affected by such nobility, and requested him to ask God's pardon for his sins. When the Messenger did so, Ikrima felt exhilarated and promised to spend for the sake of Islam double what he had spent fighting it. Ikrima fulfilled his promise at the Battle of Yarmuk, where he was wounded. Seeing his wife crying beside him in the tent, he told her: "Don't weep, for I won't die before I witness the victory." Sometime later, his uncle Hisham entered and announced the Muslims' victory. Ikrima asked to be helped to stand up, and when they did so, whispered: "O God's Messenger, have I carried out the promise I gave you?"

"Then, he recited: Make me die as a Muslim and join me to the righteous (12:101), and submitted his soul to God."

Then, he recited: Make me die as a Muslim and join me to the righteous (12:101), and submitted his soul to God.

Throughout his life, God's Messenger grieved for the misfortunes of humanity. He ceaselessly called people to God's way. During his years in Mecca, he walked the streets and visited the nearby annual fairs, always hoping to gain a few converts. Insults, derision, and torture did not deter him even once. When: *Warn your tribe of the nearest kindred* (26:214) was revealed, he invited his nearest relatives over for a meal. 'Ali later narrated the incident:

Key vocabulary

- **Derision:** the feeling that people express when they criticize and laugh at someone or something in an insulting way
- **Exhilarated:** to cause (someone) to feel very happy and excited

"God's Messenger invited his relatives to his house. After the meal, he addressed them:'God has commanded me to warn my nearest relatives. You are my tribe of the nearest kindred. I will not be able to do anything for you in the Hereafter unless you proclaim that there is no deity but God.'

"At the end of his speech, he asked who would support him. At that time, I was a boy with puny legs and arms. When no one responded, I put aside the pitcher in my hand and declared: 'I will, O Messenger of God!' The Messenger repeated the call three times, and each time only I answered him."

The Messenger persevered, enduring relentless and increasingly harsh derision, degradation, beatings, and expulsion from the fairs. He was actually stoned by children in Ta'if. Only in the twelfth year of his mission was he able to meet some Medinese at 'Aqaba (located outside of Mecca). He told them of Islam, and they accepted it. The following year, 70 Madinese became Muslims at the same place. They swore allegiance to God's Messenger and promised to support him if he emigrated to Medina. He appointed Mus'ab ibn 'Umayr to teach them Islam. This was the beginning of a new phase in his life. By the time he emigrated to Medina the following year, every household had at least one Muslim.

FURTHER REMARKS

While communicating the Message, the Prophet set an excellent example in guiding people. The Companions did their best to imitate his technique.

An important point to note is that while communicating the Message, the Prophet set an excellent example in guiding people. The Companions did their best to imitate his technique. For example, Mus'ab ibn 'Umayr's technique was so effective and sincere that even the most stubborn Madinese, such as Sa'd ibn Mu'adh, became Muslims. Sa'd's initial reaction to Mus'ab's activity was harsh. But when the latter asked him politely: "First sit and listen. If you are not pleased with what I tell you, feel free to cut off my head with the sword in your hand," Sa'd's anger subsided. He parted from Mus'ab as a new Muslim.

God's Messenger continued to send Companions to neighboring cities. He sent Talha to Duwmat al-Jandal, and Bara' ibn A'dhib to Yemen. If a Companion was not successful, although this was rare, he sent another in his place. When Khalid and Bara' could not capture the Yemenis' hearts, God's Messenger sent 'Ali. Shortly thereafter, almost all of them became Muslim.

Another important point is his conduct after the Treaty of Hudaybiyah. Some of the Companions considered various conditions dishonorable (to the Muslims). However, in the ensuing atmosphere of peace, which followed years of disruption and war, many enemies of Islam reconsidered the Message. Eventually, even such leading opponents as Khalid and 'Amr ibn al-'As accepted Islam. God's Messenger welcomed Khalid with a compliment: "I was wondering how a sensible man like Khalid could remain an unbeliever. I had a strong conviction that you would one day accept Islam."He comforted 'Amr ibn al-'As, who asked him to pray for God's forgiveness of him, and said: "Don't you know that those who accept Islam are cleansed of all their previous sins?"

- **Subside:** to move down to a lower level
- **Ensuing:** happening as a result

Say: "O people of the Book. Come to a word common between us and you that we worship none but God, that we associate nothing in worship with Him, and that none of us shall take others for lords beside God. If they turn away, say: 'Bear witness that we are Muslims.'"(3:64)

After the Treaty of Hudaybiyah, God's Messenger sent letters to the rulers of neighboring countries. He wrote to the Negus, king of Abyssinia:

> From Muhammad, God's Messenger, to Negus Ashama, King of Abyssinia.
>
> Peace be upon you! On this occasion, I praise God, the Sovereign, the Holy One free from all defects, the Giver of security, the Watcher over His creatures. I bear witness that Jesus is a spirit from God, a word from Him, whom He bestowed upon Mary, who was chaste, pure, and a virgin. I call you to God, One with no partner.

The Messenger approached Negus by first greeting him with peace; this was perhaps a sign that he was very hopeful about him. Since Negus was a Christian, God's Messenger referred to the verses in the Qur'an that are related with Jesus, peace be upon him, and his mother Mary, thus emphasizing the point of agreement between them.

Negus received the letter, and, kissing it, put it to his head as a sign of respect. After reading it, he accepted Islam without hesitation and dictated the following to his secretary:

> To Muhammad, God's Messenger, from Negus. I bear witness that you are the Messenger of God. If you command me to come to you, I will do it, but I am not in a position to make my subjects Muslim. O God's Messenger, I testify that what you say is all true.

Negus was so sincere that one day he told his confidants: "I would rather be a servant of Muhammad than a king." When he died, God's Messenger performed the funeral prayer for him in absentia.

The following letter was sent to Heraclius, emperor of Byzantium:

> From Muhammad, the servant of God and His Messenger, to Heraclius, the greatest of the Byzantines. Peace be upon him who follows the guidance. I invite you to Islam. Embrace Islam and secure salvation that God may give you a double reward. If you turn away, you will be burned with, besides your own, the sins of all those who turn away (among your people). Say: "O people of the Book. Come to a word common between us and you that we worship none but God, that we associate nothing in worship with Him, and that none of us shall take others for lords beside God. If they turn away, say: 'Bear witness that we are Muslims.'"(3:64)

The Emperor was moved by the letter. He summoned Abu Sufyan, who was then in Syria leading a Meccan trade caravan. The following dialogue took place between them:

- **Confidant:** a trusted friend you can talk to about personal and private things

- What is this man's family status?
- A noble one.
- Did any of his ancestors claim Prophethood?
- No.
- Was there a king among his ancestors?
- No.
- Do the elite or the weak mostly follow him?'
- The weak.
- Has anyone apostatized after conversion to his religion?
- So far, nobody has.
- Do his followers increase or decrease?
- They increase daily.
- Have you ever heard him tell a lie?
- No.
- Has he ever broken his promise?
- Not yet, but I don't know whether he will in the future.

Those who want their words to influence people must practice what they preach.

Although Abu Sufyan was at that time a ruthless enemy of God's Messenger, he told the truth about him except in his last words, which might raise doubts about the Messenger's future trustworthiness. The Emperor was inclined to acknowledge the faith, but seeing the reaction of the priests near to him, only concluded: "In the very near future, all these lands I am resting upon will be his." Imam Bukhari narrates that the bishop of the area accepted Islam.

God's Messenger sent letters to other kings, among them Muqawqis, the ruler of Egypt, who responded with some presents. Chosroes of Persia tore up the letter, an incident predicting his empire's end, which took place during 'Umar's caliphate.

OTHER IMPORTANT POINTS

The following three points are important in conveying the Message of Islam: intelligence, practicing what they preach, and asking for no reward.

IMAGINE

Do you ever wonder if whether or not even the largest, best-equipped group of professional educations, modern pedagogues, sociologists, psychologists, teachers and the like could achieve in 100 years anywhere in the modern civilized world even a hundredth of what God's Messenger did in 23 years in uncivilized Arabia, 14 centuries ago?

First, intelligence must be used to reach people on their own level. A Prophetic Tradition states: "We, the community of the Prophets, are commanded to address people according to their level of understanding." Those seeking to spread Islam should know how to approach and gain non-Muslims' attention. This point can be illustrated by many examples from the life of God's Messenger. For example:

God's Messenger won 'Umar's heart by appreciating his good sense. He told 'Umar: "I can't understand how a reasonable man like you can expect anything from inanimate objects like stones, wood, or soil." He also inspired confidence in 'Umar through his good conduct. His committed worship of God so influenced 'Umar that at last he came to God's Messenger, and was as obedient and reverent before him as a well-mannered child before a respected father.

One day, a young man (apparently Julaybib) asked God's Messenger for permission to fornicate, since he could not restrain himself. Those who were present reacted in various ways. Some scoffed at him, others pulled his robe, and still others readied themselves to hit him. But the compassionate Prophet drew him near and engaged him in conversation. He began by asking him: "Would you let someone do this with your mother?" to which the young man replied: "My mother and father be your ransom, O God's Messenger, I don't agree with that." The Prophet said: "Naturally, no one agrees that his mother should be a party in such a disgraceful act."

He then continued asking Julaybib the same question, but substituting daughter, wife, sister, and aunt for mother. Every time Julaybib replied that he would not agree to such an act. By the end of this conversation, Julaybib had lost all desire to fornicate. But God's Messenger concluded this "spiritual operation" with a supplication. Placing his hand on Julaybib's chest, he prayed: "O God, forgive him, purify his heart, and maintain his chastity."

Julaybib became a model of chastity. Some time later he married through the intermediation of God's Messenger. Not long after that he was martyred in a battle after killing seven enemy soldiers. When his corpse was located, God's Messenger put his hand on his knee and said: "This one is of me, and I am of him."

God's Messenger was so competent and successful in educating people that it is a conclusive proof of his Prophethood. The most uncivilized, crude, ill-mannered, ruthless, and ignorant people of that time were transformed into the most praiseworthy guides of humanity in a very short period.

The modern efforts and techniques applied to remove a bad habit such as smoking with almost no success, when compared to the Prophet's lasting success in eradicating so many bad habits and views, prove that Prophet Muhammad was without parallel or equal when it came to educating people.

Second, those who want their words to influence people must practice what they preach. If they do not, how can they expect to succeed, for it is well known that actions always speak louder than words. The Qur'an is very explicit in this matter: *O you who believe, why do you say that which you do not do? Most hateful it is in the sight of God that you say what you do not do* (61:2-3).

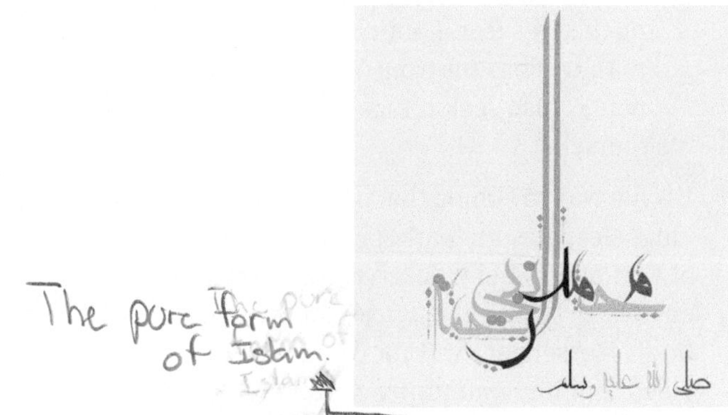

God's Messenger was the living embodiment of his mission. He was the foremost in practicing Islam, devotion to God, and servanthood to Him. It was not uncommon for those who saw him to require no other proof to believe in his Prophethood. For example, 'Abd Allah ibn Salam, the renowned Jewish scholar of Medina, believed in him at first sight, saying: "There can be no lie in this face. One with such a face can only be a Messenger of God."

'Abd Allah ibn Salam, the renowned Jewish scholar of Medina, believed in him at first sight, saying: "There can be no lie in this face. One with such a face can only be a Messenger of God."

One reason why Prophet Muhammad is still loved deeply by hundreds of millions of people, regardless of unending hostile and negative propaganda, and why people all over the world embrace Islam daily, is that he practiced what he preached.

For example, he invited people to worship God sincerely, and is himself the best example of such worship. He would spend more than half the night in prayer, crying and full of humility. When asked why he went to such lengths that his feet would swell, and did so even though he was sinless, he would answer: "Should I not be a thankful slave of God?"

- **Embodiment:** someone or something that is a perfect representative or example of an idea, practice

"Don't you agree that the world should be theirs and the Hereafter ours?"

'A'isha narrated that one night he asked her permission to get up and pray. He was so sensitive to the rights of his wives that he would seek their permission to perform supererogatory prayers. He prayed until daybreak and shed tears. He frequently recited the following verses:

> In the creation of the Heavens and the Earth, and in the alternation of day and night, are signs for those of understanding, those that remember God standing, sitting, and lying down, and reflect on the creation of the Heavens and the Earth. "Our Lord, You have not created this without meaning and purpose. Glory be to You. Protect us from the punishment of the Fire. Our Lord, those whom You will admit to the Fire You have abased; for wrongdoers there are no helpers. Our Lord, we have heard a caller calling to faith: 'Believe in your Lord!' So we believed. Therefore, Our Lord, forgive our sins and erase our evil deeds. Take our souls in death in the company of the righteous. Our Lord, grant us what You promised to us through Your Messengers, and do not abase us on the Day of Resurrection. You never break the promise." (3:190-94)

God's Messenger, like all Prophets, expected no reward for performing his mission.

Again, 'A'isha reports:

> I woke up one night and could not see God's Messenger beside me. I was jealous, lest he had gone to another of his wives. As I just got up from bed, my hand touched his feet. I noticed that he was prostrating, praying: "O God, I seek refuge in Your pleasure from Your wrath, and in Your forgiveness from Your punishment; I also seek refuge in Yourself from You. I cannot praise You as You praise Yourself."

His life was so simple that once 'Umar, upon seeing him, said: "O Messenger of God, kings sleep in soft, feather beds, while you lie on a rough mat. You are the Messenger of God and thereby deserve an easy life more than anyone else." God's Messenger answered: "Don't you agree that the world should be theirs and the Hereafter ours?" God's Messenger lived for others. He desired a comfortable life for his nation, provided that his community would not be led astray by world attractions, but himself lived a very simple life.

Third, God's Messenger, like all Prophets, expected no reward for performing his mission. He suffered hunger, thirst, and every other hardship. He was forced into exile and made the target of assaults and traps. He bore all of these simply for the good pleasure of God and the good of humanity. Abu Hurayra once saw him praying while seated and asked if he were sick. The Messenger's reply caused Abu Hurayra to cry: "I am hungry, Abu Hurayra. Hunger has left me no strength to stand up for prayer." Hunger was a common feature of Muslim life. One night, God's Messenger, Abu Bakr, and 'Umar met each other unexpectedly outside. When they asked one another why they were outside, all replied: "Hunger."

Even though most of his Companions became wealthier in later years, the Messenger and his family never changed their very simple lifestyle. Fatima, his only surviving child, did all of the housework for her family by herself. Once when captives were distributed in Medina, she asked her father for a maid. He replied:

- **Supererogatory prayers (nafila):** voluntary acts of worship that are not obligatory but important to get closer to Allah. Fasting outside of Ramadan, prayers other than five prescribed prayers are examples of such prayers

"O my daughter. I can give you nothing before I satisfy the needs of the people of the Suffa. However, let me teach you something that is better for you than having a servant. When you go to bed, say: 'Glory be to God, All praise be to God, God is the Greatest' 33 times each. This is better for your next life." (Note: Some Traditions say that the last phrase should be recited 34 times.)

When you go to bed, say: "Glory be to God, All praise be to God, God is the Greatest" 33 times each. (Some Traditions say that the last phrase should be recited 34 times.) This is better for your next life.

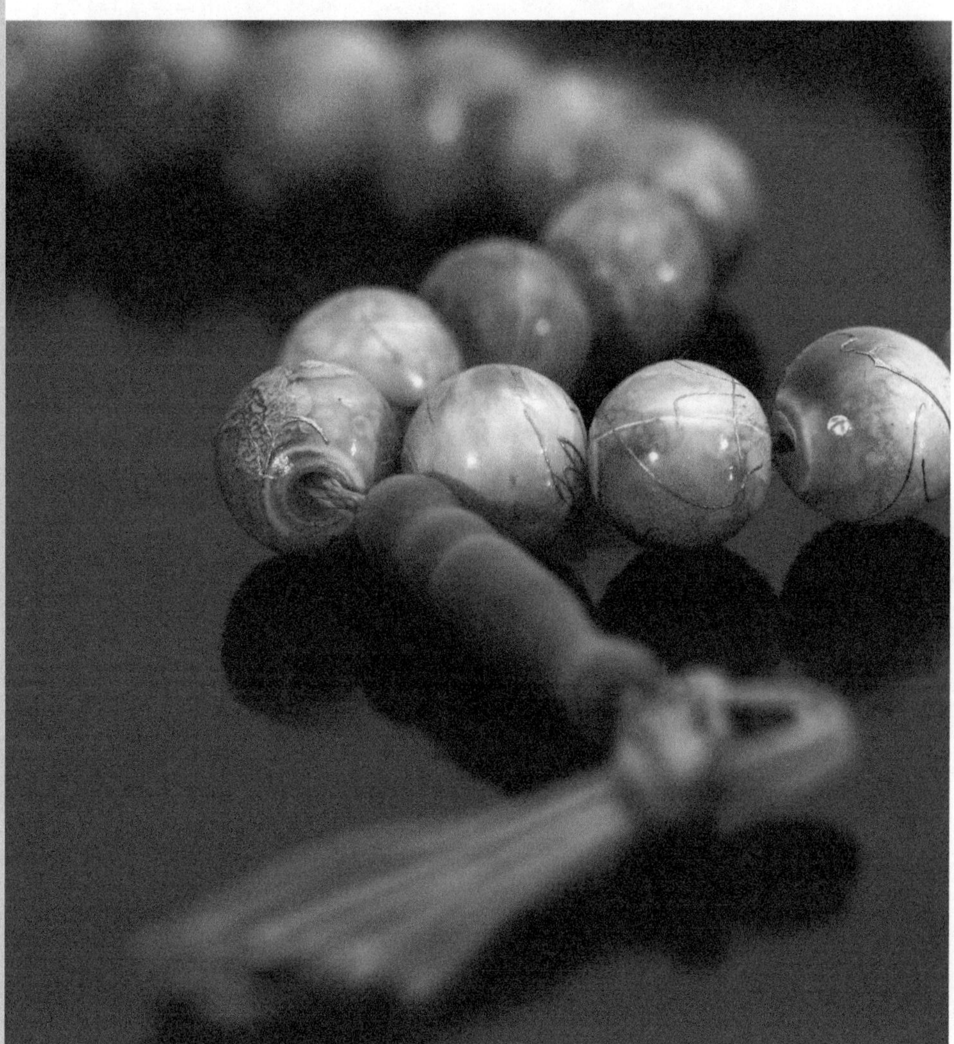

One day he saw her wearing a chain of gold and warned her: "O my daughter, do you want people to say of my daughter that she is wearing a chain of Hellfire?"

In addition to receiving no worldly benefit, God's Messenger bore many tortures. He often was beaten and left on the ground covered with dust, and only Fatima would run to his aid. Once he was being beaten at the Ka'ba, Abu Bakr ran to help him, shouting to those beating him: "Will you kill a man because he says: 'My Lord is God?'"

WHAT DID WE LEARN?

LESSON SUMMARY:

- The third attribute of Prophethood is communication of Islamic truths, otherwise known as "enjoining good and forbidding evil (amr bi-l ma'ruf wa-n nahy 'anil munkar)."
- We say Islamic truths because every Prophet came with the same Divine Religion based on submission to God, and had as his sole mission the communication of this Message.
- The Prophets dealt with people and life in a holistic manner, appealing to each person's intellect, reason, spirit, and all outer and inner senses and feelings. They never ignored or neglected any human faculties.
- Many Prophets lived with no one accepting their Message.
- Communicating the Divine Message was the most essential characteristic of God's Messenger
- While communicating the Message, the Prophet set an excellent example in guiding people
- God's Messenger was so competent and successful in educating people that it is a conclusive proof of his Prophethood.

LESSON REVIEW: INDIVIDUAL ASSESSMENT

1. What is another phrase used for communication of Islamic truths?
2. When are people able to be motivated to activity in the illuminated way of the Divine Message?
3. Are Prophets responsible for the results of their prophecies? i.e. people accepting faith? Why or why not?
4. Which verse of Qur'an shared by Prophet Muhammad to Wahshi finally brought Wahshi to Islam?
5. Essay: Define and explain the three important points of conveying the message of Islam according to the text.

ESSAY

"Trustworthiness is the cornerstone of belief." In an explanatory essay, analyze why this is a true statement. Be sure to reference the text. Your essay must be a minimum of 3 paragraphs.

LESSON VOCABULARY

- Volition
- Recluse
- Emigrant
- Alluding
- Derision
- Holistic
- Mortician
- Devoid
- Altruist
- Deception
- Ignominy
- Exhilarated
- Subsided
- Persevere
- Ensuing
- Confidant
- Embodiment
- Supererogatory prayer
- Exile

Lesson 5

Intellect (Fatanah)

THINK

The Prophetic intellect allows a Prophet to understand everything about his people and thus answer all their questions and solve their problems.

INTELLECT IS AN IMPORTANT ATTRIBUTE OF PROPHETHOOD

Intellect, in this context, has a specific meaning: a composite of reasoning power, sagacity, intelligence, sound judgment, and wisdom far surpassing the ability of ordinary people through a sublime power of understanding. It encompasses and coordinates all human abilities, whether of the heart and soul or of the mind.

A Prophetic intellect to grasp the entire meaning of the universe and humanity is needed. Islam admits reason's ultimate authority; not of human reason, which is limited by one's capacity and usually conflicts with another's, but of a Prophet's universal reason, for Islam is the name of the Divine universal order.

God manifests His Names through veils. His absolute Unity requires that we attribute effects directly to His creative Power. But His Transcendence, Grandeur, and Majesty require "natural" causes to veil His acts so that people do not ascribe to Him that which seems disagreeable to them. He raised the Prophets to communicate His Revelation. As we cannot receive Revelation directly, the Prophets functioned as a prism receiving and then reflecting Divine Revelation. They modulated the Revelation according to their audience's intellectual ability and the prevailing circumstances.

If we study the Prophet's achievements, we see that he was a statesman and commander of the highest order. As the embodiment or most comprehensive manifestation of the Divine Attribute of Speech, he is the most influential orator we have ever seen. His words, regardless of their apparent simplicity, affect everyone, regardless of their intellectual simplicity. As human knowledge increases, we see that these supposedly simple words are, in fact, like an ocean whose depth is only appreciated the more deeply one dives into it, or like a rose with petals one within the other, each one full of meanings.

His level of understanding was so sublime that Wahb ibn Munabbih, who was well-versed in the Torah and Gospels, said: "When compared to that of God's Messenger, humanity's total mental capacity and perception is like a single sand particle compared to all the sand in a vast desert."

Key vocabulary

- **Sagacity:** ability to understand difficult ideas and situations and to make wise decisions
- **Surpassing:** to a much greater degree than others
- **Prevailing:** generally current superior power or influence:
- **Statesman:** a usually wise, skilled, and respected government
- **Orator:** a person who makes speeches and is very good at making them leader

EXAMPLES OF HIS INTELLECTUAL CAPACITY

Before his Prophethood, the Ka'ba was partly ruined by rain and floods. The Quraysh restored it. However, clan warfare almost broke out over who would have the honor of restoring the sacred Black Stone to its proper place. Someone suggested that they refer the matter to whoever appeared first at the Ka'ba. To everyone's relief, this person was Muhammad. They told each other: "The Trustworthy One is coming!" After explaining the problem, he asked them to bring a piece of cloth, which he spread on the ground. Putting the Black Stone on it, he told each clan chief to hold a corner and lift the cloth. When the Black Stone was at the required height, Muhammad put it in its place. Clan warfare was thus averted.

God's Messenger always assessed a person's or an audience's spiritual and mental capacities accurately. He spoke directly to a particular individual at a particular time and under particular circumstances; he had no need for flattery or falsehood. One time Husayn, an eloquent speaker renowned for his persuasive rhetoric, sought to dissuade him from his mission. God's Messenger listened carefully to his argument and then initiated the following dialogue:

- **Eloquent:** having or showing the ability to use language clearly and effectively
- **Rhetoric:** the art or skill of speaking or writing formally and effectively especially as a way to persuade or influence people

– Husayn, how many deities do you worship?
– Eight; one in the Heavens and the others on Earth.
– Which one do you call upon when misfortune befalls you?
– The one in the Heavens.
– Which one do you call when your goods are gone?
– The one in the Heavens.

God's Messenger asked a couple of similar questions, and, upon receiving the same answer to each question, asked: "According to you, the one in the Heavens alone answers your call. Yet you continue to associate partners with Him. Isn't this what I have been preaching? There is no deity but God. Become a Muslim and be saved." This apparently simple argument defeated Husayn with his own logic.

History records no other instance of an individual forming such a virtuous community so quickly and from such unpromising people and insufficient resources.

Bedouins are often called "people of the desert." Their way of life engenders many unique experiences: the loss of a camel, forgetfulness of where items have been placed, or being caught in a sandstorm. However many deities they worship, they always ask God, the One, the Unique Creator of the universe, and Powerful over all things, for help and rescue. Their inner sense and sound conscience tell them the truth under the enchanting desert sky or in the darkness, and they then acknowledge His Oneness. This happened with Hamza, who proclaimed: "O Muhammad, I have perceived in the darkness of the desert night, that God is too great to be restricted within four walls!"

God's Messenger knew everyone's mood and thus took people "by the soul" when inviting them to Islam. For example, Ahmad ibn Hanbal reports from Abu Tamima that a Bedouin once asked God's Messenger if he was Muhammad. Receiving an affirmative answer, the Bedouin asked to what he was inviting people. The Messenger replied: "To God, the All-Majestic. I invite them to Him alone, without associating any partners with Him. He is God whom you call upon when a misfortune befalls you and He who removes it. It is to Him alone that you pray during drought and famine, and He sends rain and causes the grass to grow. It is also Him you entreat when you lose something in the vast desert, and He causes you to find it." These simple, accurate, and concise words caused the Bedouin to awake to the truth and embrace Islam on the spot.

"History records no other instance of an individual forming such a virtuous community so quickly and from such unpromising people and insufficient resources."

Prophet Muhammad used the dynamics granted to him by God so effectively that historians and sociologists still cannot fully grasp all dimensions of his revolutionary Message. Its waves have swept through the ages, and continue to attract increasing numbers of people from all over the world into the peaceful ocean of Islam.

Consider the following example. After the conquest of Mecca, many former enemies proclaimed their conversion. Naturally, it was difficult for them to acquire sincere belief so quickly. So, God's Messenger sought to "reconcile their hearts" and increase their commitment by preferring them over the Muslims when distributing the war spoils after the Battle of Hunayn.

- **Bedouin:** an Arab of the desert; nomadic Arab
- **Spoils:** money or goods taken in war; booty

"True, O God's Messenger! We are indebted to God and His Messenger!"

The spoils consisted of 24,000 camels, 40,000 sheep and goats, and 10,000 pounds of gold and silver. God's Messenger gave 300 camels and 250 pounds of gold and silver to Abu Sufyan and his family, 200 camels to Hakim ibn Hizam, and 100 camels each to Nusayr ibn al-Harith, Qays ibn Asiyy, Safwan ibn Umayya, Malik ibn Awf, Akra ibn Habis, and 'Uyayna ibn Hisn. Such generosity also did much to repair the Meccan chiefs' wounded pride.

Some younger Ansaris, despite their devotion to God's Messenger and Islam, became upset. They did not desire the spoils themselves; rather, they did not want to see such formerly staunch enemies of Islam, in their view, rewarded. This might have led to a dissident movement among the Muslims. When informed of the situation by Sa'd ibn 'Ubada, an Ansari leader, God's Messenger ordered them to assemble so he could address them. They did so, and he opened his speech in a dramatic way designed to attract and hold their attention, and to impress their souls: "O Community of the Ansar (Helpers)! I hear that you are displeased with me."

He continued in this powerful and impressive style, reminding them of God's blessings upon them through him. He asked: "Were you not in misguidance when I came to you? And has God not guided you to the truth through me? Were you not in poverty when I came to you? And has God not enriched you through me? Were you not in internal conflicts when I came to you? And has God not reconciled you through me?" They agreed to all of this, answering each question with: "True, O God's Messenger! We are indebted to God and His Messenger!"

- **Dissident:** someone who opposes and disagrees with official policy
- **Reconcile:** to cause people or groups to become friendly again after an argument or disagreement

"O Ansar! Even if you're upset with my actions, wouldn't you rather return home with God's Messenger while they return with camels and sheep? I swear by God, in Whose Hand of Power is my soul, that if all other people took a different direction than that of the Ansar, I wouldn't hesitate to go with the Ansar!"

After reminding them of these blessings, God's Messenger recounted their services to Islam, saying: "O Ansar! If you had desired, you could have answered me differently and said: 'Your people denied you, but we believed in you. You came to us with no one to defend you, but we admitted and protected you. Your people exiled you, but we embraced you. You came to us with nothing to subsist on, and we met all your needs.' If you had responded thus to me, you would have told the truth and no one would have stood up to contradict you."

He continued: "O Ansar! Even if you're upset with my actions, wouldn't you rather return home with God's Messenger while they return with camels and sheep? I swear by God, in Whose Hand of Power is my soul, that if all other people took a different direction than that of the Ansar, I wouldn't hesitate to go with the Ansar! Had it not been for the Emigration, I would have wished with all my heart to be one of the Ansar! O God, protect the Ansar and their descendants!" These words were enough for the Ansar to burst into tears, and all of them responded with one voice: "We are content with God and His Messenger! We desire nothing else!"

Although uttered on the spur of the moment, this speech both quashed a potential dissident movement and once again conquered the hearts of the Ansar.

Let's analyze this speech so that its wisdom may be better understood and appreciated.

He addressed the Ansar only, for they were the offended party. This showed them special honor, and exerted a psychological influence upon them from the outset. It also prevented any ill-will among the Muhajirun, who had been forced to emigrate to Medina, or the new Muslims of Mecca, many of whom still had to be won over.

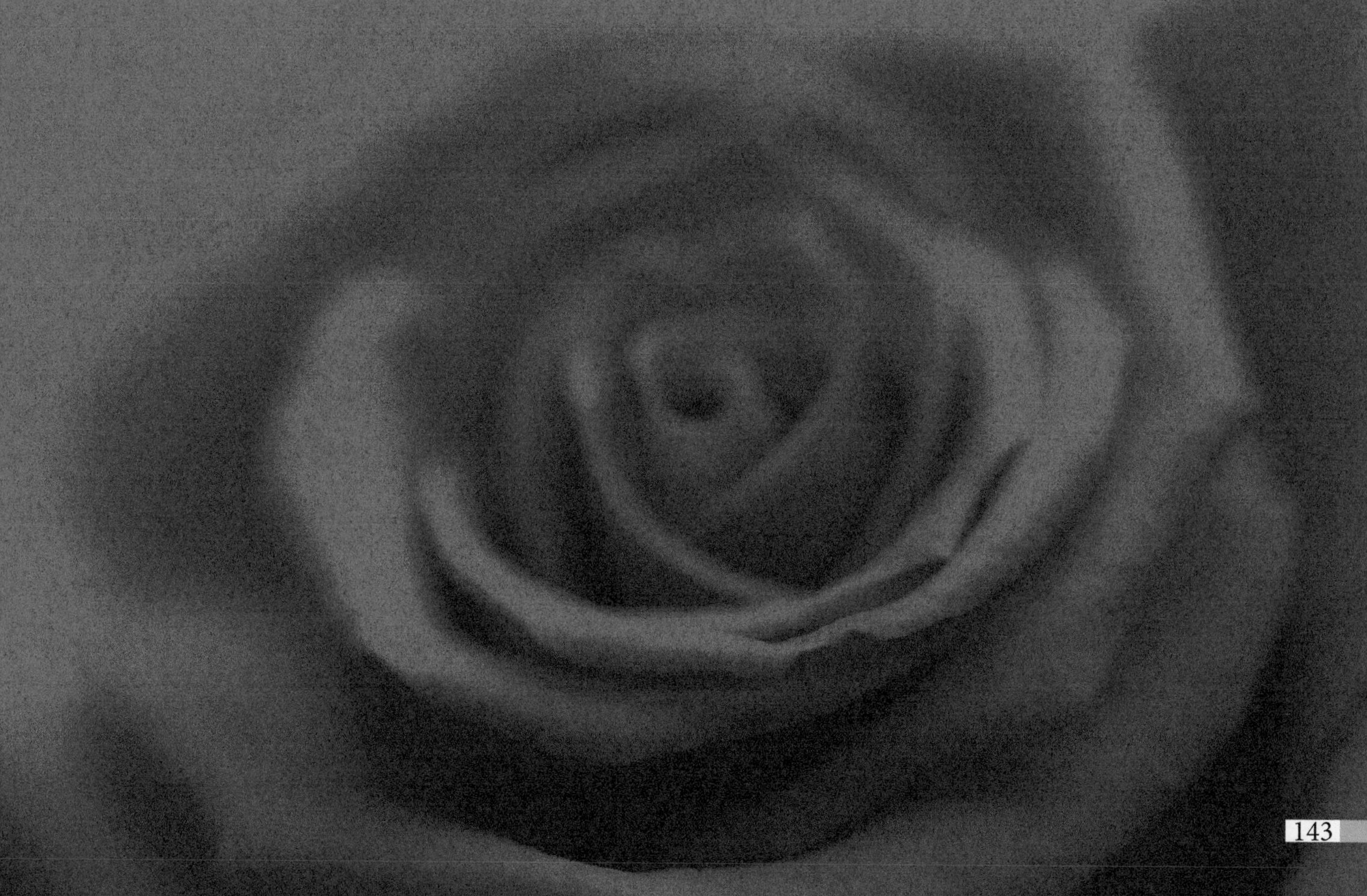

Those few examples illustrate the intellect of God's Messenger, and show that he did not speak or act of himself; rather, what he said and did carried the charge or force of one fulfilling a Divine mission.

His speech, when considered in its Arabic original, is an extraordinarily eloquent rhetorical document.

His opening was dramatic, for it was designed to win the audience's attention. Their attention never wavered, for the rest of his speech was just as dramatic and effective.

He did not resort to flattery or diplomacy. Rather, he spoke in plain sincerity, which was vital in securing the desired influence upon the listeners.

The spur-of-the-moment nature of his speech also was significant in obtaining the desired result. The freshness and force of such an unprepared address, on such occasions, is often more effective than a speech prepared in advance.

"Those few examples illustrate the intellect of God's Messenger, and show that he did not speak or act of himself; rather, what he said and did carried the charge or force of one fulfilling a Divine mission."

CONCISE SPEECH

THINK

Even today, Prophet Muhammad's words are enough to cause people to reform themselves and embrace Islam. Discuss the implications of his intellect in today's society. How has it changed the way you view common, daily issues?

Another dimension of his intellect is the very concise nature of his speech.

"Remember that he is the leader not only of those who lived during his lifetime, but of every believer to come."

He was sent to address people of every level, from ignorant seventh-century bedouins to those of the highest intellectual with scientific achievements, until the Day of Judgment. No one has yet been able to disprove what he said. Accordingly, after we scrutinize his Traditions and the Qur'an, we realize that they complement each other in style and content. Moreover, there is no contradiction between them and established scientific knowledge.

He acknowledged this as one of God's blessings and, to emphasize it as so, would sometimes say: "I am Muhammad, an unlettered Prophet. No Prophet will come after me. I have been distinguished with conciseness of speech and comprehensiveness of meaning," and: "O people, I have been honored with conciseness of speech and giving the final judgment in all matters."

As God's Messenger was unlettered, he was not influenced by his era's written culture. His conscience was so sound, his intellect so comprehensive, and his character so pure that only he could have received Divine Revelation. His mind and heart were fed by Divine Revelation exclusively. Each word and deed was a ray from that Revelation, a sign of his Messengership. Like a bright, crystal cup of clear, sweet water, his intellect was so pure that Divine Revelation entered it and emerged from it, drop by drop, in the form of words in their original clarity.

- **Concise:** expressing or covering much in few words; brief in form but comprehensive in scope
- **Scrutinize:** to examine in detail with careful or critical attention

Every Prophet was supported by miracles relevant to his time and environment. For example, Moses' miracles had to appear as magic, for magic was widespread. Jesus' miracles took the form of healing, for medicine was in wide demand. Similarly, during the time of Prophet Muhammad, four things enjoyed popularity in Arabia: eloquence and fluency in writing and speaking, poetry and oratory, soothsaying and divination, and knowledge of the past and cosmology. The Qur'an challenged all known experts in these fields and forced them to surrender. Prophet Muhammad surpassed them through his wonderful eloquence, knowledge of the cosmos, and predictions.

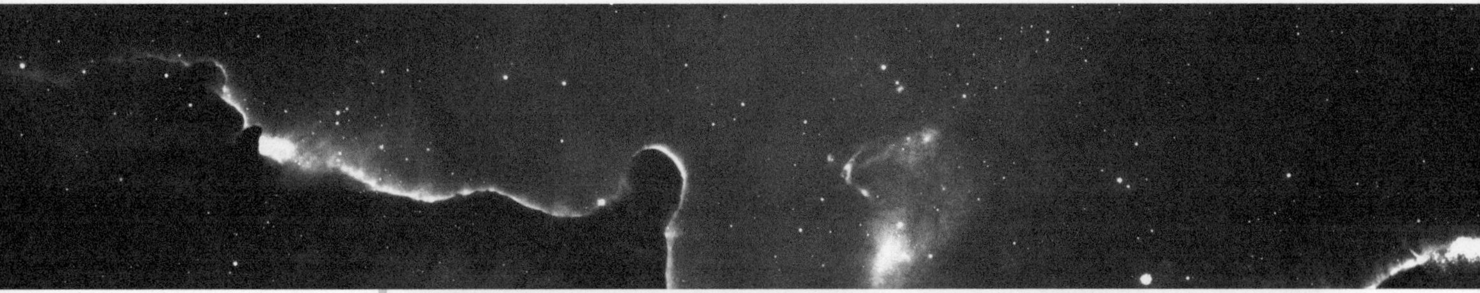

As his Prophethood is universal and will exist until the Last Day, his eloquence and linguistic style will never be surpassed. His words, together with the Qur'an, supersede all literary works. Their excellence is everlasting and becomes increasingly vivid as their deeper meanings are discovered over the course of time. His words and the Qur'an are of such extraordinary nature and so full of meaning that millions of saints and people seeking Divine knowledge have obtained perfect knowledge of the Divine Essence, Attributes, and Names through them. The hidden truths of the Unseen worlds (e.g., angels, jinn, the Hereafter, Paradise, and Hell) are unveiled through them.

SOME EXAMPLES OF INTELLECT FROM THE PROPHET

Since everything is ultimately in the hands of God, we should strive in accordance with His Commandments and seek the results only from Him.

Imam Tirmidhi relates from Ibn 'Abbas, the Scholar of the Ummah, that God's Messenger said to him:

> "O young man, let me teach you a few principles: Observe the rights of God so that God will protect you. Observe His rights so that you always will find Him with you. When you ask something, ask it from God. When you seek help, seek it from God. Know that if everyone joined together to help you, they could only do that which God already preordained for you. If everyone joined together to hurt you, they could only do that which God already preordained for you. The Pen of Destiny has been lifted, and everything has been ordained."

This hadith encourages submission to God, and belief in His Unity and the truth of Destiny. We should not conclude that it excludes human free will; rather, it stresses one's action, prayer, and need to strive for the desired results. It balances this with a warning that since everything is ultimately in the hands of God, we should strive in accordance with His Commandments and seek the results only from Him.

- **Preordained:** decided in advance and certain to happen

"Live in the world as if you were a stranger or traveler. Regard yourself as one of the dead." This succinct hadith encourages us to lead an austere, disciplined life based on awareness of God. It reminds us of our final destination by stressing this world's transience, and establishes the balance between this life and the next.

"A person is with the one whom he (she) loves." This hadith is a source of hope and consolation for those unable to adhere completely to the Divine Commandments. Those who love the Prophets and saints will be in their company in the Hereafter. Therefore, whoever desires this should love them sincerely and follow them as best as they can.

Nu'ayman, a Companion, could not stop drinking alcohol. He was punished several times. When yet another Companion reproached him, God's Messenger warned that Companion: "Don't help Satan against your brother! I swear by God that he loves God and His Messenger." Thus, those who are trying their best to reform themselves, as long as they continue to perform their obligatory duties and try to refrain from major sins, should be encouraged, not reprimanded. This is a prerequisite of their love for God and His Messenger.

God's Messenger said: "Fear God where ever you are. Do good immediately after a sinful act to erase it, and always be well-mannered in your relationship with people." This concise hadith establishes the principles of a happy life and describes the way to eternal bliss. Fear of God is the basis of every virtue and good conduct, and leads to Paradise. Through this, people can erase their sins with good deeds, and being well-mannered elevates them to the rank of perfection.

"The Muslim is one from whose tongue and hand Muslims are safe. The Emigrant is one who emigrates from what God forbids."This short hadith expresses many truths. First of all, it describes the ideal or norm by beginning with *the Muslim*, as opposed to *a Muslim*. In this way, our Prophet draws attention to the qualities of perfect Muslims, not to those who are only nominal Muslims.

The word Muslim, derived from the infinitive silm (security, peace, and salvation), comes to mean one who desires and gives peace, security, and salvation. So, the Muslims are believers who embody peace, cause no trouble for anyone, from whom all are safe, and who are the most reliable representatives of peace and security.

Our Prophet mentions the tongue before the hand, for slander, gossip, and insult often do far more damage than physical violence. If people can refrain from verbal assault, they can more easily refrain from physical assault. Moreover, self-defense against physical violence is often easier than that against gossip and slander. So, true Muslims always restrain their tongues and hands so that others will be safe from them. In the same hadith, emigration means more than leaving one's family, house, possessions, and native land for the sake of God.

To be capable of the latter, one must first emigrate from the material to the spiritual dimension of his or her being, from worldly pleasures to an altruistic life, and from selfish aims to living for a Divine cause.

- **Succinct:** using few words to state or express an idea
- **Consolation:** something that makes a person feel less sadness, disappointment, etc.

IMAGINE

Picture yourself in a situation that makes you upset, is it easy to show patience at the moment of misfortune, when it hits your heart for the very first time?

Both Bukhari and Muslim relate that God's Messenger said: "Patience is shown at the moment of misfortune."

Therefore, obeying Divine prohibitions is directly related to being a good Muslim and to sacrificing one's life in the service of people purely for the sake of God.

God's Messenger said: "The upper hand is better than the lower one." In another hadith, God's Messenger explains that the upper hand gives to the poor and needy, while the lower hand takes from others. So, besides expressing the merits of charity, this hadith encourages people to work and earn their living.

A subtle point: God's Messenger did not say the one who gives and the one who receives. Instead, he said the upper hand and the lower hand. This indicates that the act, not the person, is generally preferable. As a result, the recipient may sometimes be better than the giver.

God's Messenger said: "Patience is shown at the moment of misfortune."

In the early days of his mission, God's Messenger forbade people to visit graves, as some un-Islamic practices were still observed. After such practices vanished, he encouraged his Companions to visit graves, and did so himself, for this encourages people to improve their moral conduct and strive for the next life.

During a visit to Medina's graveyard, God's Messenger saw a woman weeping bitterly and complaining about Destiny. When he sought to console her, the woman, who did not recognize him, angrily told him to go away, for: "You don't know what misfortune has befallen me!" When she later learned his identity, she hurried after him and, finding him at home, begged his pardon. God's Messenger told her: "Patience is shown at the moment of misfortune."

Patience is a key to success and triumph. It means to accept pain, trouble, misfortune, and similar unpleasant facts without complaint, or loss of self-control, trust, or belief in God and Destiny. Sometimes one can achieve patience in difficult circumstances by changing one's attitude, place, preoccupation, or immediate conditions. Performing wudu' (ritual ablution) or praying also may help one deal with sorrow.

THERE ARE SEVERAL KINDS OF PATIENCE:

– Determination to avoid sins. This elevates one to the rank of the God-fearing, whom God takes into His care.

– Constant and regular worship of God. This causes one to acquire the rank of being a beloved of God.

– Acceptance of misfortune without complaint. This causes one to be included among the people of patience and those who put their trust in God.

– Dealing with exasperation. This means having a realistic understanding of what is required to achieve a specific result. For example, producing a loaf of bread requires that the field be cultivated, the crop harvested, the grain taken to a mill, and the dough shaped into loaves and baked in an oven. If, out of impatience or neglect, this procedure is not followed exactly and in this specific order, a loaf of bread will not be produced.

- **Triumph:** a great success or achievement
- **Exasperation:** the state of being very annoyed or upset

WHAT DID WE LEARN?

LESSON SUMMARY:

- Intellect is another important attribute of Prophethood.
- In this context, it has a specific meaning:
  a composite of reasoning power, sagacity, intelligence, sound judgment, and wisdom far surpassing the ability of ordinary people through a sublime power of understanding
- God's Messenger always assessed a person's or an audience's spiritual and mental capacities accurately
- Prophet Muhammad used the dynamics granted to him by God so effectively that historians and sociologists still cannot fully grasp all dimensions of his revolutionary Message.
- Prophet Muhammad is the leader not only of those who lived during his lifetime, but of every believer to come.
- As his Prophethood is universal and will exist until the Last Day, his eloquence and linguistic style will never be surpassed

LESSON REVIEW: INDIVIDUAL ASSESSMENT

1. What did Wahb Ibn Munabbih say in regards to the intellect of Prophet Muhammad?
2. Describe your understanding of the example given about how the Prophet averted clan warfare.
3. Why did the Prophet address the Ansar only during his speech following the distribution of spoils after the Battle of Hunayn?
4. Why is it important that Prophet Muhammad was unlettered? What did that save him from being influenced by?

ESSAY

Summarize your understanding of the Prophet's intellect and how he did not speak or act for himself, rather through his words and actions, carried the Divine mission. Use examples from the text.

LESSON VOCABULARY

- Orator
- Statesman
- Sagacity
- Surpassing
- Prevailing
- Eloquent
- Rhetoric
- Bedouin
- Spoils
- Dissident
- Reconcile
- Concise
- Scrutinize
- Preordained
- Succinct
- Consolation
- Triumph
- Exasperation

Lesson 6

Infallibility (`Isma)

INFALLIBILITY IS A NECESSARY ATTRIBUTE OF THE PROPHETS

The original Arabic word translated here as infallibility is 'isma, which means "protecting, saving, or defending." It appears in the Qur'an in several forms. For example, when Prophet Noah asked his son to board the Ark during the Flood, the son replied: I will betake myself to some mountain; it will save me from the water. Noah replied: Today there is not a saving one (active participle) from the command of God (11:43).

The wife of a high Egyptian official, named Potiphar in the Bible (Genesis 39:1), uses the same word in: *I did seek to seduce him, but he firmly saved himself guiltless* (12:32). The Qur'an calls believers to hold fast to the rope of God (the Qur'an and Islam) using the same word in a different form: *Hold fast all together to, and protect (against being divided), the rope of God* (3:103). Again, we see the same word in the verse: *God will defend (protect) you from people* (5:67).

- **Infallibility:** not capable of being wrong or making mistakes; protected from sin

"The infallibility of Prophets is an established fact based on reason and tradition."

This quality is required for several reasons:

First, Prophets came to convey the Message of God. If we liken this Message to pure water or light (13:17, 24:35), the Archangel Gabriel (who brought it) and the Prophet (who conveyed it) also must be absolutely pure. If this were not so, their impurity would pollute the Message. The hearts or souls of Gabriel and the Prophet are like polished mirrors that reflect the Divine Revelation to people, a clean cup from which people quench their thirst for the pure, Divine water.

"The infallibility of Prophets is an established fact based on reason and tradition."

Any black spot on the mirror would absorb a ray of that light; a single drop of mud would make the water unclear. As a result, the Prophets would not be able to deliver the complete Message.

But they delivered the Message perfectly, as stated in the Qur'an:

> O Messenger! Convey what has been sent to you from your Lord. If you did not, you would not have fulfilled His mission. God will defend you from people. God guides not the unbelieving people. (5:67)

> Today I have perfected your religion for you, and I have completed My favor upon you, and I have chosen and approved for you Islam as religion. (5:3)

Second, the Prophets teach their people all the commands and principles of belief and conduct. So that the people learn their religion in its pristine purity and truth, and as perfectly as possible to secure their happiness and prosperity in both worlds, the Prophets must represent and then present the Revelation without fault or defect. This is their function as guides and good examples to be followed.

> You have in the Messenger of God a beautiful pattern, an excellent example, for anyone who aspires after God and the Last Day, and who engages much in the remembrance of God. (33:21)

You have in the Messenger of God a beautiful pattern, an excellent example, for anyone who aspires after God and the Last Day, and who engages much in the remembrance of God. (33:21)

> There is for you an excellent example in Abraham and those with him ... there was in them an excellent example for you—for those who aspire after God and the Last Day. (60:4, 6)

A Prophet can do or say only that which has been sanctioned by God. If he could, he would have to repent even beyond his current lifetime. For example, Abraham will tell those who approach him for intercession on the Day of Judgment to go to Moses, saying he cannot intercede for them because he spoke allusively three times in his life. Although this is not a sin, his repentance will continue in the Hereafter.

Key vocabulary

- **Pristine:** not changed by people; left in its natural state, having its original purity
- **Allusively:** referring to something without stating it directly

Third, the Qur'an commands believers to obey the Prophet's orders and prohibitions, without exception, and emphasizes that it is not fitting for a believer, man or woman, when a matter has been decided by God and His Messenger, to have any option about their decision (33:36). It also warns believers that what falls to them when God and His Messenger have given a judgment is only to say: "*We have heard and obeyed*" (24:51). Absolute obedience to a Prophet means that all of his commands and prohibitions are correct and beyond reproach.

Prophethood is so great a favor that all Prophets bore extreme hardship while fulfilling the duty of thanksgiving, and always worried about not worshipping God sufficiently. Prophet Muhammad often implored God as follows:

> Glory be to You. We have not been able to know You as Your knowledge requires, O Known One. Glory be to You. We have not been able to worship You as Your worship requires, O Worshipped One.

The Qur'an commands believers to obey the Prophet's orders and prohibitions, without exception.

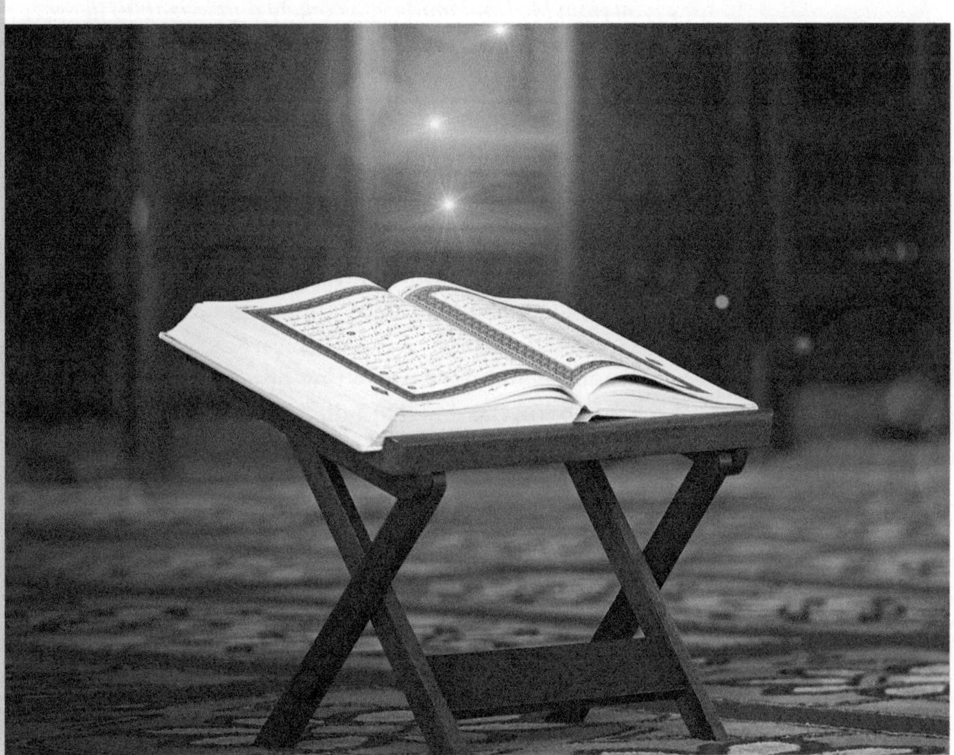

The Qur'anic verses that are sometimes understood (mistakenly) to reprimand certain Prophets for some faults or to show that they seek God's forgiveness for some sin, should be considered in this light. Besides, God's forgiveness does not always mean that a sin has been committed. The Qur'anic words 'afw (pardon) and maghfira (forgiveness) also signify a special favor and kindness, as well as Divine dispensation, in respect to lightening or overlooking a religious duty, as in the following verses:

Key vocabulary

- **Implore:** to beg sincerely or desperately, as for aid or mercy; beseech
- **Reprimand:** to express sharp disapproval or criticism in an angry and critical way
- **Dispensation:** exemption from a rule or usual requirement

If any is forced (to eat of them) by hunger, with no inclination toward transgression, God is indeed Oft-Forgiving, Most Merciful. (5:3)

If . . . you find no water, then take for yourselves clean sand or earth, and rub therewith your faces and hands. For God is All-Pardoning and Oft-Forgiving. (4:43)

Not doing something as perfectly as possible, which is required by the love of and nearness to God, is not a sin.

Fourth, sins and pardoning have different types and degrees. These are: 1. disobeying religious commandments, and forgiveness thereof; 2. disobeying God's laws of creation and life, and forgiveness thereof; and 3. disobeying the rules of good manners or courtesy, and the forgiveness thereof. A 4th type, which is not a sin, involves not doing something as perfectly as possible, which is required by the love of and nearness to God. Some Prophets may have done this, but such acts cannot be considered sins according to the common definition.

Tradition also proves the Prophets' infallibility. God says of Moses: *I cast love over you from Me (and made you comely and loveable) in order that you might be brought up under My eye* (20:39). Thus, as Moses was brought up by God Himself and prepared for the mission of Messengership, how could he possibly commit a sin?

As Moses was brought up by God Himself and prepared for the mission of Messengership, how could he possibly commit a sin?

The same is true of all other Prophets. For example, God's Messenger says of Jesus: "Satan could not touch Jesus and his mother at his birth." Jesus was protected from birth until his elevation to the Presence of God:

(Mary) pointed to the infant (Jesus). They asked: "How can we talk to an infant in the cradle?" Jesus said: "I am a servant of God. He has given me the Scripture and made me a Prophet. He has made me blessed wheresoever I may be, and enjoined on me prayer and charity as long as I live. He has made me kind to my mother, and not overbearing or a wretched rebel. So peace is on me the day I was born, the day that I die, and the day that I will be raised up to life again." (19:29-33)

Jesus, like all Prophets, was protected from sin from his birth. The Messenger, while still a child and not yet a Prophet, intended to attend two wedding ceremonies, but on each occasion was overpowered by sleep. During his youth he helped his uncles repair the Ka'ba by carrying stones. Since the stones hurt his shoulders, his uncle 'Abbas advised him to wrap part of his lower garment around his shoulders for padding. But as soon as he did so, thereby leaving parts of his thighs exposed, he fell on his back and stared fixedly. An angel appeared and warned him: "This is not befitting for you," for later he would tell people to be well-mannered and observe Divinely ordained standards of conduct, including covering the thighs. In such ways was the future Prophet protected from his people's pagan rituals and practices.

Whether by God's Will and special protection or, as will be explained below, by His showing the way to become free of error or sin, even the greatest saints who continue the Prophetic mission may be infallible to some degree.

DISCUSS

God's Messenger said "all children of Adam make faults and err, and the best of those who make faults and err are the repentant." What does this imply?

- **Transgress:** to violate a law, command, moral code, etc.; sin.

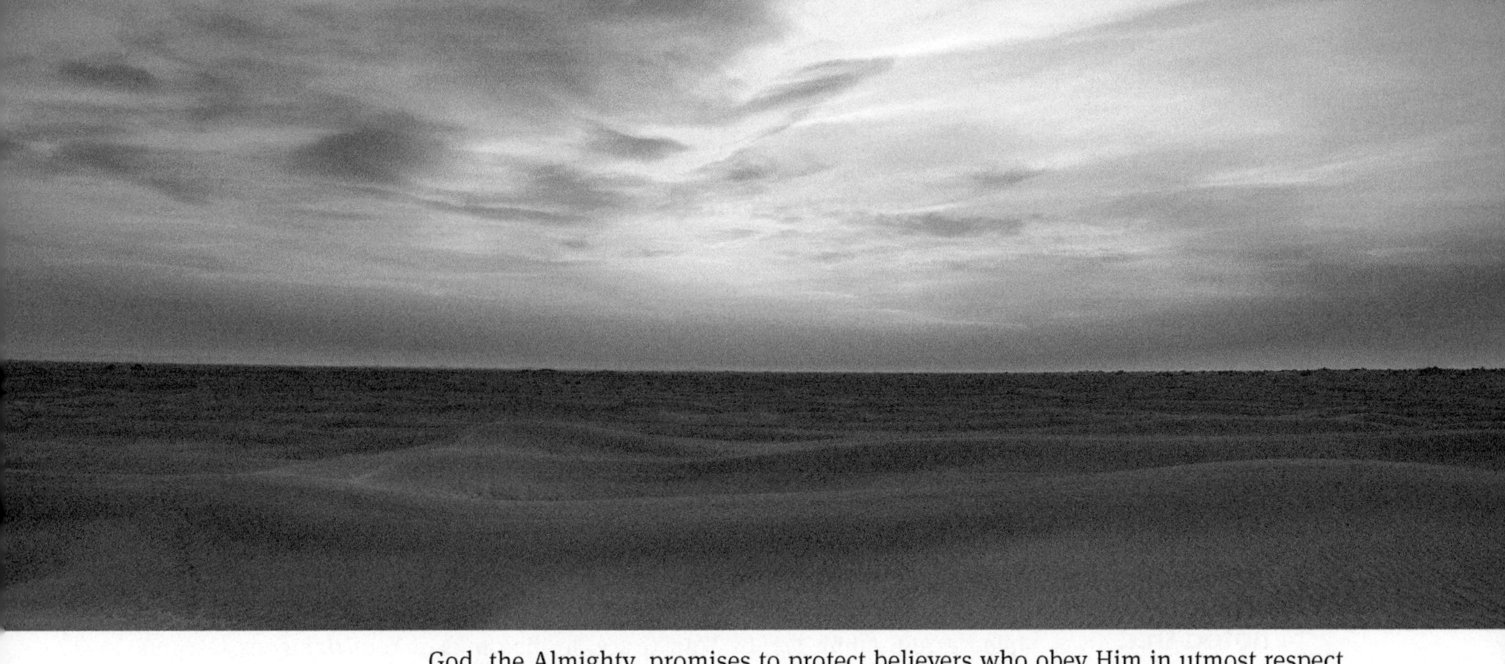

God, the Almighty, promises to protect believers who obey Him in utmost respect and deserve His protection, and to endow them with sound judgment so that they can distinguish between the truth and falsehood, and right and wrong:

> O you who believe! If you obey God in utmost respect, He will establish in you a Criterion (to judge between right and wrong), purify you of all your evils, and forgive you. God is of grace unbounded. (8:29)

God made a covenant with the believers that if they obey Him and strive to exalt His Word, by proclaiming His religion, He will help them and establish them firmly in the religion, protecting them against all kinds of deviation (47:7). This protection from enemies and committing sins depends upon their support of Islam and the struggle to spread it so that only God is worshipped, and that no partners are associated with Him in belief or worship, or in the creation and rule of the universe. If believers keep their promise, God will keep His (2:40); if they break it, God will cause them to fail (17:8).

THINK

God guides His true servants to good and protects them from evil. What does this require of you as a Muslim?

God protects His servants against sin in different ways. For example, He may place obstacles in their way, establish a "warner" in their hearts, or even cause them to suffer some injury so that they physically cannot sin. Or, He may put a verse in someone's mouth, as happened with a young man during 'Umar's caliphate.

This is how God protects His sincere servants. He says in a hadith qudsi:

> "My servants cannot draw near to me through something else more lovable to Me than performing the obligations I have enjoined upon them. Apart from those obligations, they continue to draw near to Me through supererogatory acts of worship, until I love them. When I love them, I will be their ears with which they hear, their eyes with which they see, their hands with which they grasp, and their feet on which they walk. If they ask Me for something, I will give it to them immediately. If they seek refuge in Me from something, I will protect them from it."
>
> (The servants do what is good, and refrain from wickedness. They ask God for what is good, and whatever they ask is provided. They seek refuge in God from what is bad, and God protects them according to their request.)

Key vocabulary

- **Hadith qudsi:** a sub-category of hadith, which Muslims regard as from God, but phrased by the Prophet

REMOVING DOUBTS

If the Qur'an had not been revealed, we would not be sure whether the previous Prophets were really sincere, devout, and thankful servants of God. The Qur'an frees Jesus from his followers' mistaken deification of him and from his own people's denial of his Prophethood, and explains that God had no sons and daughters. It also clears the Israelite and non-Israelite Prophets of their supposed "sins" mentioned in the Bible. It presents Jesus as a spirit from God breathed into the Virgin Mary, Abraham as an intimate friend of God, Moses as one who spoke to God, and Solomon as a king and a Prophet who prayed to Him humbly:

> O my Lord, order me that I may be grateful for Your favors, which You have bestowed on me and on my parents, and that I may work the righteousness that will please You. Admit me, by Your Grace, to the ranks of Your righteous servants. (27:19)

Solomon never worshipped idols or committed a sin. Despite being the greatest and most powerful king that ever lived, he remained a humble servant of God until his death.

Several other assertions are equally impossible to accept. For example, the Bible claims that although Prophet Isaac wanted to bless his older son Esau, he mistakenly blessed Jacob, for he could not see through his wife Rebaka's trick (Genesis 27). Also, the Bible claims that Prophet Jacob wrestled with God, who appeared to him in the form of a man (Genesis 32:24–30).

A small minority of Muslim scholars have asserted that the Prophets may have committed insignificant sins (zalla: error or lapse). To prove their assertion, they cite some examples from the lives of Adam, Noah, Abraham, and Joseph.

"It should be noted that lapses and sins have totally different definitions."

"It should be noted that lapses and sins have totally different definitions."

Sin, for example, means disobedience to God's commands. When the Prophets were faced with a question that they could not answer, they tended to wait for Revelation. On rare occasions, however, they used their own reason to decide the matter, as they were the foremost mujtahids (jurists of the highest rank who can deduce laws from the principles established by the Qur'an and the Sunna). They might have erred in their judgments or decisions. However, such errors, which were immediately corrected by God, are not sins.

Moreover, Prophets always sought God's good pleasure and tried to obtain whatever was best. If, for some reason, they could not obtain the best but had to settle for the better, a very rare event, this does not mean that they sinned.

So, a Prophet's preference of what is better instead of the best is not a sin. However, because of his position before Him, God might sometimes reproach him mildly.

PROPHET ADAM

Adam was in the Garden before his worldly life. While therein, God told him and his wife Eve not to eat of the fruit of a particular tree. They disobeyed Him in this matter, and so were expelled from the Garden and commanded to live on earth.

Although Qur'anic interpreters differ on what the prohibited fruit was, it was most probably the human inclination toward the opposite sex. Satan approached Adam and Eve, saying that it was a tree of eternity and of a kingdom that would never decay, the fruit of which had been prohibited to them (20:120). Most probably knowing that they were mortal, Adam and Eve must have desired eternity through offspring, as such a desire is inherent in people.

This can also be deduced from the following verses:

> Then Satan whispered to them so that he might show to them that which was hidden from them of their shame. He said: "Your Lord forbade you this tree only lest you should become angels or become immortal." And he swore to them (saying): "Truly, I am a sincere adviser to you." Thus did he lead them by a deceit. When they tasted of the tree, their shame was shown to them and they began to cover (by placing) on themselves some leaves of the Garden. . . (7:20–22)

Even if we accept Adam's eating of the forbidden fruit as a lapse, it is difficult to regard it as deliberate or sustained disobedience or revolt against God, which might lead us to see the Prophets as fallible. First, Adam was not a Prophet while in the Garden. Second, this lapse was the result not of willful disobedience, but merely some sort of forgetfulness. Concerning this, the Qur'an says: *We had made a covenant with Adam before, but he forgot, and we found on his part no firm resolve* (20:115).

Sins committed because of forgetfulness will not be accounted for in the Hereafter. The Prophet said: "My community is exempt from being questioned about forget-

IMAGINE

Suppose you must decide whether to recite the Qur'an in 10 days while giving due attention to each verse, or recite it in 7 days to express your deep love of the Word of God. If you choose the first option without knowing that God's greater pleasure lies in the second, you cannot be considered guilty of a sin.

ting, unintentional errors, and what they are compelled to do." The Qur'an teaches us this prayer: *Our Lord, don't condemn us if we forget or fall into error* (2:286).

Adam and Eve turned to God immediately after their lapse and, in sincere repentance.

Adam did not make this lapse deliberately. Although some have read into this verse Adam's lack of determination to fulfill his covenant with God, the context does not allow such an interpretation. Adam and Eve turned to God immediately after their lapse and, in sincere repentance, entreated Him: *Our Lord, we have wronged our own selves. If you don't forgive us and don't bestow Your Mercy upon us, we certainly shall be among the lost* (7:23).

Destiny had a part in Adam's lapse. God had destined him to be His vicegerent on Earth, even before his creation and settlement in the Garden. This is explicit in the Qur'an:

> Behold, your Lord said to the angels: "I will make a vicegerent on Earth." They asked: "Will you make therein one who will make mischief and shed blood, while we celebrate Your praises and glorify You?" He said: "I know what you know not." (2:30)

God's Messenger also points to that truth in a hadith:

> "Adam and Moses met each other in Heaven. Moses said to Adam: 'You are the father of humanity, but you caused us to come down to Earth from the Garden.' Adam replied: 'You are the one whom God addressed directly. Did you not see this sentence in the Torah: Adam had been destined to eat of that fruit 40 years before he ate of it?'"

After reporting this meeting, God's Messenger added three times: "Adam silenced Moses."

Adam's life in the Garden and his trial were preliminaries he had to pass through before his earthly life. He passed these tests. Being chosen and rescued from the swamp of sin and deviation, he was made a Prophet and honored with being the father of thousands of Prophets, including Prophet Muhammad, and millions of saints: Then his Lord chose him; He relented toward him, and rightly guided him (20:122).

PROPHET NOAH

Prophet Noah called his people to the religion of God for 950 years. When they insisted on unbelief and persisted in their wrongdoing, God told him to build the Ark. After completing this task, Noah placed therein, according to God's command, a male and female of each animal, all his family members (except for those whom God already had said He would punish), and the believers (11:40).

When the Ark was floating through the mountain-high waves, Noah saw that one of his sons had not boarded the Ark. He called to him, but his son rejected his call, saying: I will betake myself to some mountain and it will save me from the water (11:43). When Noah saw his son drowning, he called out to God: *My Lord, my son is of my family! Your promise is true, and You are the Most Just of Judges* (11:45). God replied: *O Noah, he is not of your family, for his conduct is unrighteous. Do not ask of Me that of which you have no knowledge. I give you counsel, lest you should act like the ignorant* (11:46).

Some scholars have regarded Noah's appeal as a sin. However, it is difficult to agree with them. Noah is mentioned in the Qur'an as one of the five greatest Prophets, and is described as resolute and steadfast. He thought his son was a believer.

Noah immediately turned to Him and sought refuge with Him, lest he should ask Him for that of which he had no knowledge.

It is well known that the religion of God tells us to judge according to outward appearances. Thus, those who profess belief and appear to perform the religious duties of primary importance (e.g., prescribed prayers and alms-giving) are treated as believers.

Apparently, Noah's son hid his unbelief until the Flood, for it was Noah himself who had prayed beforehand: "*O my Lord. Forgive me, my parents, and all who entered my house in faith, and all believing men and believing women, and grant to the wrongdoers no increase but perdition*" (71:28).

God accepted his prayer and told him to board the Ark with his family, except those who had already deserved punishment because of their willful insistence on unbelief. Noah's wife was among those who drowned. Noah did not ask God to save her, for he either knew or was informed that she was an unbeliever. He must have thought his son was a believer. As such, he felt compelled to express, in a manner befitting a Prophet, his astonishment that God had let him drown. This is why God replied to him as He did (11:46).

Noah, like every other Prophet, was kind-hearted and caring. Every Prophet sacrificed himself for the good of humanity and made tireless efforts to guide people toward the truth and true happiness in both worlds. Concerning Prophet Muhammad's attitude in this respect, God says: *You would nearly kill yourself following after them, in grief, if they believe not in this Message* (18:6).

Noah appealed to his people for 950 years, never once relenting. It is natural for a Prophet, a father, to show disappointment when he learns that his son is among the unbelievers who have been condemned to punishment in both worlds. But since God is the Most Just and Most Compassionate, Noah immediately turned to Him and sought refuge with Him, lest he should ask Him for that of which he had no knowledge:

> O my Lord, I seek refuge with You, lest I should ask You for that of which I have no knowledge. Unless You forgive me and have mercy on me, I shall be lost. (11:47)

So also did We show Abraham the inner dimensions of, and the metaphysical realities behind, the Heavens and the Earth, that he might have certainty. (6:75)

Abraham, the "intimate friend of God," was one of the greatest Prophets. God's Messenger took pride and pleasure in his connection with him, saying: "I am the one whose coming Abraham prayed for and Jesus gave glad tidings of, and I resemble my forefather Abraham more than anyone else."

He was thrown into fire because of his belief in One God, and the fire became, by God's Will and Power, coolness and a means of safety for him.

Like all Prophets, Abraham never even thought of worshipping that which was not God. Despite this fact, various erroneous and untrue stories have found their way into some Qur'anic commentaries. They have come from a misunderstanding of the following verses:

> When the night covered him over, he saw a star and said: "This is my Lord." But when it set, he said: "I don't love those that set." When he saw the moon rising in splendor, he said: "This is my Lord." But when it set, he said: "Unless my Lord guides me, I surely will be among those who go astray." When he saw the sun rising in splendor, he said: "This is my Lord; this is the greatest (of all)." But when the sun set, he said: "O my people, I am free from your ascribing partners to God. I have set my face toward Him Who created the Heavens and the Earth, a man of pure faith and one by nature upright. I am not among those who associate part-

ners with God." (6:76–79)

These verses clearly show that Abraham tried, by way of analogy, to convince his people that no heavenly body could be God. Abraham lived among the Chaldeans of northern Mesopotamia, a people who knew a great deal about heavenly bodies and who worshipped them, along with many other idols. Abraham first argued with his father, telling him that no idol was worthy of worship: Abraham once said to his father Azar: "Do you take idols for gods? Surely I see you and your people in manifest deviation" (6:74).

It is a great mistake to infer from some verses that Abraham took heavenly bodies as God in the early phase of his life.

Since Azar was the local idol maker, Abraham began his mission by opposing him. After that, he sought to guide his people to the truth. Since they had a great knowledge of heavenly bodies, God instructed him in such matters and showed him various hidden metaphysical realities so that he might attain complete certainty in belief and convince his people of their deviation:

> So also did We show Abraham the inner dimensions of, and the metaphysical realities behind, the Heavens and the Earth, that he might have certainty. (6:75)

While traveling in mind and heart through heavenly bodies, Abraham began by telling his people that a star could not be God because it sets. Although the superstitious might read fortunes into it or attribute some influence to it, true knowledge shows that it rises and sets according to God's laws, and that its light is extinguished in the broader light of day. So why should anyone worship stars?

His second step in this analogy was to show that the moon, although looking brighter and bigger than a star, could not be God. This is because it sets like a star, changes its shape from hour to hour, and depends on some other heavenly body for its light. At this point, Abraham openly declared that his Lord had guided him, and that those who did not worship only Him had gone astray.

Abraham's final analogy showed that the sun could not be worshipped as God, for despite its size and light, it also disappears from sight. Thus, worshipping created phenomena is pure folly. After rejecting the worship of creation, Abraham declared his faith:

> I have set my face toward Him Who created the Heavens and the Earth, a man of pure faith and one by nature upright. I am not among those who associate partners with God. (6:79)

So, it is a great mistake to infer from these verses that Abraham took heavenly bodies as God in the early phase of his life.

Abraham's second supposed fault or lapse is that he appealed to God to show him how He revives the dead. Concerning this, the Qur'an says:

> Behold! Abraham said: "My Lord, show me how You give life to the dead." He asked: "Do you not believe?" He said: "Yes, but to set my heart at rest." (2:260)

In a hadith, God's Messenger says that 70,000 veils separate God from humanity. This implies that our journey toward God is endless, and that people have different

- **Revive:** to bring back to life after death.

Abraham used allusions in three occasions. In other words, he chose to divert his audience's attention to something else by making indirect references to the truth.

degrees of knowledge and understanding as well as varying capacities for spiritual and intellectual satisfaction. Since God is infinite, unbounded in His Attributes and Names, each individual can obtain only some knowledge of Him and attain some degree of satisfaction (according to his or her capacity).

Abraham had one of the greatest capacities, and therefore needed to increase in knowledge of God every day to attain full spiritual satisfaction. The Prophets, like every other human being, were in a constant process of spiritual and intellectual growth. Considering each previous stage of growth inadequate, they incessantly pursued further degrees of conviction. For this reason, God's Messenger asked God's forgiveness about 100 times a day and frequently entreated Him, saying:

> Glory be to You, we have not been able to know You as Your knowledge requires, O Known One! Glory be to You, we have not been able to worship You as Your worship requires, O Worshipped One!

Abraham's whole life was a constant struggle against unbelief and polytheism. On only three occasions did he ever use allusions. In other words, he chose to divert his audience's attention to something else by making indirect references to the truth. He did this either to avoid harassment or explain a religious truth in simpler terms. Since, however, some scholars consider these allusions to be lies, we must clarify them here.

The first allusion: When his people wanted him to accompany them to their religious celebration, he cast a glance at the stars and said he was sick.

Abraham was not physically sick, but the grief that he might be associated with his people's falsehoods was preying on his mind and soul. It was impossible for him to

- **Allusion:** mention of something with indirect reference or an implication.

worship idols; rather, he was determined to destroy them. Once, to avoid participating in their ceremonies, he told them he was sick and, after they left, smashed their idols. This was not a lie, for he truly was sick of their idols and idolatry. This is why he did what he did. The Qur'an praises him for this:

> Among those who followed Noah's way was Abraham. He came unto his Lord with a pure, sound heart. He said to his father and his people: "What do you worship? Do you desire a falsehood, gods other than God? What, then, is your opinion of the Lord of the Worlds?" Then he cast a glance at the stars, and said: "I am indeed sick!" So they turned away from him and departed. Then he turned to their gods and asked: "Why don't you eat (of the offerings before you)? Why don't you speak?" Then he turned upon them, striking them with might (and breaking them). (37:83-93)

Abraham never lied. If he had done so, he would have been reproached by God.

In conclusion, Abraham never lied. If he had done so, he would have been reproached by God. However, the Qur'an never mentions that God reproached him for lying. On the contrary, his allusions are mentioned where God praises him in the Qur'an.

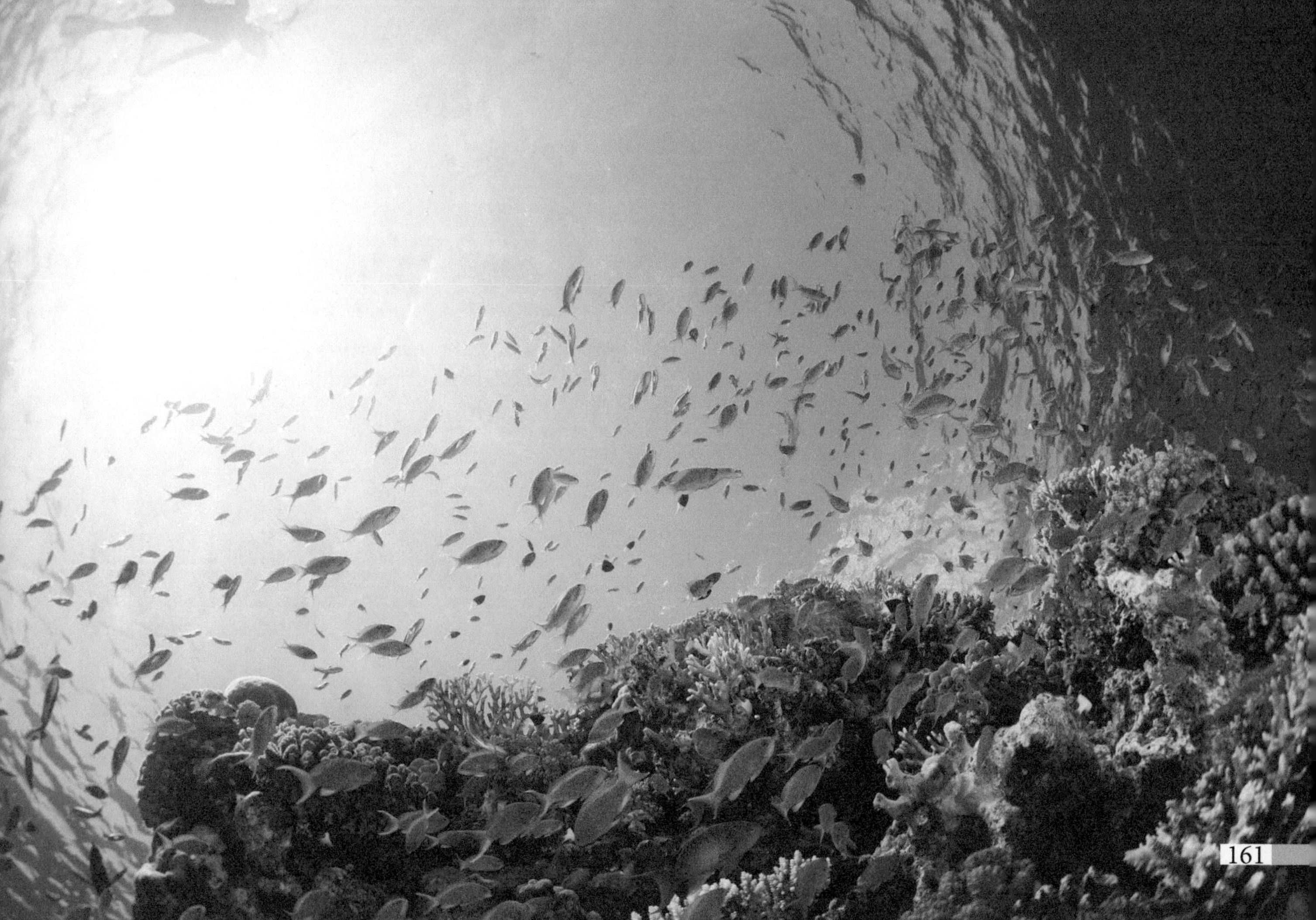

WHAT DID WE LEARN?

LESSON SUMMARY:

- Infallibility is a necessary attribute of the Prophets.
- The infallibility of Prophets is an established fact based on reason and tradition:
  First, Prophets came to convey the Message of God
  Second, the Prophets teach their people all the commands and principles of belief and conduct
  Third, the Qur'an commands believers to obey the Prophet's orders and prohibitions, without exception, and emphasizes that it is not fitting for a believer, man or woman, when a matter has been decided by God and His Messenger, to have any option about their decision (33:36)
  Fourth, sins and pardoning have different types and degrees
- If the Qur'an had not been revealed, we would not be sure whether the previous Prophets were really sincere, devout, and thankful servants of God.

LESSON REVIEW: INDIVIDUAL ASSESSMENT

1. Define the word 'isma.
2. Why must Prophets be infallible?
3. What are some ways Prophet Muhammad was protected from his people's pagan ritual practices?
4. What is the difference between sin and lapse?

ESSAY

Infallibility is a necessary attribute of all Prophets. Using examples from the text, write a persuasive essay convincing the reader of the infallibility of Prophets with proof in both reason and tradition.

LESSON VOCABULARY

- Pristine
- Allusively
- Dispensation
- Hadith Qudsi
- Allusion
- Revive

ابيث ححح دد

Saktin Quran

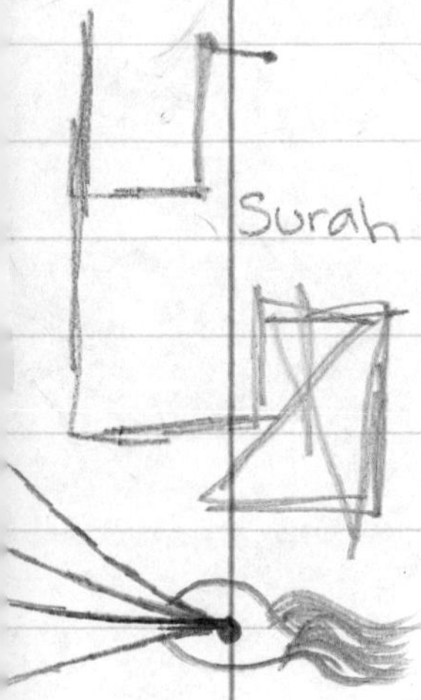

Surah kaf - ولم يجعل له عوجا* قيما لينذر بأساً

Wakf in Quran

"م"

"لا"

لازم وقف

لازم أو قف

"ج" "جائز"

صلى

"جائز"

"قلى"

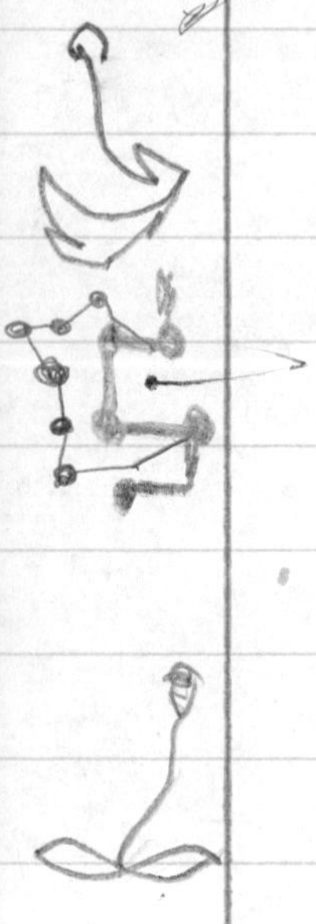

Yasin 13

يس | تَبْدِيلًا

Sikki ldimghn

* Gozumde biten nursun
* kalbinde olan bir melexsin

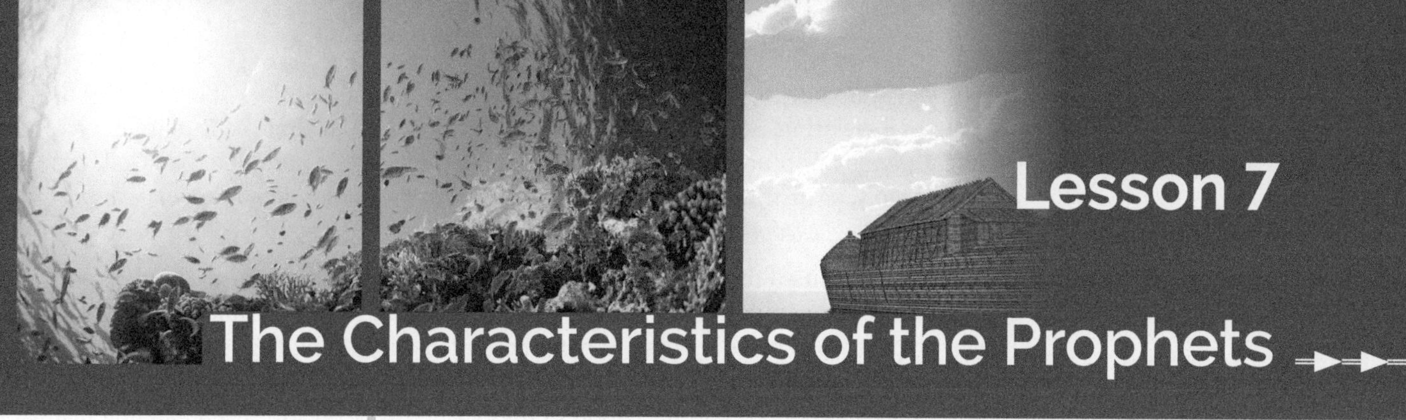

Lesson 7

The Characteristics of the Prophets

Now that you have learned the Essentials of Prophethood, this lesson will summarize the characteristics of the Prophets in five categories:

1. Total dependence on revelation and submission to God
2. Trustworthiness and asking no wage
3. Complete sincerity
4. Calling people wisely and with kindness
5. Calling humanity to God's Unity

All the Prophets were specially brought up through God.

Although every Prophet was intelligent and endowed with a comprehensive understanding and a pure soul, these play no role in God's choice of a Prophet. Most Prophets, including Prophet Muhammad, were unlettered and therefore taught by God. Prophet Muhammad, despite his illiteracy, was blessed with knowledge of the past and the future, and insight into every branch of knowledge. He did not attend any school or have any human teachers, yet even his enemies admitted (and still do) that he displayed perfect justice in family affairs, perfect competency in state administration, and perfect command of armies.

"All the Prophets were specially brought up through God."

PROPHETHOOD IS DISTINGUISHED BY DIVINE REVELATION

> And thus have We revealed to you a spirit of Our command. You would not have known what the Book was, and what faith was. But We have made it a light whereby We guide whom We will of Our servants. And you, surely you guide unto a straight path. (42:52)
>
> As a result, Prophets never spoke on their own accord: Nor does he speak of (his own) desire. It is naught but a Revelation revealed (53:3–4).

Prophet Muhammad, particularly when asked about the essentials of belief, would wait for Revelation. Sometimes the polytheists asked him to alter the Qur'an. But as it is a Divine Scripture whose wording and meaning belong completely to God, he would reply, as instructed by God: *Say: "It is not for me to alter it of my own accord. I follow nothing, except what is revealed to me"* (10:15).

Prophets submitted themselves wholly to God, and fulfilled their mission solely because God commanded them to. They never compromised or deviated from their way in order to achieve success. When confronted with threats or seductive offers, they replied with words similar to those of the Prophet: "If you were even to put the sun in my right hand, and the moon in the left, I will never give up preaching my cause." He knew that the Qur'an is the Word of God, and so bore all hardship and opposition.

TRUSTWORTHINESS AND ASKING NO WAGE

Prophets were completely trustworthy and asked no wage for their services. This very important characteristic is mentioned five times in Surah al-Shu'ara'. All Prophets said the same thing: "I am for you a trustworthy Messenger, so serve God, and obey me. I ask of you no wage for this; my wage falls only upon the Lord of the worlds" (26:107–9, 125–27, 143–45, 162–64, 178–80).

THINK

Those who intend to spread the values of Islam should follow these practices. Any message based on an impure intention, regardless of eloquence, will have no effect on people. This point is frequently emphasized in the Qur'an: Follow those who ask of you no wage, and are themselves rightly guided (36:21). What does this imply about the importance of intention?

Prophets never thought of material gain, spiritual reward, or even Paradise—they strove only for God's good pleasure and to see humanity guided to the truth. Prophet Muhammad was the foremost in this respect. As he devoted his life to humanity's welfare in this world, he will do so in the Place of Gathering. While everybody else will care only about themselves, he will prostrate before God, pray for the Muslims' salvation, and intercede with God on behalf of others.

Imam Busiri expresses the altruism, sincerity, and patience of God's Messenger in vivid language: "Mountains desired to run on his either side in heaps of gold, but he refused." The Messenger once said: "A day comes when I am hungry so as to endure it with patience; on another day I am full to praise my Lord, acquiring thus the reward of both patience and praising."

'A'isha reported that sometimes no food was cooked for four successive days in their house. Abu Hurayra also reports: "Once I went into the Prophet's room. He was praying while seated and groaning. I asked him if he was ill. He replied that he was too hungry to stand. I began to sob bitterly, but he stopped me, saying: "Don't cry, for one who endures hunger here will be safe from God's torment in the next."

One day he told Gabriel: "It has been several days since someone has lit a fire to cook food in the house of Muhammad's family." An angel appeared and asked: "O Messenger of God, God greets you and asks if you would like to be a Prophet-king or a Prophet-slave?" He turned to Gabriel, who recommended humility.

The Prophet raised his voice and replied: "I wish to be a Prophet-slave, who entreats God in hunger one day and thanks Him in satisfaction the next."

God's Messenger used to eat with slaves and servants. Once a woman saw him eating and remarked: "He's eating as if he were a slave." God's Messenger responded: "Could there be a better slave than me? I am a slave of God."

God's Messenger is, by virtue of being a slave of God, our master and that of creation, as eloquently stated by Galip Dede:

An exalted king, the King of the Messengers, O my Master.

You are an endless source of help for the helpless, O my Master. God honored you by swearing by your life in the Qur'an, O my Master. In the Divine Presence, you are the greatest, O my Master.

You are the beloved, lauded and praised one of God, O my Master. Our "eternal" king you are, sent to us by God, O my Master.

"I wish to be a Prophet-slave, who entreats God in hunger one day and thanks Him in satisfaction the next."

COMPLETE SINCERITY

Another indispensable characteristic is sincerity, which in this context means "purity of intention, to do everything solely for the sake of God."

God also mentions sincerity as the foremost attribute of the Prophets: *And mention Moses in the Book; he was made sincere, and he was a Messenger, a Prophet* (19:51).

We worship God only because we are His servants and He has told us to do so. Obeying Him allows us to secure His approval and be rewarded in the Hereafter. Said Nursi, the great twentieth century Turkish thinker, said: "Do what you do only for God's sake, start for God's sake, work for God's sake, and act within the sphere of God's good approval."

DISCUSS

We are told to worship God sincerely: They were commanded only to serve God, making the religion His sincerely, people of pure faith, and to perform the prayer, and pay the alms (98:5). What is the difference between sincere and insincere worship?

God's Last Prophet worshipped God so sincerely that people could say: "No one can remain as humble as he was at the beginning of his career or quest after attaining its height. Prophet Muhammad was an exception to this." He is so great and sublime that we still stand out of respect for him, although he used to warn his Companions: "When I come upon you, don't stand up as the Persians do (for their elders)."

Although his Companions had complete respect for him, he considered himself a poor slave of God. On the day he conquered Mecca, he was the same as when he humbly had begun his mission. At the outset of his mission, he would sit and eat with the poor and slaves. As he entered Mecca in triumph, he rode a mule in such deep submission and humility before God that his forehead touched its pack-saddle.

Key vocabulary

- **Pack-saddle:** a seat for a rider on the back of a horse or other animal.

He was prostrating before God and taking refuge in Him from being a tyrannical, haughty conqueror.

God's Messenger had one intention: to please God and worship Him sincerely. He worshipped Him at a level of perfect goodness (*ihsan*) and sincerity, as he himself stated in a famous Tradition: "Perfect goodness or virtue is to worship God as if you were seeing Him, and while you see Him not, yet truly He sees you."

CALLING PEOPLE WISELY AND WITH KINDNESS

Another attribute of Prophets is calling people to the way of God with wisdom and fair exhortation. They never resorted to demagogy and dialectics, but acted and spoke with wisdom. God ordered His Last and Greatest Messenger: *Call to the way of your Lord with wisdom and fair exhortation, and reason with them in the best way* (16:125).

People are more than just minds or hearts. We are complex beings with many faculties, including the mind, intellect, heart, and soul. All of our faculties, even the innermost ones, require satisfaction. The Prophets addressed all of them.

Those taught by the Prophets acquired certainty, and their view of things differed from those with limited external sight and devoid of insight and spiritual vision. Their conviction of religious truths was unshakable, and they were continually fed with Divine Revelation. They combined speech with action, knowledge with practice, and action with contemplation. 'Ali ibn Abi Talib, among others, would say: "If the veil of the Unseen were lifted up, my certainty would not increase." There was no further degree of certainty left for them to attain.

The education given by the Prophets to their disciples, or the function of the Prophets, is described precisely in the Qur'an:

> We have sent among you, of yourselves, a Messenger, to recite Our signs to you and to purify you, and to teach you the Book and Wisdom, and to teach you what you know not. (2:151)

Call to the way of your Lord with wisdom and fair exhortation, and reason with them in the best way (16:125).

Key vocabulary

- **Exhortation:** advise or warn somenone earnestly

"The cornerstone of the Prophetic mission was to preach Divine Unity."

IMAGINE

Allah tells us to judge according to outward appearances. Thus, those who profess belief and appear to perform religious duties of primary importance (prescribed prayers, alms-giving, etc.) are treated as believers. This is why Prophet Muhammad treated the hypocrites as if they were Muslims. Is this an easy thing to do?

CALLING HUMANITY TO GOD'S UNITY

"The cornerstone of the Prophetic mission was to preach Divine Unity."

All Prophets concentrated on this basic principle: *O my people, serve God: You have no god other than He* (11:84).

God has sent at least one Prophet to every people. The fact that all of them, regardless of time or place, agree on one basic principle shows that they did not speak or act on their own; rather, they did no more than teach the Message received from God. Philosophers and thinkers, no matter how great they may be, disagree among themselves because they depend on their own intellect and findings. Frequently, the same philosophical or sociological school contains different opinions.

Such a disagreement was out of question among the Prophets, and this is another evidence that they were taught by a Single, Eternal Teacher—God—and not guided by defective human reasoning. Such a unity of belief is also a strong evidence of Divine Unity, the fundamental principle of their mission, as declared by Prophet Muhammad: "The most meritorious of the words spoken by me and the Prophets before me is:

'There is no god but God, He is One, having no partners.'

Key vocabulary

- **Meritorious:** deserving honor or praise

WHAT DID WE LEARN?

LESSON SUMMARY:

- The characteristics of the Prophets are in five categories:
  1. Total dependence on revelation and submission to God
  2. Trustworthiness and asking no wage
  3. Complete sincerity
  4. Calling people wisely and with kindness
  5. Calling humanity to God's Unity
- All the Prophets were specially brought up through God
- Sincerity is the foremost attribute of the Prophets
- The cornerstone of the Prophetic mission was to preach Divine Unity
- Prophets never thought of material gain, spiritual reward, or even Paradise—they strove only for God's good pleasure and to see humanity guided to the truth.

LESSON REVIEW: INDIVIDUAL ASSESSMENT

1. What are the five characteristics of the Prophets?
2. Will sins committed because of forgetfulness be accounted for in the hereafter? Why or why not?
3. What was the phrase all Prophets said in Surah Al-Shu-ara?
4. What is the definition of sincerity in the text?

ESSAY

Now that you've read the characteristics and essentials of Prophethood, write a narrative essay detailing the essential and/or characteristic that made the biggest impact on you and why.

LESSON VOCABULARY

- Pack-saddle
- Exhortation
- Meritorious

Lesson 8

The Miracles of the Prophets

THINK

It may even be said that like spiritual and moral attainments material attainments and wonders also were first given to mankind as a gift by the hand of miracles.

What first gave man the gift of the ship, which was a miracle of Noah, and the clock, a miracle of Joseph , was the hand of miracles.

Just as the All-Wise Qur'an sends the Prophets to man's communities as leaders and vanguards in respect of spiritual and moral progress, so too it gives each of them some wonders and makes them the masters and foremen in regard to mankind's material progress. It commands men to follow them absolutely. Thus, just as by speaking of the spiritual and moral perfections of the prophets, it is encouraging people to benefit from them, so too in discussing their miracles it is hinting encouragement to attain to things similar to them and to imitate them.

"Thus, what first gave man the gift of the ship, which was a miracle of Noah , and the clock, a miracle of Joseph , was the hand of miracles."

Messengers also became the forerunners in scientific knowledge and progress by miracles. The miracles of a Prophet worked, by God's leave, usually concerned the science that was being studied the most at his time. So, just as the miracles left the scientist of that time helpless creating something similar, they also marked the final point of progress which that science would be able to realize by the Last Day.

Since scholars have agreed that each of the Qur'an's verses contains numerous aspects of guidance and instruction, then the verses of the miracles of the Prophets, which are the most brilliant of the Qur'an's verses, are not each historical stories, but comprise numerous meanings of guidance.

By giving the encouragement to humanity, it urges him forward towards their goals.

1. The subjugating of the air: Solomon's miracle.

"And to Solomon, We (subjugated) the wind: its morning course covered the distance of a month's journey (at normal pace), and its evening course, a month's journey." (34:12)

This describes one of Solomon's miracles, the subjugating of the air, says: *"Solomon's traversed the distance of two months in one day by flying through the air."* Thus, it is suggesting in this that the road is open for man to cover such a distance in the air.

DISCUSS

How does mentioning the Prophet's miracles and tracing the limits of science and industry specify the final goals of humankind?

Key vocabulary

- **Vanguards:** group of people who are the leaders of an action or movement in society
- **Subjugating:** to get something under complete control

You too may find the cure for every illness in the pharmacy of My wisdom. Work and find it! If you seek, you will certainly find it!"

2. Extracting treasures under the earth: Moses' miracle.

> So We said "Strike the rock with your staff." Then gushed forth there-from twelve springs, (2:60)

This explains a miracle of Moses. This verse indicates that the treasures of Mercy concealed under the earth may be profited by utilizing simple tools. In places hard as rock even, the water of life may be extracted with a staff. Thus, through this meaning the verse says to man: "You may find the Mercy, the water of life, with a staff. In which case, come on, work and find it!' And in meaning Almighty God says through the verse's allusive tongue: "O man! Since I gave to the hand of one of my servants who trusted in Me such a staff that it draws the water of life from wherever he wishes, if you too rely on the laws of My Mercy, you may obtain an implement resembling it or close to it. So, come on and do so!" Thus one of the most important contributions to man's progress is the creation of an implement that causes water to gush forth from most of the places it is struck. This verse traces farther goals and limits, and ends beyond that. Just as the previous verse specified final points far ahead of today's airplanes.

3. Remedies for the ill: Jesus' miracle.

> "And I heal the blind from birth and leper, and I revive the dead, by God's leave."(3:49)

This concerns a miracle of Jesus . Just as the Qur'an explicitly urges man to follow Jesus' high morals, so too it allusively encourages him towards the art of medicine, in which he was the master. Thus, this verse indicates this: "Remedies may be found for even the most chronic illnesses. In which case, O man! And O calamity-afflicted sons of Adam! Don't despair! Whatever the ill, its cure is possible. Search for it and you will find it. It is even possible to give a temporary color of life to death." And in meaning Almighty God is saying through the figurative of this verse: "O man! I gave two gifts to one My servants who abandoned the world for Me. One was the remedy for spiritual sicknesses, and the other the cure for physical sicknesses. Thus, dead hearts were raised to life through the light of guidance. And sick people who were as though dead found health through his breath and cure. You too may find the cure for every illness in the pharmacy of My wisdom. Work and find it! If you seek, you will certainly find it!"

4. The softening the iron and copper: David's and Solomon's miracles.

And We made the iron soft for him (34:10)

And We gave him wisdom and sound judgment in speech and decision, (38:20)

And "We caused molten copper to flow for him (like fountain)" (34:12)

These indicate that the softening of iron is one the greatest of Divine bounties, through which is shown the virtue of one of the greatest Prophets. Indeed, softening iron, that is, making it soft like dough, smelting copper, and finding minerals and extracting them is the origin and the source, and basis, and foundation of all man's material industries. And so, this verse indicates: "A great bounty bestowed on a great Prophet and Divine Vicegerent on Earth in the form of a great miracle was the softening of iron. And making it soft like dough and fine like a thread and smelting copper are the means to most of the general industries." Since wisdom was given to the tongue of one who was both Prophet and Vicegerent, that is to one who was both a spiritual and material leader, and craft and industry were given to his hand, just as it is explicitly urging towards the wisdom on his tongue, so too there is a sign that it is also encouraging towards the craft in his hand.

5. Transport of things from distance: Solomon's miracle.

> Said one who had the knowledge of the Book: "I will bring it to you in the twinkling of an eye!' Then when (Solomon) saw it placed firmly before him..., (27:40)

This points to another wondrous event: in order to attract Belkis' throne to him, one of Solomon's ministers who was versed in the science of attraction said: "I'll have the throne here before you can blink your eyes." Thus the verse suggests that is possible to make things present from long distances, either themselves or their forms. And it is a fact that Almighty God bestowed this on Solomon, who was honored with kingship as well as prophethood, in the form a miracle so that as a means to his innocence and justice he might himself, in person, be informed of all the regions of his extensive realm and see the state of his subjects and hear of their illnesses. That is to say, while Belkis' throne was in Yemen, it was itself present in Damascus, or its form was present, it was seen. And for sure the forms of the man around the throne were present and their voices heard. This indicates in magnificent fashion to the attraction of forms and sounds from long distances, and in effect says:

"O Kings and Rulers! If you wish to act with pure justice, try to see and understand the face of the earth in all its details, like Solomon. For, by rising to the level of being informed whenever he wishes about every part of his realm, a just ruler and king who cherishes his subjects his saved from being made answerable, and may act with complete justice." And Almighty God in effect says the following through the allusive tongue of the verse:

> "O Sons of Adam! I gave one of My Servants a broad realm, and in order to act completely justly within it, I allowed him to know personally of all situations and events that occurred there. And since I have given all men, by their natures, the ability to be vicegerent of the earth, I gave them also the capacity to see, consider, and understand the face of the earth in accordance with that ability, since My wisdom required it. If individuals do not attain to that point, as a race man may attain to it. And if they do not reach it physically, the saint may reach it in meaning. In which case, you may benefit from this great bounty. Come on, let's see you do it! On condition you do not neglect your duties of worship, work to turn the face of the earth into a garden every part of which you may see, and the sounds of every corner of which you may hear. Heed the decree of the Most Merciful: *It is He Who has made the earth manageable for you, so traverse its tracts and enjoy of the sustenance which He furnishes, but unto Him is the Resurrection.'* (67:15)"

Thus, the above mentioned verse alludes to the farthest limit in much further advances in the attraction of forms and sounds, one of man's finest arts, and hints encouragement.

6. Subjugating Jinn & Devils: Solomon's miracle.

And others (of the rebellious jinn) linked together in fetters...(38:38), And of the evil ones were some who dived for him, and did other work besides..... (21:82)

Solomon subjugated the jinn, devils, and evil spirits, and preventing their evil, employed it beneficial matters, and they say: the jinn, the most important inhabitants of the earth after man who are conscious, may serve man. Contact may be made with them. Devils too may be compelled to give up their enmity and whether they want to or not, made to serve.

7. Mass communication. David's miracle.

We made the mountains to glorify (their Lord) along with him in the afternoon and bright morning. (38:18)

O you mountains! Sing you back the Praises of God with him! and you birds! And We made the iron soft for him. (34:10)

We have been taught the speech of birds (27:16)

Almighty God gave David's praises and glorification such a strength and a sound so loud and agreeable that they brought the mountains to ecstasy, which, each like a huge gramophone or a man, formed a circle on the horizon around the chief reciter and also declared the glorifications.

Whatever David said, they repeated. Mountains have a collective personality and corporate identity, and offer glorifications and worship in a way suitable to it. That is to say, just as all mountains recite glorifications in the tongue of men through the mystery of echo, so too they glorify the All-Glorious Creator in their own particular tongues.

8. Communication with the animals: David and Solomon's miracles.

And the birds gathered (in assemblies) (38:19) We have been taught the speech of birds, (27:16)

Almighty God bestowed on David and Solomon knowledge of the tongues of the bird species, and of the tongues of their abilities, that is, of the things for which they would be useful. Yes, since it is the truth and since the face of the earth is a laden table of the Most Merciful, which was set up in honor of man, most of the other animals and birds that benefit from the table may be subjugated to man and serve him. Man employs some of the smallest of them, the honeybee and silkworm, and through Divine inspiration has opened up a mighty way of benefit. By employing pigeons in various tasks, and making birds like parrots speak; he has added fine things to the virtues of human civilization. In the same way, if the tongues of ability of other birds and animals were known, there are many species that could be employed in the important tasks like their brothers, the domesticated animals.

IMAGINE

Every mountain with caves can speak with man in man's language like a parrot, by means of an echo. You say: "All praise be to God!" to the mountain before you, and the mountain will say: "All praises be to God!", exactly the same as you. Since Almighty God has given this ability to mountains, for sure it can be made to develop, and that seed may sprout.

Key vocabulary

- **Fetters:** someone that prevents someone or something from moving or acting freely
- **Gramophone:** an old fashioned record player

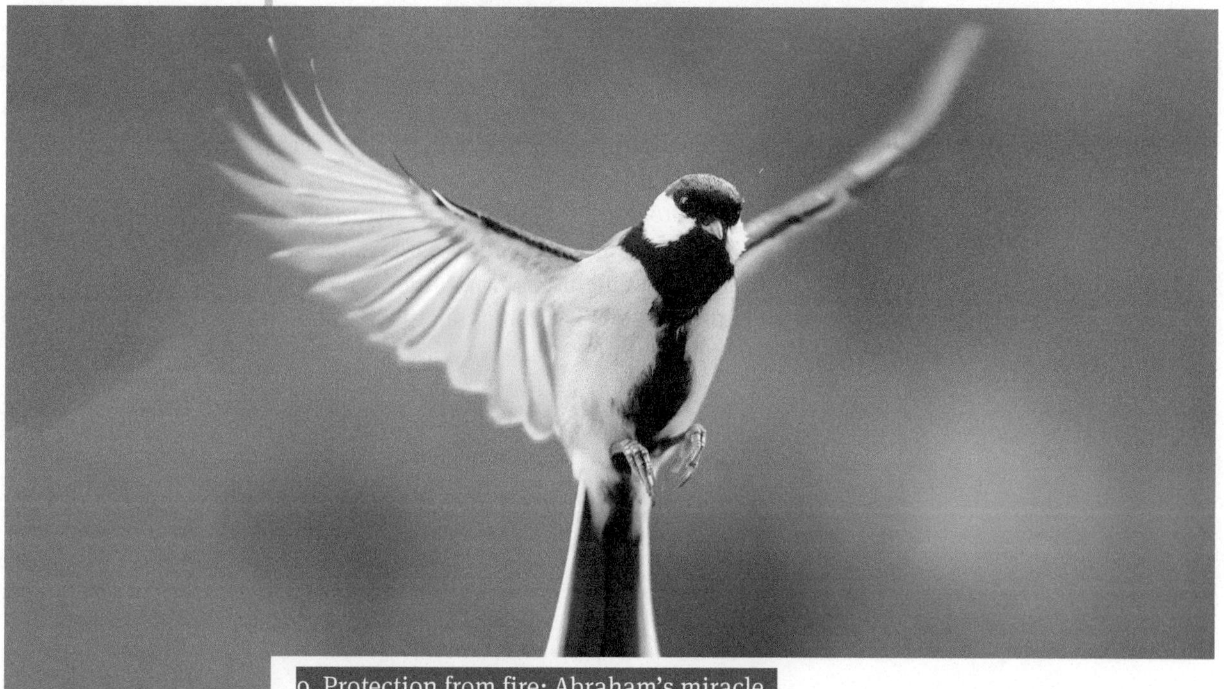

9. Protection from fire: Abraham's miracle.

We said: "O fire! Be cool and (a means of) safety for Abraham, (21:69)

This is one of Abraham's miracles and has three subtle indications:

The First: Like other natural causes, fire does not act according to its own wishes and nature, blindly, but it performs a duty under a command. Thus it did not burn Abraham , for it was commanded not to burn him.

The Second: There is a degree of heat, which burns through its coldness. That is, it has an effect similar to burning. Through the word, Be cool!, Almighty God is saying to the coldness: "Do not burn with your coldness, the same as your heat!' That is to say, through its coldness, fire at that degree displays an affect like burning. It is both fire, and cold. Indeed, in natural science, there is a degree of fire, the state of 'white heat', the heat of which does not spread to its surroundings. Since it attracts the heat around itself, with this sort of cold it freezes surrounding liquids like water, and in effect burns them through its cold. Thus, intense cold is a category of fire, which burns through its cold.

The Third: Like there is an immaterial substance like belief, which is an obstacle to the effects of Hellfire and affords security from it, an armor like Islam, so too there is a physical substance which prevents the effects of a worldly fire. For as is required by the Name of the All-Wise, since this world is the abode of wisdom, Almighty God carries out His works under the veil of causes. Therefore, like the fire did not burn Abraham's body, neither did it burn his garments; He gave them a state, which resisted fire.

10. Teaching of the Names: Adam's miracle

And he taught Adam the Names, All of them (2:31)

Adam's greatest miracle is the teaching of the Divine Names. Like the miracles of the other Prophets, each alludes to a particular human wonder. The Miracle of Adam, the father of all the Prophets, indicates almost explicitly to the final points of all human attainment and progress, their final goals. Through this verse, Allah is saying in meaning: "O Sons of Adam! Since proof of their superiority over the angels in the question of vicegerency, I taught your forefathers all the Names; you too, since you are his sons and inheritors of his abilities should learn all the Names and show your worthiness before all creatures.

WHAT DID WE LEARN?

LESSON SUMMARY:

- Just as the All-Wise Qur'an sends the Prophets to man's communities as leaders and vanguards in respect of spiritual and moral progress, so too it gives each of them some wonders and makes them the masters and foremen in regard to mankind's material progress
- In discussing their miracles, the Qur'an is hinting encouragement to attain to things similar to them and to imitate them.
- Craftsmen take a prophet as the patron of their craft.

LESSON REVIEW: INDIVIDUAL ASSESSMENT

1. What is encouraged through the discussion of the Prophets and their miracles in regards to humankind?
2. Explain why it is not correct to view the stories of the Prophets in the Qur'an as solely historical accounts.
3. What was the miracle of Moses mentioned in the text?
4. Explain how our modern airplane is described through the Qur'an in the text.

ESSAY

Write an essay detailing the miracles of the Prophets found in this text. Since there are many more miracles found in Qur'an, but not mentioned here, describe how you will read Qur'an differently to look for some of these miracles.

LESSON VOCABULARY

- Vanguards
- Gramophone
- Fetters

BELIEF IN LIFE AFTER DEATH

CHAPTER 6

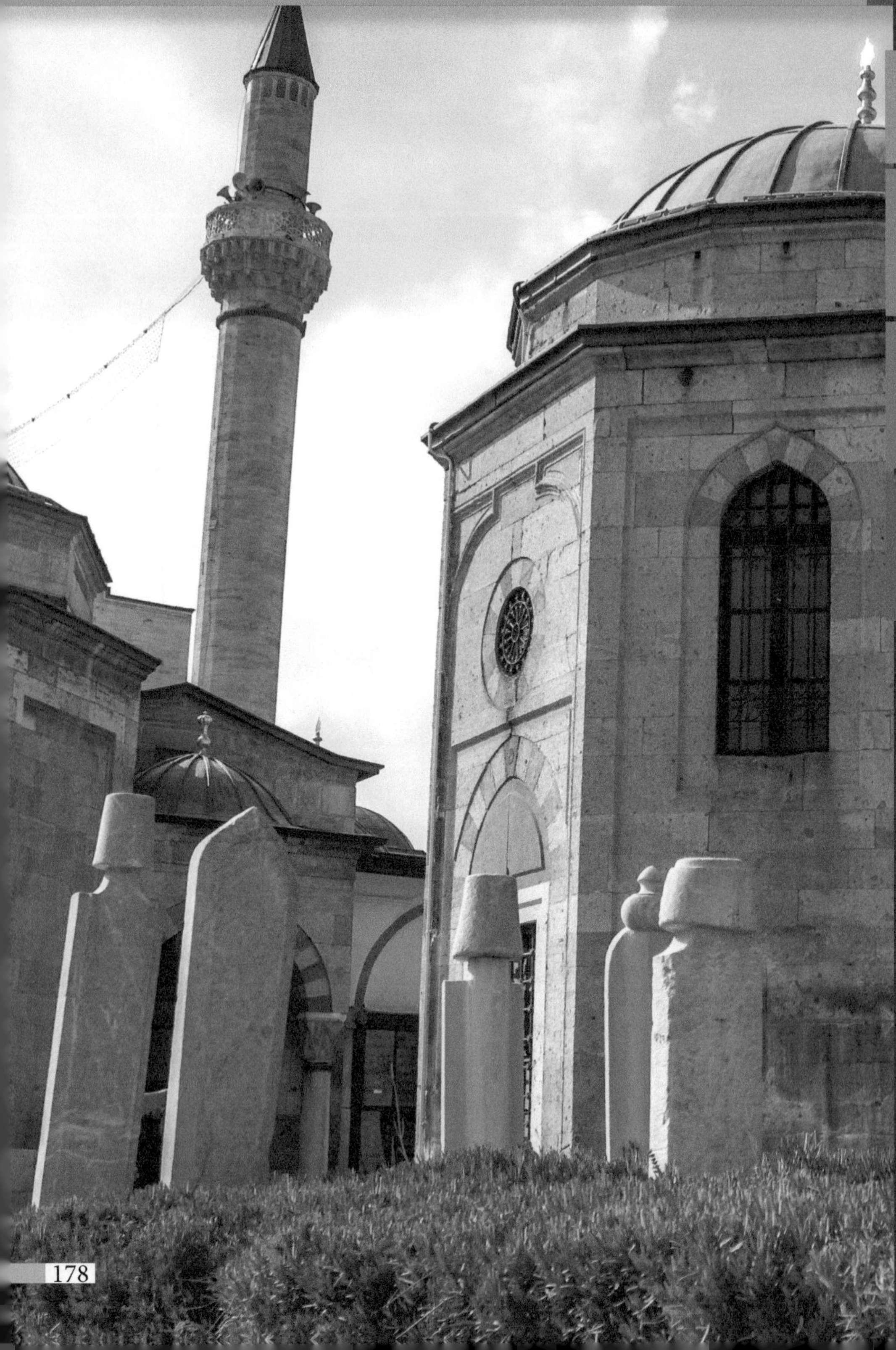

It is an obvious fact that true justice can never be achieved on earth.

Lesson 1
Introduction

BELIEF IN LIFE AFTER DEATH IS ONE OF THE MOST IMPORTANT ARTICLES OF FAITH

Life after death is an answer to the deepest prayers of the human soul.

True justice can never be achieved on earth.

Faith in the hereafter gives humanity hope and strength to endure the burdens of worldly life. Life after death is an answer to the deepest prayers of the human soul. Resurrection and eternal life is a promise given to humankind by the Almighty Himself. The Divine Names of Allah necessitate the existence of a realm of justice, reward and punishment.

Without Judgment Day and life after death, this world would be a realm of injustice, tyranny, disappointment and delusion. Those who have not been apprehended for their crimes on earth could not be punished and those who live a life of piety and righteousness could not be rewarded.

"It is an obvious fact that true justice can never be achieved on earth."

We live in a world where some indulge themselves in the pleasures of wealth and prosperity whilst others struggle to find a morsel of food. The human justice system does not always favor the truth as it operates with ambiguities and loopholes. Since Allah is Just, this alone requires the establishment of a Day of Judgment where everyone is dealt with fairly. Without doubt, Allah hears the desperate screams of millions of people who cry out for justice.

There is also the reality that pleasure and pain are intermingled in this life, hence true pleasure can never be experienced in the presence of pain. Statistically, on average a human being experiences six months of pleasure in his/her life. According to a research, we spend 25 years of our lives sleeping. Eight hours of sleep a day means one third of our daily lives, therefore, an individual who lives to the age of 75, has spent 25 years of his/her life sleeping.

When we remove activities such as education, work, daily chores, illnesses, dealing with problems, time spent in the restroom and showering, and the burdens of old age from the remaining 50 years, we are left with no more than six months of pleasure. The results of this research clearly state that the world we live in is not a realm of gratification or entertainment, but a world of testing. Moreover, there are many who do not even live long enough to experience adulthood. There are also those who suffer throughout their lives, struggling with poverty, sickness and oppression. Considering all of the above, without the establishment of the hereafter, this temporary life would contradict the Mercy, Compassion and Justice of Allah.

THINK

Considering all of the above, without the establishment of the hereafter, this temporary life would contradict the Mercy, Compassion and Justice of Allah.

Key vocabulary

- **Morsel:** a small piece
- **Ambiguities:** something that does not have a single clear meaning
- **Gratification:** to make someone happy or satisfied
- **Resurrection:** coming to life after death

THE KING AND HIS PALACE ANALOGY

Imagine a generous King who invites the entire inhabitants of a poor village to his palace. All the guests arrive to the King's palace where they are welcomed with a magnificent feast and entertainment. They enjoy and indulge themselves for 75 hours in the King's palace. During the program the King distributes bags of gold coins to his servants. Everyone is happy and full of bliss. At the conclusion of the program, the guests are taken out of the palace one by one and hanged in the garden. Can any person of logic claim that the King is a compassionate, merciful, and generous ruler?

DISCUSS

Is it reasonable to claim that the King in the analogy is a compassionate, merciful, and generous ruler?

On the contrary, he would be a merciless tyrant who gave his servants a sample of his wealth and bounties and then condemned them to death.

Just as in the analogy above, human beings are transitory guests in this great palace we call earth. Like the villagers who enjoyed 75 hours of pleasure in the palace, we enjoy 75 years of life on this planet. We benefit from the bounties and pleasures of this world until such a time that death takes everything away from us. However, unlike the story above, the King of this world is not a tyrant. On the contrary, He is the All-Compassionate, the All-Merciful, the All-Munificent and the All-Generous Allah. His treasures are limitless. His power has no boundaries. His existence is eternal in the past and everlasting in the future. He has created human beings so that they would recognize His Might, observe His magnificent art and benefit from His Mercy and Compassion.

Key vocabulary

- **Transitory:** lasting only for a short time

Therefore, eternal power necessitates eternal observers; eternal Mercy and Compassion necessitates eternal beneficiaries; eternal wealth necessitates eternal recipients; eternal Munificence necessitates eternal gratefulness and Exalted Justice necessitates the establishment of a realm where everyone is dealt with fairly. Accordingly, all human beings will certainly be resurrected and held accountable for their lives spent on this transient world of assessment. Consequently, they will either be rewarded for their good deeds or punished for their evil.

Although, there are countless proofs and evidences to the establishment of a life after death, the Holy Qur'an and the presence of the noble Messenger of Allah is the greatest evidence to the hereafter. Along with these two unquestionable authentic proofs there are other solid evidences such as the previous Divine Books, Prophets and thousands of saints and scholars who all claimed the very same thing: "There is life after death." Moreover, history verifies that all of these individuals who make the very same claim has never lied or even exaggerated in their lives.

QUESTION:

Since one-fifth of the Holy Qur'an talks about the life after death and the noble Messenger have informed us about the Day of Judgment, we have no reservations about its existence. However, some people find it difficult to comprehend the concept of resurrection and a life after death. What can we say to them?

ANSWER:

Obviously, it is difficult to comprehend a life that we have not seen or experienced, however, some evidences of a life after death can be physically observed in this life. For example; imagine a baby still in his/her mother's womb. Just for arguments sake, let us say, we had the opportunity to establish a conversation with this baby. Assuming that the baby also possesses the ability to understand us, we tell him/her about the reality of this world. We explain to him/her that the world he/she is currently in is a temporary abode from where he/she will soon come out to a bigger and larger world. We describe to him/her things that exist in this world, such as the sun, the moon, trees, ocean, rivers, flowers, millions of different life forms. Furthermore, let us say that we talk to him/her about jets, cars, trains, ships and technology. Could he/she have any concept or even imagine such things?

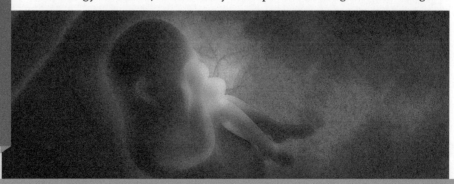

IMAGINE

Imagine a baby still in mother's womb and we had the opportunity to talk with the baby and the baby has the ability to understand us, tell him/her about the reality of the world we live in. How much can he/she comprehend without seeing this world?

Key vocabulary

- **Munificence:** very generous

The only world he/she has experienced for the past nine months is the tiny space in the womb hence for him/her no other world exists. The world to which he/she would soon be arriving is incomprehensible.

Human beings who were created for eternity and a realm of everlasting life are no different to a baby in the womb. In comparison to the life after, this world is like the mother's womb. Hence, imagining a world of eternity seems a difficult task for us. However, just as the baby realizes the existence of this world upon his/her birth, we will realize the existence of the hereafter upon our death. Furthermore, there are many signs and indications that the intellect can detect even in this life.

In comparison to the life after, this world is like the mother's womb.

Key vocabulary

- **Eternity:** endless time, a life state that never ends after death

WHAT DID WE LEARN?

LESSON SUMMARY:

- Belief in life after death is one of the most important articles of faith.
- It is an obvious fact that true justice can never be achieved on earth.
- The human justice system does not always favor the truth as it operates with ambiguities and loopholes
- Human beings are transitory guests in this great palace we call earth
- All human beings will certainly be resurrected and held accountable for their lives spent on this transient world of assessment
- One-fifth of the Holy Qur'an talks about the life after death and the noble Messenger have informed us about the Day of Judgment

LESSON REVIEW: INDIVIDUAL ASSESSMENT

1. What would this world turn into without Judgement Day and life after death?
2. What fraction of the Qur'an speaks about life after death?
3. According to the text, how much of our lives, on average, do we spend sleeping?
4. How does the analogy of the baby help you understand the concept of life after death?

ESSAY

Why is it impossible for true justice to be achieved on earth?

LESSON VOCABULARY

- Morsel
- Ambiguities
- Gratification
- Transitory
- Munificence
- Resurrection
- Eternity

Lesson 2
The Signs & Indications of Life After Death

SO WHAT ARE THE SIGNS AND INDICATIONS OF LIFE AFTER DEATH?

Giving life to inanimate matter is one of Allah's Attributes. We observe this every day in nature.

Once again, the answer lies in the baby allegory. During his/her time in the mother's womb the baby feeds through the umbilical cord, therefore, does not need a mouth. Also, the baby does not need eyes, ears, hands and feet in the womb, because he/she has no use for them. If the baby had the necessary intelligence to think and ponder, he/she would use his/her logic and contemplate: "Why do I possess eyes when it is dark in here? Why do I have feet when I cannot walk? Why do I have a mouth when I am being fed through my stomach?" This line of questioning will lead to the reality that the baby will indeed have use for all of the organs mentioned above, but in some other realm for which he/she is being prepared. This is quite a valid argument, because everything Allah has created comes with a corresponding counterpart or an opposite. For example, the creation of nose indicates scent; the creation of ears indicates sound; the creation of eyes indicates light and so on...

THINK

We all want to live forever, we all want everlasting wealth and health; we all want eternal youth and prosperity. Unfortunately, none of these properties exist here.

However, there are some things in this life for which we fail to find a counterpart. For example, we all want to live forever, we all want everlasting wealth and health; we all want eternal youth and prosperity. Unfortunately, none of these properties exists here. But according to the reality above, Allah creates everything with a corresponding item. A famous scholar once said, "If He did not want to give, He would not have given the feeling of want." Since these sensations, feelings, wishes and desires of eternity exist in all human beings; their counterparts will also be created. Consequently, Allah wanted to give, hence He has created the feeling of want.

Allah wanted to give, hence He has created the feeling of want.

Another significant point about resurrection is Allah the Almighty exhibits samples of resurrection before our very eyes each year during springtime. All trees and plant life that transform into mere logs and dried out strands comes back to life during spring, blossoming with exquisitely colorful flowers and fruits. Moreover, the indication of resurrection is also manifested to us through the seeds of plants, which evidently die out and decompose upon entering the dark soil of the earth. Yet, their death gives birth to a brand new life.

Giving life to inanimate matter is one of Allah's Attributes.
We observe this every day in nature.

Key vocabulary

- **Inanimate:** not capable of life

DISCUSS

Which one is harder? To create anything from scratch or to reproduce it again once it is created in the first place?

By the will of Allah, life emerges from non-living matter such as carbon atoms, amino acids, nucleic acids and proteins. As mentioned previously, the notion of easy and difficult does not apply to Allah, however, for arguments sake, we would like to point out that creating something out of nothing and for the first time would plausibly be considered as more difficult than reproducing it.

The notion of easy and difficult does not apply to Allah

Let us explain this with another analogy: Imagine an electronics wizard who walks into a room packed with a large audience, carrying a bag filled with thousands of tiny electronic components.

He then opens the bag and within minutes, he puts the tiny components together and constructs a network of computer systems. He then, pulls everything apart, dismantling the entire system into tiny pieces. Can anyone in the room argue that this person is incapable of putting the same system together again and making it work?

Certainly not! Simply because he has already proven that he has the ability and capability to construct and built extremely complex systems.

Key vocabulary

- **Plausibly:** realistically, believable

IMAGINE

Imagine just as a general who reassembles an entire army which had taken a rest break, with one commandment, the All-Powerful will too bring together the decomposed components of all human beings who had died and resurrect them on the promised Day of Judgment.

"An existing product points to its maker and it is the greatest evidence that the maker has the talent and the power to reproduce it."

The example above is closely related to an incident that took place during the time of the noble Messenger of Allah. A man came up to the noble Prophet holding a chinbone of a dead camel in his hand. He asked with sarcasm, "Who will give life to this"? The Holy Qur'an answered his question with a verse from Surah Yasin:

وَضَرَبَ لَنَا مَثَلًا وَنَسِيَ خَلْقَهُ قَالَ مَنْ يُحْيِي الْعِظَامَ وَهِيَ رَمِيمٌ ﴿٧٨﴾
قُلْ يُحْيِيهَا الَّذِي أَنْشَأَهَا أَوَّلَ مَرَّةٍ وَهُوَ بِكُلِّ خَلْقٍ عَلِيمٌ ﴿٧٩﴾

And he coins a comparison for Us, having forgotten his own origin and creation, saying, "Who will give life to these bones when they have rotted away?" Say: "He Who produced them in the first instance will give them life. He has full knowledge of every creation."

An existing product points to its maker and it is the greatest evidence that the maker has the talent and the power to reproduce it.

The Holy Qur'an provides the most perfect answer to those who doubt resurrection. Do they not look at their own origin? Indeed, those who doubt resurrection should look at the origin of all life forms on earth and the origin of the universe. It is the Omnipotent Allah, the Almighty Allah who created the universe and the life forms that dwell in it. He then, exhibited His grand art to those who has the ability to think and comprehend. Obviously, creating everything and giving life to the dead is within the limits of His Power and Wisdom. Just as a general who reassembles an entire army which had taken a rest break, with one commandment, the All-Powerful will too bring together the decomposed components of all human beings who had died and resurrect them on the promised Day of Judgment.

The Holy Qur'an instructs us to scrutinize our own origin. Although, there have been many scientific theories and proposal regarding the origin of life on earth, no scientist or thinker has provided answers to the metaphysical link between non-living matter and living organisms.

Key vocabulary

- **Scrutinize:** to examine carefully, especially in a critical way

DISCUSS

The Holy Qur'an provides the most perfect answer to those who doubt resurrection. Do they not look at their own origin?

Whoever created the mosquito's eye, created the sun. Whoever ordered the flea's stomach, ordered the solar system.

The raising to life of all animate beings at the resurrection of the dead can be no more difficult for divine power than restoring to life a fly in the spring, after the heavy death like sleep of winter.

For pre-eternal power, it is essential that; it doesn't change; impotence cannot penetrate it; obstacles cannot intervene in it; everything, easy or hard is the same in relation to it.

Whoever created the mosquito's eye, created the sun.
Whoever ordered the flea's stomach, ordered the solar system.

Nature resembles a printing press, not the printer. It is embroidery, not the Embroiderer. It is passive, not active. It is a pattern, not a source. It is an order, and not the Orderer. It is a law, not a power. It is a code of laws proceeding from a will, not an external reality.

Whoever created the first time from nothing will recreate in the Hereafter.

Pre-eternal power, which does not leave ants without a prince or bees without a queen, certainly does not leave mankind without prophets. As the Splitting of the Moon was a miracle of Muhammad for men in the Manifest World, so his Ascension was a supreme miracle before the angels and spirit beings in the World of the Inner Dimensions of Things.

"And indeed, the home of the Hereafter - that is the (eternal) life,
if only they knew."(29:64)
Whoever created the first time from nothing will recreate in the Hereafter.

WHAT DID WE LEARN?

LESSON SUMMARY:

- The allegory of the baby in the womb can be used to see the signs & indications of life after death
- Everything Allah has created comes with a corresponding counterpart or an opposite.
- Those who doubt resurrection should look at the origin of all life forms on earth and the origin of the universe
- Giving life to inanimate matter is one of Allah's Attributes. We observe every day in nature

LESSON REVIEW: INDIVIDUAL ASSESSMENT

1. Describe two examples of things in this world that we have no counterpart for.
2. What is the greatest evidence that the maker has the talent and the power to reproduce something?
3. When does Allah exhibit resurrection before our very eyes?
4. In the text, which Attribute of Allah is mentioned?

ESSAY

Describe what you understand from "if He did not want to give, He would not have given the feeling of want" and how it relates to belief in life after death.

LESSON VOCABULARY

- Inanimate
- Scrutinize
- Plausible

Lesson 3
The Benefits of Believing in Resurrection

Belief in the Resurrection prevents young people from wasting their lives in transitory and trivial things, and gives hope to the elderly as they move closer to the grave.

After belief in God, belief in the Resurrection has the primary place in securing a peaceful social order.

The Qur'an declares:

In whatever affair you may be, and whichever part of the Qur'an you recite, and whatever deed you do, We are witness over you when you are deeply engrossed therein. Not an atom's weight in the Earth and in the heaven escapes your Lord, nor is there anything smaller or greater, but it is in a Manifest Book. (10:61)

God has full knowledge and awareness of all our deeds, intentions, thoughts, and imaginings. Those who understand this (and act accordingly) will find true peace and happiness in both worlds. A family and community composed of such individuals would feel that they were living in Paradise.

Belief in the Resurrection prevents young people from wasting their lives in transitory and trivial things, and gives hope to the elderly as they move closer to the grave.

It also helps children endure the death of loved ones. Children who believe that they will be reunited with their deceased loved ones in a far-better world find true consolation in the Resurrection. Everyone, regardless of age, gender, and any other artificial human-devised difference, needs belief in the Resurrection as much as they need air, water, and bread.

As this belief leads people to a life of peace, intellectuals who seek public peace and security should emphasize it. Those who are convinced of what the Qur'an declares—*Whoever does an atom's weight of good shall see it, and whoever does an atom's weight of evil shall see it* (99:7-8)—live a responsible life, and a community composed of such people finds true peace and happiness. When this belief is inculcated in the hearts of young people, they will no longer be a harmful social element, but rather will seek to serve their nation and humanity.

THINK

Why should those who do not believe that they will be called to account strive to live and honest, upright life? But those of us who are convinced of this final reckoning, certainly try to live a disciplined life?

Key vocabulary

- **Inculcated:** make something to be learned and implanted by teaching and repeating it over and over again

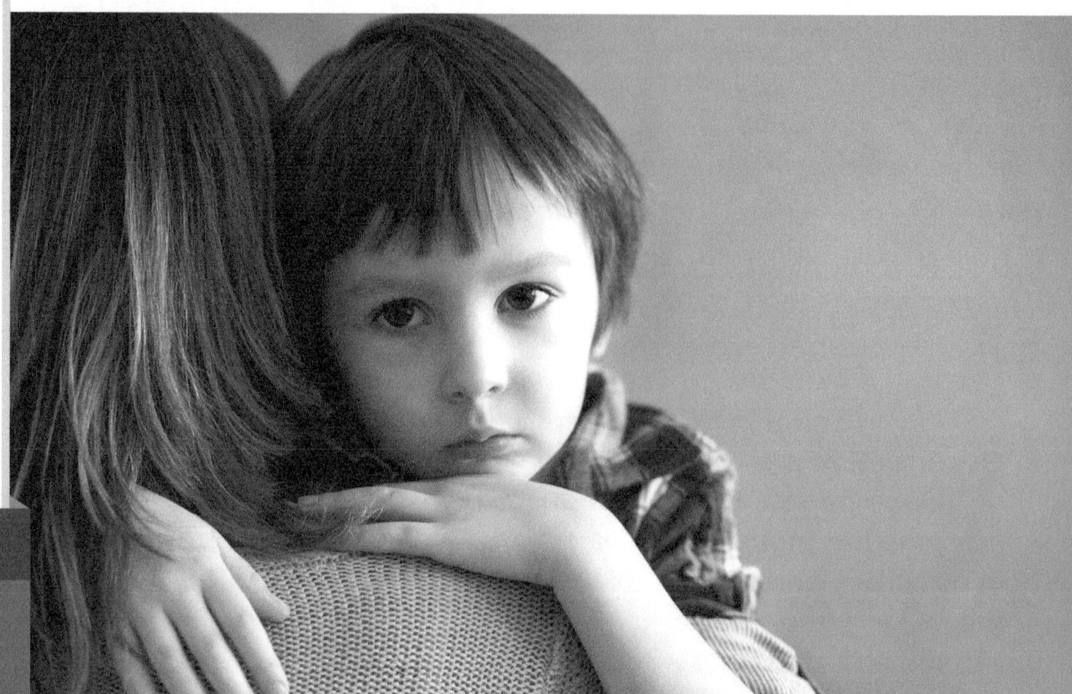

DISCUSS

What else other than belief in the Resurrection and reunion with deceased loved ones can compensate for the loss of parents, brothers, sisters, and friends?

Children are very sensitive and delicate. Extremely susceptible to misfortune, they also are easily affected by what happens to them and their families. When they lose a family member or become orphans, their world is darkened and they fall into deep distress and despair. So, what else other than belief in the Resurrection and reunion with deceased loved ones can compensate for the loss of parents, brothers and sisters, and friends?

Children will find true consolation only when they are convinced that their beloved ones have flown to Paradise, and that they will be reunited with them.

How can you compensate the elderly for their past years, their childhood and youth that have been left behind? How can you console them for the loss of their loved ones who preceded them in death? How can you remove the fear of death and the grave from their hearts? How can you make them forget death, which they feel so deeply? Will more and newer worldly pleasures console them? Only convincing them that the grave, which seems to them like an openmouthed dragon just waiting to devour them, is really a door to another and much better world, or simply a lovely waiting room opening onto that world, can compensate and console them for such losses.

In its inimitable style, the Qur'an voices such feelings through Prophet Zachariah: *This is a mention of your Lord's mercy unto His servant Zachariah; when he invoked Him with a secret, sincere call, saying: "My Lord, my very bones have become rotten and my head is shining with gray hair. My Lord! I have never been disappointed in my prayer to You."* (19:2-5)

Key vocabulary

- **Consolation:** the act of lessening sadness and giving relief.

"Do not be afraid of death, for death is not eternal extinction. It is only a change of worlds, a discharge from your life's distressing duties, a passport to an eternal world where all kinds of beauty and blessings wait for you.

Fearing that his kinsmen would not be sufficiently loyal to his mission after his death, Prophet Zachariah appealed to his Master for a male heir to his mission. This is the cry of all old people. Belief in God and the Resurrection gives them the good news: "Do not be afraid of death, for death is not eternal extinction. It is only a change of worlds, a discharge from your life's distressing duties, a passport to an eternal world where all kinds of beauty and blessings wait for you. The Merciful One Who sent you to the world, and has kept you alive therein for so long, will not leave you in the grave's darkness and dark corridors opening onto the other world. He will take you to His Presence, give you an eternal and ever-happy life, and bless you with all the bounties of Paradise."

Only such good news as this can console the elderly and enable them to welcome death with a smile.

Only such good news as this can console the elderly and enable them to welcome death with a smile.

Our free will, which we use to direct our life, makes us unique among all creatures. Free will is the manifestation of Divine Mercy and, if used properly, will cause us to be rewarded with the fruits of Mercy. Belief in the Resurrection is a most important and compelling factor urging us to use our free will properly and not to wrong or harm others.

The Qur'an declares: Those who fear to stand before their Lord and curb the desires of the carnal self, Paradise will be their dwelling place (79:40-41).

Young people have a transforming energy. If you let them waste it in triviality and indulgence, you undermine your own nation's future.

Sahl ibn Sa'd narrates that God's Messenger was told of a young man who stayed at home for days. The Messenger went to visit him. When the young man saw him appear unexpectedly, he threw himself into the Messenger's arms and died instantly. The Messenger told those around him: "Lay out your friend's corpse. Fear of Hell frightened him deeply. I swear by Him in Whose hand my life is that God will surely protect him from Hell."

The Qur'an declares: *Those who fear to stand before their Lord and curb the desires of the carnal self, Paradise will be their dwelling place* (79:40-41).

In a hadith qudsi, God says: "I will not unite two securities, nor two fears."
In other words, those who fear His punishment here will be protected from His punishment there, while those who do not fear His punishment here will not be saved from it there.

'Umar said, upon seeing a young man bravely protesting and resisting an injustice: "Any people deprived of the young are doomed to extinction."

Young people have a transforming energy. If you let them waste it in triviality and indulgence, you undermine your own nation's future.

Belief in the Resurrection stops young people from committing atrocities and wasting their energies on passing pleasures, and directs them to lead a disciplined, useful, and virtuous life.

Belief in the Resurrection also consoles the sick. A believer with an incurable illness thinks: "I am dying; no one can prolong my life. Everyone must die. Fortunately, I am going to a place (Paradise) where I will recover my health and youth, and enjoy them forever." Secure in this knowledge, all beloved servants of God, Prophets, and saints welcome death with a smile. The Last Prophet said during the final minutes of his life: "O God, I desire the eternal company in the eternal world." He had informed his Companions the day before: "God let one of His servants choose between enjoying the beauty of this world as long as he wishes and what is with Him. The servant chose what is with Him." That servant was the Messenger himself. The Companions understood whom he meant and burst into tears.

Similarly, when 'Umar ruled over a vast area stretching from the western frontiers of Egypt to the highlands of Central Asia, he prostrated himself before God and sighed: "I can no longer fulfill my responsibility. Let me die and be taken to Your Presence." Such a strong desire for the other world, the world of eternal beauty, and being blessed with the vision of the Eternally Beautiful One caused the Prophet, 'Umar, and many others to prefer death to this world.

The world is a mixture of good and evil, right and wrong, beauty and ugliness, and oppressors and oppressed. Many instances of wrong (appear to) go unnoticed, and numerous wronged people cannot recover their rights. Only belief in being resurrected in another world of absolute justice consoles the wronged and oppressed, and dissuades them from seeking vengeance. Similarly, those stricken with affliction and misfortune find consolation in the Resurrection, because they believe that whatever befalls them purifies them, and that anything lost in a catastrophe will be restored in the Hereafter as a blessing, just as if they had given these items as alms.

Key vocabulary

- **Triviality:** something that is not important

Belief in the Resurrection changes a house into a garden of Paradise.

Belief in the Resurrection changes a house into a garden of Paradise.

IMAGINE

Imagine a house where the young pursue their pleasures, children have nothing to do with religious sentiment and practices, parents are engrossed in procuring all fantasies of life, and grandparents life in a nursing home and console themselves with pets since there are no grandchildren around whom they can love and who can show them the respect they desire – life in such a house is difficult to bear.

Belief in the Resurrection reminds people of their familial responsibilities, and as they implement these duties, an atmosphere of mutual love, affection, and respect begins to pervade the house.

Such a belief-based family life makes its members feel that they are already living in Paradise. Similarly, if a country orders itself according to this same belief, its inhabitants would enjoy a life far better than what Plato imagined in his *Republic* or al-Farabi (Alpharabios) in his *Al-Medinat al-Fadila* (The Virtuous City). It would be like Medina in the time of the Prophet or the Muslim lands under 'Umar's rule.

To have a better understanding of how the Prophet built that society, we provide several examples of his sayings concerning the Resurrection and the afterlife:

Since God created them, the children of Adam have not experienced an event more terrible than death. However, death is easier than what will follow it. They will suffer such terror that sweat will cover their bodies until it becomes like a bridle around their chins, until it grows into something like a sea on which, if desired, vessels could be sailed.

Key vocabulary

- **Sentiment:** feelings of love and sympathy
- **Engrossed:** to hold complete interest or attention to something

People will be resurrected in three groups: those who combined fear of God with expectation (fearing His punishment but never despairing of His mercy and forgiveness), those who (because they frequently "faltered") will try to go to Paradise "mounted on a mule" in twos, threes, fours ... or tens. The rest will be resurrected into Fire; (since they constantly pursued sins worthy of Hellfire), if they want to sleep in the forenoon, Hell will go to sleep with them; when they reach night, Hell will reach night with them; when they reach morning, Hell will reach morning with them, and when they reach evening, Hell will reach evening with them.

God's Messenger made sure that his Companions understood exactly what Hell was, and roused in them a great desire for Paradise by conveying its good tidings to them. As a result, they lived in great consciousness of Divine reward and punishment. They were so sensitive to religious obligations and the rights of people that, for example, two of them once appealed to the Messenger to solve a disagreement. After hearing them, the Messenger said:

I am a human being like you, so I will judge according to what you say. It is possible that one of you speaks more convincingly and I may judge in his favor. However, God will judge rightly in the Hereafter according to the truth of the matter. The wrongdoer will meet his due punishment, while the innocent will meet his reward.

This was enough for each Companion to concede his claimed right. The Messenger advised them: "Divide the disputed goods in half, and then draw lots. Each one should consent to his share wholeheartedly and without regret."

This was enough for each Companion to concede his claimed right. The Messenger advised them: "Divide the disputed goods in half, and then draw lots. Each one should consent to his share wholeheartedly and without regret."

Sa'd ibn Rabi' was severely wounded at the Battle of Uhud. In his last breath, he whispered to Muhammad ibn Maslama, who brought him greetings from the Messenger: "Take my greetings to God's Messenger. By God, I sense the fragrance of Paradise behind Mount Uhud."

God will judge rightly in the Hereafter according to the truth of the matter. The wrongdoer will meet his due punishment, while the innocent will meet his reward.

WHAT DID WE LEARN?

LESSON SUMMARY:

- After belief in God, belief in the Resurrection has the primary place in securing a peaceful social order.
- Belief in the Resurrection prevents young people from wasting their lives in transitory and trivial things, and gives hope to the elderly as they move closer to the grave.
- Children will find true consolation only when they are convinced that their beloved ones have flown to Paradise, and that they will be reunited with them
- Belief in the Resurrection changes a house into a garden of Paradise
- Belief in the Resurrection reminds people of their familial responsibilities, and as they implement these duties, an atmosphere of mutual love, affection, and respect begins to pervade the house.

LESSON REVIEW: INDIVIDUAL ASSESSMENT

1. What are the 3 groups that people will be resurrected in?
2. How can belief in the Resurrection change a house into a garden of paradise?
3. Why are young people in particular by protected by belief in life after death?
4. How does belief in the afterlife allow the elderly and sick to welcome death with a smile?

ESSAY

In your own words, what does Allah mean when He said in a hadith qudsi: I will not unite two securities or two fears?

LESSON VOCABULARY

- Inculcated
- Triviality
- Sentiment
- Engrossed
- Consolation

Lesson 4

Qur'anic and General Arguments

The Qur'an argues for the Resurrection. To impress upon our hearts the wonder of what the Almighty will accomplish in the Hereafter, and to prepare our minds to accept and understand it, the Qur'an presents the wonder of what He accomplishes here.

For example, the following Qur'anic verse stresses God's Power and, by mentioning specific instances of It, calls us to have strong belief in our meeting with Him in the Hereafter:

> God is He Who raised the heavens without any pillars that you can see, then He established Himself upon the Throne (of authority; having shaped the universe and made it dependent upon certain laws, He exercises His absolute authority over it), and subjected the sun and the moon (to His command); each runs (its course) for an appointed term. He regulates all affairs, he sets out the signs of the truth in detail, that you may have certainty in the meeting with your Lord (on Judgment Day). (13:2)

"The First Origination of the Universe and Humanity Indicate Their Second Origination"

The Qur'an presents the phenomenon of the universe's creation, which it defines as *the first origination* (56:62), while describing the raising of the dead as *the second origination* (53:47), to prove the Resurrection.

The Qur'an makes analogies between the Resurrection and His deeds in this world, and sometimes alludes to His deeds in the future and in the Hereafter, in such a way that we can become convinced of that which we cannot fully understand. It also shows similar events here and compares them to the Resurrection. One example is as follows:

> Has human not considered that We have created him from a drop of (seminal) fluid? Yet, he turns into an open, fierce **adversary** (selfishly disputing against the truth). And he coins a comparison for Us, having forgotten his own origin and creation, saying, "Who will give life to these bones when they have rotted away?" Say: "He Who produced them in the first instance will give them life. He has full knowledge of every creation (and of everything He has created, He knows every detail in every dimension of time and space)." He Who has made for you fire from green tree, and see, you kindle fire with it. Is not He Who has created the heavens and the earth able to create (from rotten bones) the like of them (whose bones have rotted under the ground)? Surely He is; He is the Supreme Creator, the All-Knowing. (36:77-81)

THINK

Look at the prints of God's Mercy: How He gives life to the soil after its death.

The Qur'an likens the universe to a book unfolded. At the end of time, its destruction will be as easy for God as rolling up a scroll. As He unfolded it at the beginning, He will roll it up and, manifesting His absolute Power without any material cause, will re-create it in a much better and different form:

> The Day when We will roll up the heaven as written scrolls are rolled up. We will bring the creation back into existence as easily as We originated it in the first instance. This is a binding promise on Us, and surely We fulfill whatever We promise. (21:104)

Key vocabulary

- **Adversary:** an enemy or opponent

"In many verses, the Qur'an warns us that we were created to achieve specific goals, not to do whatever we want."

DISCUSS

Paradise and Hell are the two opposite fruits growing on the tree of creation's two branches, the two results of the chain of creation, the two cisterns being filled by the two streams of things and events, and the two poles to which beings flow in waves. They are the places where Divine Grace and Divine Wrath manifest themselves, and will be full of inhabitants when Divine Power shakes up the universe.

The Qur'an likens the Resurrection to reviving soil in spring following its death in winter, and mentions how God disposes of atoms and molecules while creating us in stages. Dried-out pieces of wood blossom and yield leaves and fruits similar, but not identical, to those that existed in previous years. Innumerable seeds that had fallen into soil now begin to germinate and grow into different plants without confusion. God's raising the dead on the Day of Judgment will be like this:

> And among His signs is this: you see the earth lying low and barren; but when We send down water upon it, it stirs and swells (with life). He Who will bring the dead to life. Surely He has full power over everything. (41:39)

> O humankind! If you are in doubt about the Resurrection, (consider that) We created you from earth, and the material origin of every one of you is earth. Then (We have created you) from a drop of (seminal) fluid, then from a clot clinging (to the womb wall), then from a (chew of) lump in part shaped and in part not shaped, and so do We clarify for you (the reality of the resurrection). And We cause what We will to rest in the wombs for an appointed term, then We bring you out as (dependent) infants, then (We provide what is necessary and appropriate) so that you may attain your age of full strength. Among you some are caused to die (during this period of growth and afterwards), and some are kept back to the most miserable state of old age, ceasing to know anything after once having some things. You see (as another proof and sign for resurrection) earth dry and lifeless, and suddenly, when We send down the (known, blessed) water on it, it stirs and swells and grows every pleasant pair of vegetation. That is so because God is the Truth, and He it is Who gives life to the dead, and He is powerful over all things. (22:5-6)

"In many verses, the Qur'an warns us that we were created to achieve specific goals, not to do whatever we want."

As we are responsible beings, whatever we do is recorded. Our creation from a drop of fluid through several stages, the utmost care shown to our creation and the importance attached to us, demonstrate that we have great responsibilities. After death, we will be called to account for our lives. In addition, our creation through stages is a manifest evidence for God's Power, Who raises the dead to life.

> Does man think he will be left to himself uncontrolled (without purpose)? Was he not a drop of fluid which gushed forth? Then he became a clinging clot; then He shaped and fashioned, and made of him a pair, the male and female. Is He then not able to raise the dead to life? (75:36-40)

A close analysis of the universe's functioning shows that two opposed elements are prevalent and firmly rooted everywhere. These elements result in good and evil, benefit and harm, perfection and defect, light and darkness, guidance and misguidance, belief and unbelief, obedience and rebellion, and fear and love. The resulting continual conflict causes enough alteration and transformation to produce the elements of a new world. These opposite elements eventually will lead to eternity and materialize as Paradise and Hell. The eternal world will be made up of this transitory world's essential elements, which then will be given permanence.

In this world, oppressors depart without paying, and the oppressed are still humiliated. Such wrongs will be brought before the Supreme Tribunal, for God would be unjust and imperfect if He allowed them to be ignored. Indeed, God sometimes punishes the guilty in this world. The suffering endured by previous disobedient and rebellious peoples teaches us that everyone is subject to whatever correction God Almighty's Splendor and Majesty chooses to apply. So, as declared in the verse: Keep apart on this day, O you criminals (36:59), God's absolute Justice requires that He separate the good from the wicked in the Hereafter and treat each group accordingly.

UNIVERSAL WISDOM REQUIRES THE RESURRECTION

God is absolutely free to do what He wills, and no one can call Him to account. Being All-Wise, He acts with absolute purposiveness and wisdom, and never does something that is in vain, futile, or pointless.

When we analyze ourselves, as well as our nature, physical and spiritual identity, structure and body, we realize that we were created for certain important purposes. Nothing in our body is **superfluous**. The same is true of the universe, which is also viewed as a macro-human being by many Muslim scholars, for each part of it manifests great purposes and innumerable instances of wisdom.

We long for eternity and desire eternal life—some of our senses or feelings cannot be satisfied with something less.

So Divine Wisdom requires the existence of an eternal world.

We are unique, for we contain some aspect of all that exists in the universe. Our mental and spiritual faculties represent angelic and other spiritual worlds, such as the world of symbols or immaterial forms. But due to our inborn capacity to learn and to our free will, we can excel even beyond the angels. Our physical or biological being represents plants and animals. Although contained in time and space, our spiritual faculties and such other powers as imagination, allow us to transcend them. Despite our unique and priceless value when compared with other members of creation, some of us die at birth and some others quite young.

DISCUSS

If we could choose between eternal life with severe hardship during this life and eternal nonexistence after a short luxurious life, we would most probably choose the former, maybe even preferring eternal existence in Hell to eternal nonexistence.

In addition, we long for eternity and desire eternal life—some of our senses or feelings cannot be satisfied with something less. If we could choose between eternal life with severe hardship during this life and eternal nonexistence after a short luxurious life, we would most probably choose the former, maybe even preferring eternal existence in Hell to eternal nonexistence. The All-Merciful and All-Wise did not condemn us to eternal nonexistence or implant within us the desire for eternity to make us suffer while trying to fulfill an impossible, yet heart-felt, desire. So Divine Wisdom requires the existence of an eternal world.

"This World Cannot Judge Our Actual Worth"

Although we have a small physical body, our mental and spiritual faculties allow us to embrace the universe. Our acts are not restricted only to this world, and therefore cannot be bound by time and space. Our nature is so universal that even the first man's acts affects the last man's life and character and all of existence. Restricting us to a physical entity, a very short lifespan, and a limited part of space, as materialists do, shows a complete misunderstanding and lack of appreciation of what each of us really is.

Key vocabulary

- **Superfluous:** unnecessary

Even if nothing required the Resurrection, the necessity of weighing our deeds would require an infinitely just and sensitive balance to be established.

This world's scales cannot weigh the intellectual and spiritual value of the Prophets and their achievements, or the destruction caused by such monsters as Pharaoh, Nero, Hitler, and Stalin. Nor can they weigh the true value of sincere belief and moral qualities. What is the proper reward for a martyr who has sacrificed everything for the sake of God, or for such universal human values as justice and truthfulness; or for a believing scientist whose dedicated research results in an invention that benefits all people until the Last Day?

Only the other world's delicate scales, which account for an atom's weight of good and evil, can weigh such deeds accurately: *We set up a just balance for the Day of Resurrection. Thus, no soul will be treated unjustly. Even though it be the weight of one mustard seed, We shall bring it forth to be weighed; and Our reckoning will suffice* (21:47). Even if nothing required the Resurrection, the necessity of weighing our deeds would require an infinitely just and sensitive balance to be established.

IMAGINE

How could He not reward believers who seek His protection as Master and Sovereign, believe in His Wisdom and Justice, and obey them through worship? Would He allow those who deny His Wisdom and Justice, who rebel against or ignore Him, to remain unpunished?

All of God's Acts have a purpose, and sometimes several purposes. Based on this fact, His universal Wisdom requires the Resurrection. If It did not, we would have to deal with the following issues, among others. The Majestic Being manifests the Sovereignty of His being Master via the universe's inclusive and perfect order and purposiveness, justice and balance.

As this impermanent world contains hardly any of His Wisdom and Justice with respect to humanity, most unbelievers depart unpunished and most believers unrewarded. Thus, God's Justice is necessarily deferred to a Supreme Tribunal, where each individual will be rewarded or punished in full.

DIVINE MERCY AND MUNIFICENCE REQUIRE THE RESURRECTION

We notice that the more needy and helpless a creature is, the better it is nourished. For example, during the first stages of human life, we are nourished in the best way and without effort on our part both before and immediately after birth. As we pass through childhood, youth, and adulthood, becoming ever more aware of our personal strength and willpower, we try to meet our own needs as well as those of our family members, often with great difficulty.

Similarly, foxes and other animals that rely on their power and cunning are barely nourished despite much effort and toil, while fruit-worms live on the best food and quite easily, and plants take their food without effort. Such examples clearly show that One absolutely Merciful and Munificent rules, sustains, and maintains all creatures.

GOD'S MERCY AND MUNIFICENCE ARE ETERNAL

An Eternal One manifests Himself eternally and requires the existence of eternal beings. His eternal Mercy and Munificence demand eternal manifestation and thus eternal beings on whom to confer eternal bounties. But our world is only temporary, and millions of its living creatures die each day. What can such a fact indicate, other than this world's final and complete death?

For a blessing to be real, it must be constant. Without an eternal life in which we can satisfy our desires eternally, all of God Almighty's bounties bestowed upon us would change into pain and sorrow. Therefore, after destroying this world, God will transform it into an eternal one that can receive the comprehensive manifestations of His Mercy and Munificence without obstruction, one in which we can satisfy all our desires eternally.

THE RESURRECTION IN REVEALED SCRIPTURES

The Qur'an, the last of the heavenly Scriptures, has four main themes: God's Existence and Unity, the Resurrection and afterlife, Prophethood, and worship and justice. It emphasizes the Resurrection far more than all previous Scriptures.

Despite the distortion it has suffered, the Torah still has verses concerning the Resurrection. The Gospel came to restore this corruption and to affirm what had remained intact. However, it also was distorted. Not long after Jesus' departure from this world, about 300 Gospels appeared and were circulated. Their internal contradictions and those with other Gospels led to many distortions that only grew over time. However, there are still some Gospel passages about the Resurrection and the Hereafter, such as the following:

Qur'an emphasizes the Resurrection far more than all previous Scriptures.

> Blessed are the poor in spirit, for theirs is the kingdom of heaven... Blessed are the merciful, for they will be shown mercy. Blessed are the pure in heart, for they will see God...Blessed are those who are persecuted because of righteousness, for theirs is the kingdom of heaven... Rejoice and be glad, because great is your reward in heaven. (Matthew 5:3, 7-8, 10, 12) Woe to the world because of the things that cause people to sin! Such things must come, but woe to the man through whom they come! If your hand or your foot causes you to sin, cut it off and throw it away. It is better for you to enter life maimed or crippled than to have two hands and two feet and be thrown into eternal fire. And if your eye causes you to sin, gouge it out and throw it away. It is better for you to enter life with one eye than to have two eyes and be thrown into the fire of Hell. (Matthew 18:7-9)
>
> The dead will be raised physically and spiritually. According to the context, the Qur'an mentions either spiritual or bodily resurrection. For example: O soul at peace! Return unto your Lord well-pleasing and well-pleased! Enter among My (righteous) servants. Enter My Paradise! (89:27-30).

These verses mention the soul's return to its Lord. Many other verses describe the Resurrection and the other world in such material or physical terms that we must accept that it also will be physical. The Qur'an discusses the truth of Paradise and Hell, either in detail or in brief, in 120 places. While describing these realms and explaining who deserves which one, it stresses the combination of our soul and our body.

The people of Paradise will live in magnificent palaces set in gardens full of splendid trees, beneath which will flow rivers of honey, pure water, milk, and other beverages.

For example, the faces of the people of Paradise will shine with happiness, and they will find prepared for them whatever they desire. They will be together with their spouses and family members who deserve Paradise. The people of Paradise will live in magnificent palaces set in gardens full of splendid trees, beneath which will flow rivers of honey, pure water, milk, and other beverages.

On the other hand, the people of Hell will suffer great remorse and burn in fire. When their skins are scorched or burned completely, they will be exchanged for new ones. In addition, those bodily parts with which they sinned will witness against them.

Hell, because of its terror, warns people to reject unbelief and sin, and Paradise urges those with sublime feelings to strive for perfection. And so the Qur'an mentions both Paradise and Hell as a favor or grace:

> This is Hell, which the disbelieving criminals deny. They will go round between it(s fire) and hot, boiling water. Then (o humankind and jinn), which of the favors of your Lord will you deny? But for him who lives in awe of his Lord, being ever conscious of His seeing Him, and of the standing before his Lord (in the hereafter), there will be two Gardens. Then (o humankind and jinn), which of the favors of your Lord will you deny? (55:43-47)

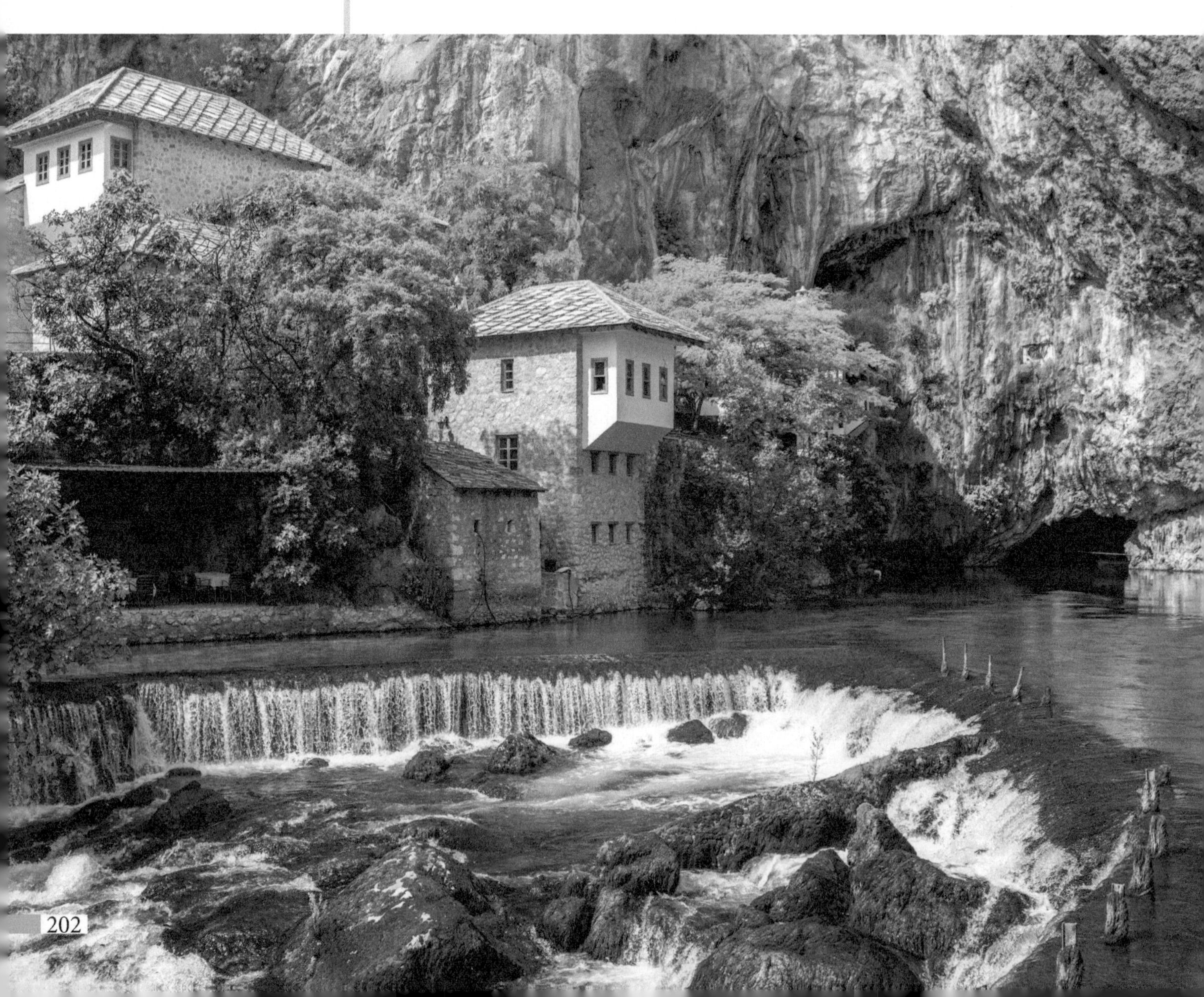

WHAT DID WE LEARN?

LESSON SUMMARY:

- The Qur'an argues for the Resurrection
- The Qur'an presents the phenomenon of the universe's creation, which it defines as the first origination (56:62), while describing the raising of the dead as the second origination (53:47)
- In many verses, the Qur'an warns us that we were created to achieve specific goals, not to do whatever we want.
- This World Cannot Judge Our Actual Worth
- Divine Mercy and Munificence Require the Resurrection

LESSON REVIEW: INDIVIDUAL ASSESSMENT

1. What does the Qur'an define as the first origination?
2. In your opinion, why does the Qur'an warn us that we were created to achieve specific goals?
3. Did all revealed scripture contain verses about the resurrection? Why or why not? Site some specific examples.
4. Why can't this world judge our actual worth?

ESSAY

How would you convince a friend who doesn't believe in life after death? Write your thoughts in a letter addressed to that friend proving its existence using specific examples from this chapter.

LESSON VOCABULARY

- Adversary
- Superfluous

CHAPTER REVIEW

- In your opinion, why does the Qur'an warn us that we were created to achieve specific goals?
- What is the greatest evidence that the maker has the talent and the power to reproduce something?
- What would this world turn into without Judgment Day and life after death?

ESSAY

Throughout the chapter you have learned many proofs of the Resurrection and belief in life after death. Write an essay describing your understanding of these things. Be sure to cite specific examples from your text. Your essay must have three specific proofs.

BELIEF IN DESTINY AND DIVINE DECREE

CHAPTER

7

Allah has recorded everything that occurred in the past, present and that will occur in the future

Lesson 1
Introduction

BELIEF IN DESTINY IS THE SIXTH PRINCIPLE OF THE SIX ARTICLES OF FAITH

Belief in destiny is an obligatory principle for all Muslims. One's faith cannot be complete without belief in destiny. However, destiny is one of the most controversial topics of faith. The notion of destiny and fate has always been a confusing concept for both believers and nonbelievers alike. Some scholars have even suggested that it is a profound matter that should not be meddled around with so extensively. Conversely, in order to possess a strong faith, one needs to satisfy both his/her heart and intellect. Therefore, we will attempt to shed light onto some perplexing issues of destiny.

Key vocabulary

Profound: requiring deep thought or wisdom

Controversial: causing much debate and discussion

Perplexing: confusing, difficult to understand

Understanding destiny runs parallel to understanding the concept of space and time. Space and time are created entities that co-exist. Moreover, they exist simultaneously, which means the past, present and the future with their corresponding space exist at the same instant. However, all of Allah's creatures are trapped within their own space and time. In simple terms, for us, the past is past and the future has not arrivedyet. Yet, for Allah, they all exist at the very same time. The reason for this is; Allah is not restricted by space or time. They are all His creations; therefore, He has the power and knowledge to observe the past, present and future altogether.

According to Islamic teachings, Allah has recorded everything that occurred in the past, present and that will occur in the future. The space and time explanation above authenticates that this is quite easy for Him since He observes everything simultaneously. He has knowledge of all that occurs at the same instant. The concept of easy and difficult does not apply to Allah, but we have used it here so that the issue could be comprehended with simplicity. Everything that has occurred, is occurring and will occur is recorded in a book titled Kitabul Qadr, the book of destiny. This means whatever occurs in the entire universe, including everything that occurs throughout the lives of all human beings is recorded in this book. Even the exact amount of breaths that a person will take and the number of times his/her heart will beat throughout his/her life is recorded in this Divine book of destiny.

QUESTION: If Allah has prewritten everyone's destiny then is it just to hold someone accountable for his crimes or rebellion when he had no other option but to fulfill his destiny?

ANSWER: Yes, it is just and fair because the offender has made the decision using his/her own free will. In order to illuminate this, we should take a look at the following analogy:

Let us assume that a scientist has developed the technology to look into the future and he has decided to browse into the future of his neighbor. Using his equipment, he observes everything that his neighbor will do within the next 24 hours. During his observations he realizes that ten hours into his future, the neighbor will commit a serious crime. The scientist records everything he observes. His observations become a reality and the neighbor is apprehended for the crime.

According to this metaphor, can the offender blame the scientist for the crime he has committed by claiming that he had already recorded his actions prior to the crime being committed and therefore he had written and decided his destiny, when he faces court and punishment? Certainly not, because the offender acted on his own free will. Therefore, the scientist cannot be held accountable for his prior knowledge of the events that would eventually take place. Consequently, having prior knowledge of something is not the same as enforcing it.

THINK

In simple terms, for us, the past is past and the future has not arrived yet. Yet, for Allah, they all exist at the very same time. The reason for this is; Allah is not restricted by space or time. They are all His creations; therefore, He has the power and knowledge to observe the past, present and future altogether.

HOW COULD DESTINY AND FREEWILL CO-EXIST?

'Knowledge depends on the evident (actuality) but the evident does not depend on knowledge.'

We make the intention and Allah creates the action.

Destiny exists so that human beings do not ascribe success and accomplishments to themselves; free will exists so that human beings do not refuse responsibility for their actions and deeds. For example, it is Allah Who grants various talents to human beings; however, it is free will that encourages human beings to develop and improve their given talents. Being a champion athlete requires hard work but the potential to become a champion was granted by Allah. This means that Allah creates human beings with the potential to do good or evil. However, the choice is left to the individual. It is free will that enables us to improve ourselves yet the process of improvement is created by Allah. In a sense, we could say that we make the intention and Allah creates the action.

In order to grasp a better understanding of destiny and free will, one must first comprehend the meaning of the following principle: 'Knowledge depends on the evident (actuality) but the evident does not depend on knowledge.'

For example, our local newspapers inform us about the exact time that the sun will rise the next day. This information provided to us is knowledge. The rising of the sun at that given time is the evident. The rising of the sun does not depend on the information provided to us by the newspapers but the information given to us by the newspapers depends on the actual time of the sunrise. What this means is the sun would have risen at that particular time, whether the information was available or not. Yet, the information provided to us by the observatories can be considered as the sun's destiny. Similarly, with His infinite knowledge, Allah knows everything that will occur in the future therefore, He has recorded everything that would occur in His Divine book of destiny. There is however, a slight distinction: not only does Allah possess information about the future, but He also creates it.

DOES THIS MEAN THAT WE CAN CHANGE OUR DESTINY?

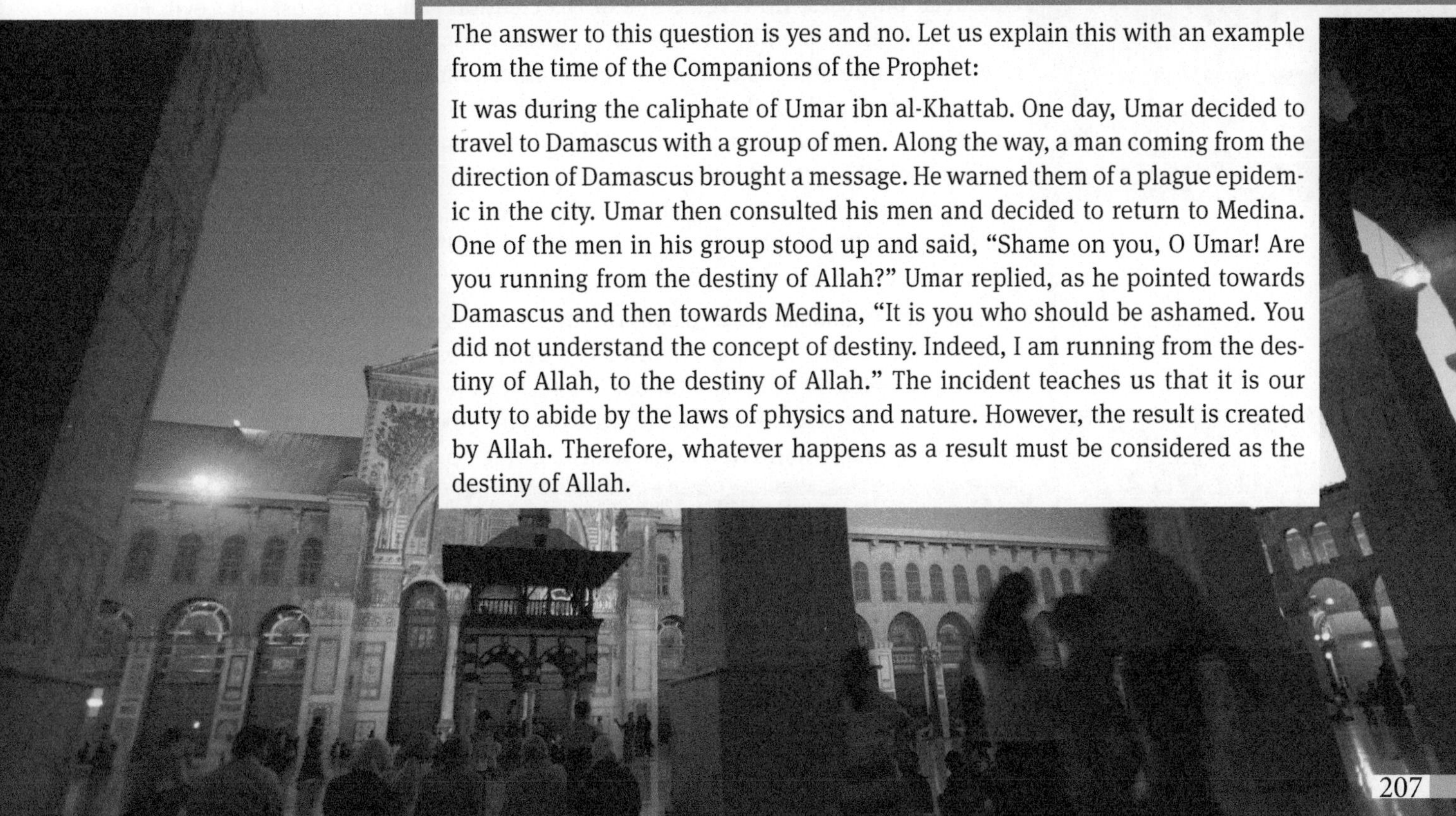

The answer to this question is yes and no. Let us explain this with an example from the time of the Companions of the Prophet:

It was during the caliphate of Umar ibn al-Khattab. One day, Umar decided to travel to Damascus with a group of men. Along the way, a man coming from the direction of Damascus brought a message. He warned them of a plague epidemic in the city. Umar then consulted his men and decided to return to Medina. One of the men in his group stood up and said, "Shame on you, O Umar! Are you running from the destiny of Allah?" Umar replied, as he pointed towards Damascus and then towards Medina, "It is you who should be ashamed. You did not understand the concept of destiny. Indeed, I am running from the destiny of Allah, to the destiny of Allah." The incident teaches us that it is our duty to abide by the laws of physics and nature. However, the result is created by Allah. Therefore, whatever happens as a result must be considered as the destiny of Allah.

Allah can see our future at the same time as He sees our present. Therefore, He already knows what our choices will be.

IMAGINE

Imagine that this book in your hand contains the entire existence from the beginning of time until the end. For instance, the first page of the book represents the creation of the universe, last page signifies the end of the universe, and the current page you are reading is the universe at its current stage and time.

"This means, changing our decisions in life does not change the information Allah has recorded in the book of destiny. The reason for this is Allah can see our future at the same time as He sees our present. Therefore, He already knows what our choices will be."

Imagine that the book you are currently holding in your hand contains the entire existence from the beginning of time until the end. For instance, the first page of the book represents the creation of the universe and last page signifies the end of the universe. Let us say that the current page you are reading is the universe at its current stage and time.

Everything that exists—including all human beings living on this planet now—is trapped in the current page you are reading. Therefore, we cannot go to the previous pages nor can we move to the following pages. Our destiny lies in the following pages yet we have no knowledge of it. However, Allah the Almighty observes all pages at the same instant and simultaneously. Therefore, He knows all that will occur, for He has recorded it all. However, His knowledge of our destiny does not remove our responsibility of being virtuous human beings. For everything we commit and every act we perform in the future, we will use our free will and therefore we will be held accountable. There is another important point that one should never forget; Allah is the Creator of all that exists, including the future. This means that using free will to decide on a certain act does not mean accomplishing it. The human potency does not go beyond a mere decision. It is Allah who creates our wishes if He wills. Consequently, we decide and He creates, if He wills. We make the intention and the attempt but we cannot interfere with the result. Evidently, we are not the creators of even our own actions. Our responsibility lies in our intentions and decisions. It is Allah who creates everything and anything.

DOES THIS MEAN THAT ALLAH ALSO CREATES EVIL?

THINK

The creation of evil is not evil, but the acting of evil is evil.

"The creation of evil is not evil, but the acting of evil is evil."

What this means is Allah creates certain properties so that they may serve many beneficial purposes. However, some of His creation can also be used for evil. For example, Allah created fire so that we can use it for light, heat energy and so on. However, if a person casts another person into a blazing fire, would he have the right to claim that Allah has created an evil like fire? The creation of fire is not evil but using it for an evil purpose is evil. Moreover, sometimes incidents that seem as evil to us may in fact conceal a Divine purpose. Since we do not possess the power to look into the future or on some occasions we fail to see the bigger picture, we can interpret certain occurrences as evil, even though they may have occurred for a Divine purpose or for a blessed cause.

It is our duty as human beings to obey the laws of nature were created by Allah. However, we need to understand that Allah also creates the results. For example, if we are ill, we need to seek remedy or cure for our illness. However, we should also acknowledge that our recovery depends on Allah's decision. An important Islamic scholar explains that submission to Allah's will does not mean giving up on causes.

Key vocabulary

Potency: the strength or effectiveness of something

Munificence: very generous

True submission is achieved through precaution and obedience to the causes created by Allah.

True submission is achieved through precaution and obedience to the causes created by Allah.

Once, a Companion of the noble Prophet came to the mosque riding a camel. He dismounted his camel and asked the Prophet, "Should I tie him up or should I submit to Allah's will?" The noble Messenger of Allah replied, "Secure your camel and then submit to the will of Allah." It is quite clear that human beings need to use their free will and the causes provided to them in order to accomplish what is best in life. However, results need to be left to Allah and should never be questioned after they occur. Belief in destiny is also a great remedy for some psychological disorders such as depression, fear of future and anxiety. Being assured of the fact that our future is in the hands of Allah the Almighty, provides a certain sense of tranquility and serenity in the mind and heart.

The statement of a great historical commander is the best example for this. Jalaladdin Khwarazm-Shah was a commander who had never lost a battle. One day, as he prepared for another battle, one of his viziers came to him and said, "O sire, today you will be victorious again!" The great commander replied, "I shall go into battle all prepared because this is my duty. However, victory belongs to Allah. It is He who will decide on whether we win or lose!"

This means that using their free will, human beings need to show effort to succeed in life, but should never interfere in Allah's decision because the result is His destiny. It is this concept of destiny that enables human beings to endure the pains and sufferings of life while it provides hope and optimism about the future.

Final word: Destiny and free will are the two realities that co-exist. It is destiny that prevents human beings from developing pharaoh-like egos and arrogance. It is also free will that protects human beings from refusing or denying responsibility or accountability for their actions.

WHAT DID WE LEARN?

LESSON SUMMARY:

- Belief in destiny is the sixth principle of the six articles of faith.
- Belief in destiny is an obligatory principle for all Muslims
- Everything that has occurred, is occurring and will occur is recorded in a book titled Kitabul Qadr, the book of destiny
- Destiny exists so that human beings do not ascribe success and accomplishments to themselves; free will exists so that human beings do not refuse responsibility for their actions and deeds
- The creation of evil is not evil, but the acting of evil is evil
- True submission is achieved through precaution and obedience to the causes created by Allah
- Destiny and free will are the two realities that co-exist. It is destiny that prevents human beings from developing pharaoh-like egos and arrogance. It is also free will that protects human beings from refusing or denying responsibility or accountability for their actions.

LESSON REVIEW: INDIVIDUAL ASSESSMENT

1. In what book is everything that has occurred, is occurring and will occur in the future written in? What is its name?
2. How could destiny and free will coexist?
3. Does the existence of destiny relieve humans of our duty to live righteously?
4. Can we change our destiny? Why or why not?

ESSAY

Explain in detail you understanding of space and time in relation to Allah. Include examples from the text.

LESSON VOCABULARY

- Profound
- Potency
- Profound

Lesson 2
Divine Decree & Destiny

BELIEF IN DESTINY IS THE SIXTH PRINCIPLE OF THE SIX ARTICLES OF FAITH

Destiny means to predetermine or preordain, while Decree means to implement or put into effect.

The Arabic word translated as destiny is *qadar*. In its derivations, this word also means determination, giving a certain measure and shape, dividing, and judging. Muslim scholars of Islam define it as Divine measure, determination, and judgment in the creation of things.

Before discussing Divine Decree and Destiny further, consider the following relevant verses:

> "With Him are the keys of the Unseen. None knows them but He. He knows what is on land and in the sea. Not a leaf falls but He knows it, not a grain in the darkness of the soil, nor anything green or drey, but it is (recorded) in a Manifest Book (Kitabun Mubin)." (6:59)

> "Surely it is We Who bring the dead to life. We record what they send ahead (of their lives to the Hereafter) and what they leave behind (of good and evil). All things we have kept in a Manifest Record (Imamun Mubin)." (36:12)

> "They say (questioning with derision): "When is this promise (of gathering) to be fulfilled, if you are truthful (in your claim)?" Say: "The knowledge (of that, and true and knowledge of all things) is with God. And I am but a plain warner." " (67:25-26)

In one sense, Decree and Destiny mean the same thing. In another sense, however, Destiny means to predetermine or preordain, while Decree means to implement or put into effect. To be more precise, Destiny means that everything that exists, from subatomic particles to the universe as a whole, is known by God Almighty. His Knowledge includes all space and time, while He Himself is absolutely free from both. Everything exists in His Knowledge, and He assigns certain shape, life span, function or mission, and certain characteristics to each and every thing.

The Manifest Record includes all things and events in the universe.

Consider the following analogy: Authors have full and exact knowledge of the books they will write, and arrange its contents before writing it. In this sense, Destiny is almost identical with Divine Knowledge, or is a title of Divine Knowledge. Therefore it is also called the "Supreme Preserved or Guarded Tablet" (or the "Manifest Record").

Because we have free will and are enjoined to follow religious obligations and refrain from sin and wrong deeds, we cannot ascribe our sins to God.

IMAGINE

A seed contains the future life of the plant that will grow from it. The plant's life also ends in seeds, each of which may be regarded as the plant's memory. The new plants that will grow from those seeds will be almost identical with the original plant.

DISCUSS

Why is belief in Destiny one of the essentials of faith?

WHY IS BELIEF IN DESTINY ONE OF THE ESSENTIALS OF FAITH?

Our self-conceit and weak devotion leads us to attribute our accomplishments and good deeds to ourselves and to feel proud of ourselves. But the Qur'an explicitly states: *God creates you and what you do* (37:96), meaning that Divine Compassion demands good deeds and the Power of the Lord creates them. If we analyze our lives, eventually we realize and admit that God directs us to good acts and usually prevents us from doing what is wrong.

In addition, by endowing us with sufficient capacity, power, and means to accomplish many things, He enables us to realize many accomplishments and good deeds. As God guides us to good deeds and causes us to will and then do them, the real cause of our good deeds is Divine Will. We can "own" our good deeds only through faith, sincere devotion, praying to be deserving of them, consciously believing in the need to do them, and being pleased with what God has ordained. Given this, there is no reason for us to boast or be proud; rather, we should remain humble and thankful to God.

On the other hand, we like to deny responsibility for our sins and misdeeds by ascribing them to Destiny. But since God neither likes nor approves of such acts, all of them belong to us and are committed by acting upon our free will. God allows sins and gives them external forms, for if He did not, our free will would be pointless. Sins are the result of our decision, through our free will, to sin. God calls and guides us to good deeds, even inspires them within us, but free will enables us to disobey our Creator. Therefore, we "own" our sins and misdeeds. To protect ourselves against sin and the temptations of Satan and our carnal, evil-commanding self, we must struggle to remove or discipline our inclinations toward sin through repentance and asking forgiveness for them. In addition, we must direct and exhort ourselves to do good deeds through prayer, devotion, and trust in God.

In short, because we have free will and are enjoined to follow religious obligations and refrain from sin and wrong deeds, we cannot ascribe our sins to God. Divine Destiny exists so that believers do not take pride in their "own" good deeds but rather thank God for them. We have free will so that the rebellious carnal self does not escape the consequences of its sins.

A second, important point is that we usually complain about past events and misfortune. Even worse, we sometimes despair and abandon ourselves to a dissolute lifestyle, and might even begin to complain against God. If we relate past events and misfortunes to Destiny, we can feel relief, security, and consolation.

Key vocabulary

Consolation: something that makes a person feel less sadness

God is completely beyond our abilities of comparison and conception, and so we can acquire only some knowledge of His Attributes and Names, not of His Divine Essence, by meditating on and studying His acts and creatures. To understand His acts, sometimes we have to resort to comparisons. We know this is allowed, because of the following verse in the Holy Qur'an: *God's is the highest comparison* (30:27).

We may get a glimpse of the relationship between Divine Decree and Destiny and Divine Knowledge by pondering the following comparisons:

Suppose an extremely skillful man, who is an engineer, an architect and a builder, wants to build a magnificent house. First, he must determine what type of house he wants (the house exists in his mind). Then, he draws the blueprints (the house exists as an actual design or plan). After this, he builds the house according to the blueprints (the house acquires a material existence). As people can see the house, its image is recorded in numerous memories.

Even if this house is completely destroyed, it lives on in these memories and in the builder's mind and plan (the final form of the house's existence, which has acquired some kind of perpetuity).

Even if the book is destroyed and vanishes, it continues to live in the memories of those who read or heard of it, and in the author's own mind.

Before writing a book, an author must have its full content or knowledge of its full meaning in his/her mind (the book exists as knowledge or meaning). To make this knowledge or meaning visible and known, he/she must express it in words. Before doing this he/she must arrange it (a "blueprint"), and then write it down (material existence). Even if the book is destroyed and vanishes, it continues to live in the memories of those who read or heard of it, and in the author's own mind.

Key vocabulary

- **Perpetuity:** the state of continuing forever or a very long time

Nothing exists beyond the scope of Divine Will.

Such existence—existence in the mind—is the thing's essential existence. Even if the thing in question is not put into words or practice, its knowledge or meaning exists in the mind. Therefore, although knowledge or meaning needs matter to be seen and known in this world, they are the essence of existence, upon which material existence depends.

Likewise, God has full and exact knowledge of the universe and all its contents. This is stated in the Qur'an many times.

For example:
It may be that you dislike a thing although it is good for you, and love a thing although it is bad for you. God knows, but you know not. (2:216)

Say: "Whether you hide what is in your breasts or reveal it, God knows it. He knows all that the heavens and the Earth contain; and He has power over all things." (3:29)

With Him are the keys of the Unseen. None but He knows them. And He knows what is in the land and the sea. Not a leaf falls but He knows it; not a grain amid the darkness of the soil, nothing of wet or dry, but (it is) in a Manifest Book. (6:59)

Say: "If the ocean were ink for the words of my Lord, assuredly the ocean would be used up before the words of my Lord were finished, even if We brought another (ocean) like it, for its aid." (18:109)

DIVINE WILL

No leaf falls and no seed germinates unless God wills it to do so.

God registers everything in His Knowledge in a record containing each thing's unique characteristics, life span, provision, time and place of birth and death, and all of its words and actions. All of this takes place by Divine Will, for it is through Divine Will that everything and event, whether in the realm of Divine Knowledge or in this world, is known and given a certain course or direction.

"Nothing exists beyond the scope of Divine Will."

For example, a baby in the womb may have many questions: whether it will be a live being, whether it will exist or not, when and where it will be born and die, and how long it will live, to mention just a few. All beings are completely unique in complexion and countenance, character, likes and dislikes, and so on, although they are formed from the same basic elements. A particle of food entering a body, whether an embryo or fully developed, also faces countless alternatives as to its final destination. If a single particle destined for the right eye's pupil were to go to the right ear, this would result in an anomaly.

Thus, the all-encompassing Divine Will orders everything according to a miraculously calculated plan, and is responsible for the universe's miraculous order and harmony. No leaf falls and no seed germinates unless God wills it to do so.

Key vocabulary

Provision: the act of process of providing or supplying something

Countenance: the look and appearance of a person's face.

The existence of Divine Will does not negate human free will.

Our free will is included in Divine Will. However, our relation with Divine Will differs from that of other beings, for only we (and the jinn) can choose as a consequence of having free will. Based on His knowledge of how we will act and speak, God Almighty has recorded all details of our life. As He is not bound by the artificial division of time into past, present, and future, what we consider predetermination exists in relation to us, not to God Himself. For Him, predetermination means His eternal knowledge of our acts.

In summary: Divine Will dominates creation, and nothing can exist or happen beyond Its scope. It is also responsible for the universe's miraculous order and harmony, and gives everything and event specific direction and characteristics.

"The existence of Divine Will does not negate human free will."

"God is the absolute owner of sovereignty, and thus does what He wills."

CREATION

There are two aspects of the relation between Divine Decree and Destiny and creation.

First, as a determining and compelling factor, Destiny is absolutely dominant everywhere, except where our free will has a part. Everything occurs according to its measure and determination, judgment and direction.

"God is the absolute owner of sovereignty, and thus does what He wills."

No one can call Him to account for His acts. Being absolutely Just and Wise, and absolutely Merciful and Compassionate, He does only good and never wrongs His creatures.

We cannot interfere with the universe's operation. The sun always sends heat and light independent of us, the Earth rotates on its axis and around the sun, days and months pass, seasons and years come and go, and we have no control over nature. There are innumerable instances of wisdom in all of God's acts, all of which benefit us.

Key vocabulary

- **Negate:** to cause something to be not effective

So, we must study and reflect on His acts to discover their wisdom.

In the creation of the heavens and the Earth, and in the alternation of night and day, there are signs for men of understanding. Those that remember and mention God standing, sitting, and lying down, and reflect upon the creation of the heavens and the Earth: "Our Lord! You have not created this in vain. Glory be to You! Protect us from the punishment of the Fire." (3:190-91)

We should reflect on what happens to us. *God never wills evil for His creatures, for whatever evil befalls you is from yourself* (4:79). In other words, our sins are the source of our misfortunes. God allows misfortunes to strike us so that our sins will be forgiven or so that we will be promoted to higher ranks. But this does not mean that God, for a reason known only to Him, sometimes overlooks our sins and does not punish us.

The second aspect of this relationship concerns the religious injunctions and prohibitions, which relate to human free will. While Divine Destiny is absolutely dominant in those areas in which our free will has no part (e.g., creating and controlling all things and beings, as well as animate and inanimate bodies, planetary movements, and all natural events or phenomena), It takes our free will into consideration.

God creates all things and events, including all our deeds, because He has honored us with free will and prepared an eternal abode for us. Although He desires that we always do what is good and insistently invites us to it, He does not refrain from giving eternal, physical existence to our bad choices and evil acts even though He is displeased with them.

IMAGINE

In the creation of the heavens and the Earth, and in the alternation of night and day, there are signs for men of understanding.

God never wills evil for His creatures, for whatever evil befalls you is from yourself (4:79).

Key vocabulary

Injunction: law, ordering to do certain things or refrain from them

WHAT DID WE LEARN?

LESSON SUMMARY:

- The Arabic word translated as destiny is qadar
- Muslim scholars of Islam define it as Divine measure, determination, and judgment in the creation of things.
- Destiny means that God Almighty knows everything that exists, from subatomic particles to the universe as a whole.
- The exact measure and balance, order and harmony in the universe clearly show that everything is determined and measured, created and governed by God
- The Manifest Record includes all things and events in the universe
- The Manifest Book is another title for Divine Will and God's creational and operational laws of the universe.
- The existence of Divine Will does not negate human free will.

LESSON REVIEW: INDIVIDUAL ASSESSMENT

1. What is the Arabic word for destiny?
2. What is the definition of destiny?
3. Why we cannot ascribe our sins to God?
4. What is the difference between destiny and divine decree?

ESSAY

Why is belief in Destiny one of the essentials of faith? Use examples from the text.

LESSON VOCABULARY

- Lucid
- Consolation
- Perpetuity
- Provision
- Countenance
- Negate
- Injunction

Lesson 3
Human Free Will

HUMAN FREE WILL EXISTS BECAUSE:

If we could not choose our actions and were compelled to do them by a superior power, why should we feel remorse and seek forgiveness for anything?

We feel remorse when we do something wrong. We beg God's forgiveness for our sins. If we trouble or harm someone, we ask that person to excuse us. These actions show that we choose to act in a particular way.

"If we could not choose our actions and were compelled to do them by a superior power, why should we feel remorse and seek forgiveness for anything?"

We choose to move our hands, speak, or stand up to go somewhere. We decide to read a book, watch television, or pray to God. We are not forced to do anything, nor are we somehow remotely controlled by an invisible, superior power.

We hesitate, reason, compare, assess, choose, and then decide to do something. For example, if our friends invite us to go somewhere or do something, we first go through a mental process and then decide whether we will accompany them or not. We repeat this very process maybe 100 times a day.

When we are wronged, we sometimes sue the one who wronged us. The court does not ascribe the crime to a compelling superior power like Destiny, and neither do we. The accused does not excuse himself or herself by blaming that power. Virtuous and wicked people, those who are promoted to high social ranks and those who waste their time, those who are rewarded for their good acts or success and those who are punished for their crimes—all of this proves that each of us has free will.

Without free will, human reason and other faculties have no meaning.

Only the insane are not held responsible for their acts. Human reason and other mental faculties require us to decide and act freely; the results seen in our lives prove the truth of this assertion.

"Without free will, human reason and other faculties have no meaning."

Animals have no will power, and so act under God's guidance ("instinct," according to materialistic science). For example, bees always build hexagonal hives. Since they have no will power, they never even try to build triangular hives or a nest. But we consider many alternatives before acting or speaking.

Key vocabulary

Assertion: making a statement, expressing an opinion

We also are free to change our minds, which we do when confronted with emergencies or new, better proposals. This also indicates our free will.

THINK

God takes our free will into account when dealing with us and our acts, and then uses it to create our deeds

THE NATURE OF OUR FREE WILL

Our free will is not visible and has no material existence. However, such factors do not render its existence impossible. Everyone has two (physical) eyes, but we also can see with our third (spiritual) eye. We use the former to see things in this world; we use the latter to see things beyond events and this world. Our free will is like our third eye, which you may call insight. It is an inclination or inner force by which we prefer and decide.

We will and God creates. A project or a building's plan has no value or use unless you start to construct the building according to it, so that it becomes visible and serves many purposes. Our free will resembles that plan, for we decide and act according to it, and God creates our actions as a result of our decisions. Creation and acting are different things. God's creation means that He gives actual existence to our choices and actions in this world. Without God's creation, we cannot act. To illuminate a magnificent palace, we must install a lighting system. However, the palace cannot be illuminated until we flick the switch that turns on the lights. Until we do so, the palace will remain dark. Similarly, each man and woman is a magnificent palace of God. We are illuminated by belief in God, Who has supplied us with the necessary lighting system: intellect, reason, sense, and the abilities to learn, compare, and prefer.

God takes our free will into account when dealing with us and our acts, and then uses it to create our deeds. Thus we are never victims of Destiny or wronged by Fate. However insignificant our free will is when compared with God's creative acts, it is still the cause of our deeds.

God makes large things out of minute particles, and creates many important results from simple means. For example, He makes a huge pine tree from a tiny seed, and uses our inclinations or free choice to prepare our eternal happiness or punishment.

To better understand our part, and that of our will power, in our acts and accomplishments, consider the food we consume. Without soil and water, air and the sun's heat, none of which we can produce or create despite our advanced technology, we would have no food. We cannot produce even a corn seed. We did not create our body, one single part of which cannot control, or establish itself.

IMAGINE

For example, if we had to wind our heart like a clock at a fixed time every morning, how long would we survive?

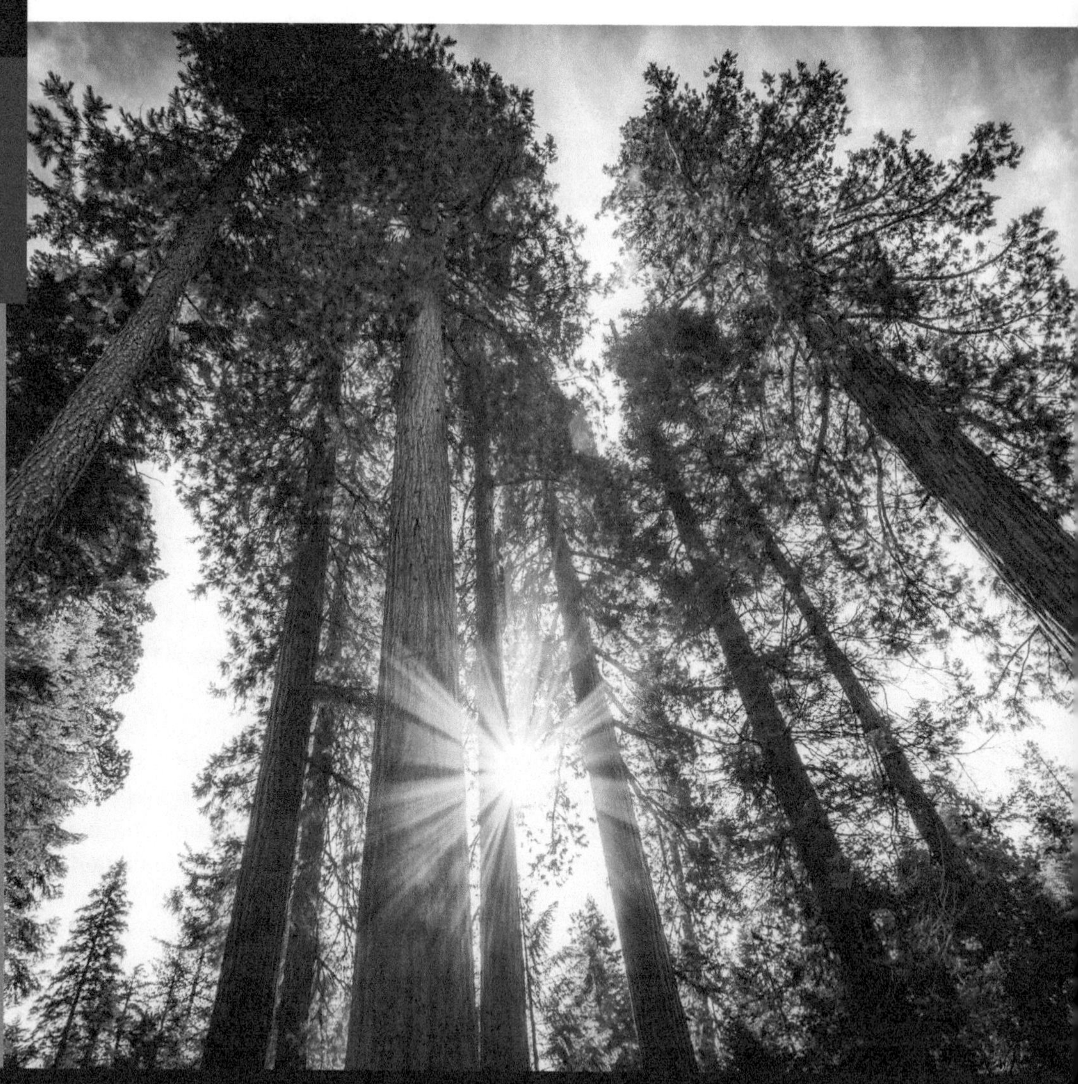

Obviously, almost all parts of the whole complex and harmonious universe, which is a most developed organism, work together according to the most delicate measures to produce a morsel of food. Thus, the price of that morsel is almost as much as the price of the whole universe. How can we possibly pay such a price, when our part in producing that morsel is utterly negligible, consisting of no more than our own effort?

Can we ever thank God enough for even a morsel of food? If only a picture of grapes were shown to us, could all of us work together and produce it? No. God nourishes us with His bounty, asking very little in return.

If He told us to perform 1,000 *rak'ah*s (units) of prayer for a bushel of wheat, we would have to do so. If He sent a raindrop in return for one rak'ah, we would have to spend our whole lives praying. If you were left in the scorching heat of a desert, would you not give anything for a single glass of water?

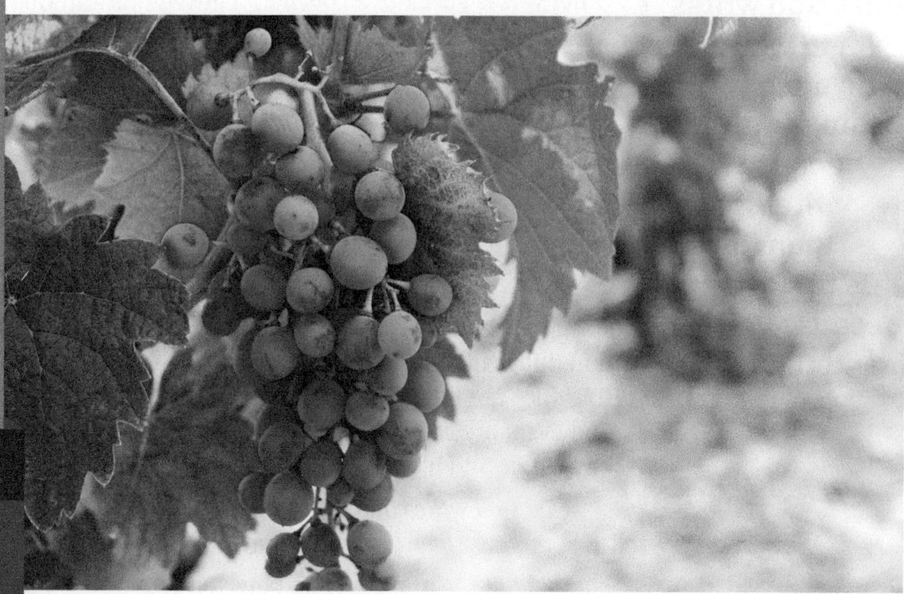

DISCUSS

How can we thank Him enough for each bodily limb? When we see sick and crippled people in hospitals, or when we ourselves are ill, we understand how valuable good health is. But can we ever thank Him enough for this blessing?

The worship God Almighty orders us to perform is, in fact, for our personal benefit and spiritual refinement, as well as for a good personal and collective life. Furthermore, if we believe in and worship God, He rewards us with infinite happiness and bounties in Paradise.

In summary: Almost everything we have is given to us for practically nothing, and our part in the bounty we enjoy here is therefore quite negligible. Similarly, our free will is equally negligible when compared with what God Almighty creates from our use of it. Despite our free will's weakness and our own inability to really understand its true nature, God creates our actions according to the choices and decisions we make through it.

Key vocabulary

Refinement: to make it pure.

DIVINE DESTINY IS COMPATIBLE WITH HUMAN FREE WILL

What God writes and what we do are exactly the same; not because God writes it and then forces us to do it, but because we will it and then do it.

Throughout history, people have tried to distinguish or reconcile Divine Will and human free will. Some have denied free will, while others have claimed that we create our own deeds and thereby ignore Destiny. However, as Islam is the middle way in everything, it proclaims that Divine Destiny dominates existence, including the human realm, but that we can use our free will to direct our lives.

The Qur'an expresses the true nature of this relation as follows: *This (Qur'an) is a reminder unto the worlds, unto whomever among you wills to walk straight. You do not will, unless God wills, the Lord of the Worlds* (81:27-29). These verses attribute absolute will to God Almighty, but do not deny human free will. Another verse reads: *God creates you and whatever you do* (37:96).

Other verses speak of a covenant between us and God, and openly declare that we direct history: *Fulfill (your part of) the covenant so that I fulfill (My part of) the covenant* (2:40); *If you help God('s religion), He will help you and will make your foothold firm* (47:7); and *God changes not the condition of a people unless they change what is in their hearts* (13:11).

Except for humanity and jinn, both of whom have free will and must account for their acts, Divine Destiny is the only absolutely dominant factor in existence.

To reconcile Destiny and human free will, consider the following: Destiny is a title for Divine Knowledge. God's Knowledge comprehends everything within and beyond time and space. If your knowledge allows you to know beforehand that a certain thing will happen at a certain future time, your "prediction" will come true. But this does not mean that your foreknowledge caused it to happen. Since everything and event are comprehended in God's Knowledge, He writes what will happen at a given time and place, and it does so.

"What God writes and what we do are exactly the same; not because God writes it and then forces us to do it, but because we will it and then do it."

For example: A train travels between two cities. Considering its speed and characteristics, the railway's condition, the distance between the two cities, as well as the number of stations along the way and how much time must be spent in each, a timetable can be prepared. Does this timetable cause the train to travel?

In an analogous way, Destiny and human free will are not mutually exclusive. We are neither dried leaves blown by the wind of Destiny nor completely independent of it. As Islam always follows the middle way, it explains the true relationship between Destiny and our free will: we will and do something, and God creates it.

In the view of Destiny, cause and effect cannot be separated. It is destined that this cause will produce that effect. But we cannot argue that killing someone is all right because the victim was destined to die at that time or place, and would have died anyway even if he or she had not been shot. Such an argument is baseless, since the

Key vocabulary

Reconcile: to cause people or groups to become friendly again after an argument or disagreement

victim is actually destined to die as a result of being shot. The argument that the victim would have died even without being shot would mean that this death was senseless. How would we explain such a death?

> Remember that there are not two kinds of Destiny, one for the cause and the other for the effect. Destiny is one.

SUMMARY

Divine Destiny, also called Divine determination and arrangement, dominates the universe but does not cancel or negate our free will.

We may summarize the discussion so far in seven points:

1. Divine Destiny, also called Divine determination and arrangement, dominates the universe but does not cancel or negate our free will.
2. Since God is beyond time and space and everything is included in His Knowledge, He encompasses the past, present, and future as one undivided and united point. For example: If you are in a room, your view is restricted to the room. If you look from a higher point, you can see the whole city. As you rise higher and higher, your vision continues to broaden. The Earth, when seen from the moon, appears to be a small blue marble. It is the same with time.
3. Since all time and space are included in God's Knowledge as a single point, God recorded everything that will happen until the Day of Judgment. Angels use this record to prepare a smaller record for each individual.
4. We do not do something because God recorded it; God knew beforehand what we would do it and recorded it.
5. There are not two destinies: one for the cause, the other for the effect. Destiny is one and relates simultaneously to the cause and the effect. Our free

Key vocabulary

Rancor: feeling of dislike and hatred towards someone believing treating unfairly

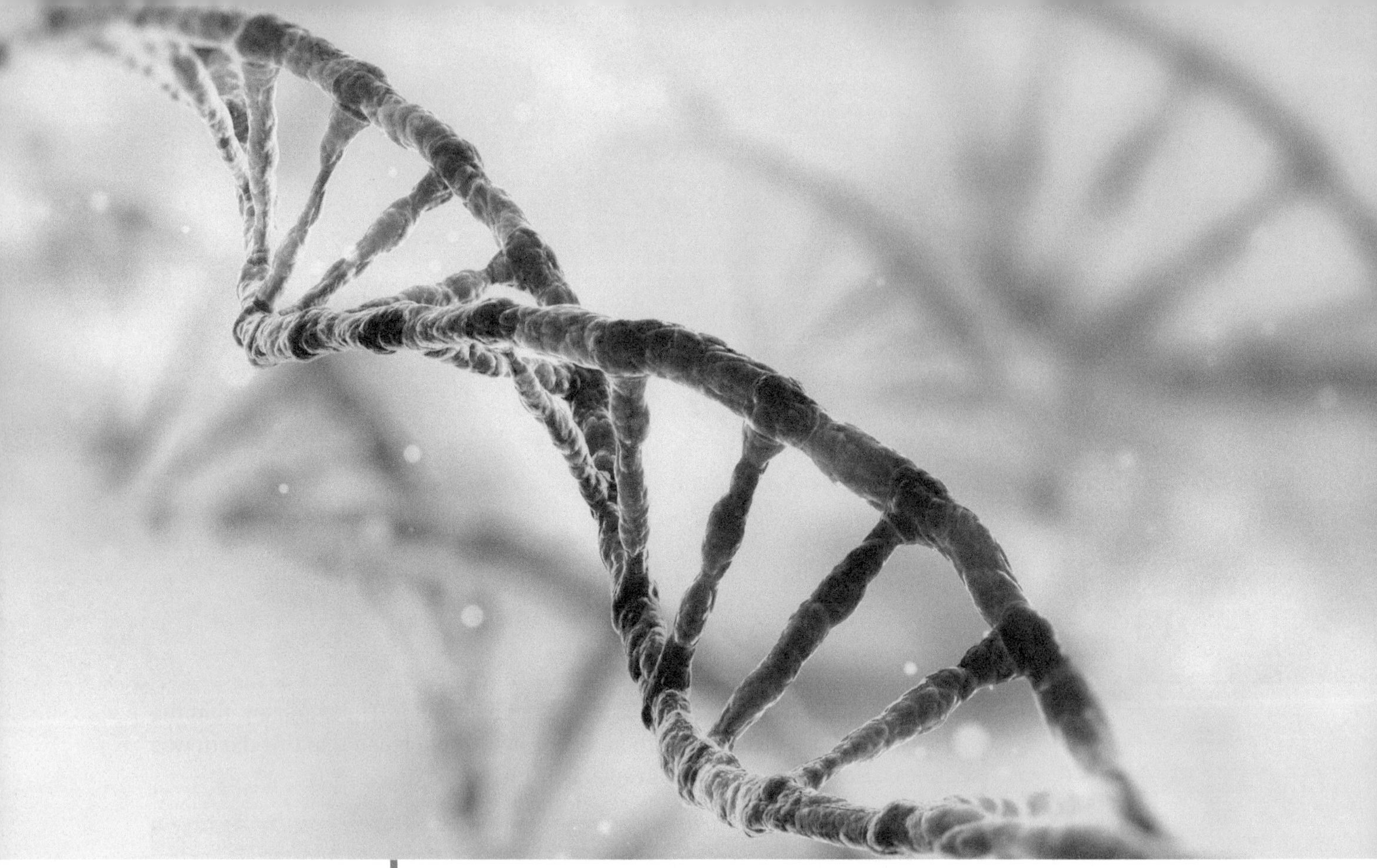

We do not do something because God recorded it; God knew beforehand what we would do it and recorded it.

will, which causes our acts, is included in Destiny.

6. God guides us to good things and actions, and allows and advises us to use our willpower for good. In return, He promises us eternal happiness in Paradise.
7. We have free will, although we contribute almost nothing to our good acts. Our free will, if not used properly, can destroy us. Therefore we should use it to benefit ourselves by praying to God. This will make it possible for us to enjoy the blessings of Paradise, a fruit of the chain of good deeds, and attain eternal happiness. Furthermore, we always should seek God's forgiveness so that we might refrain from evil and be saved from the torments of Hell, a fruit of the accursed chain of evil deeds. Prayer and trusting in God greatly strengthen our inclination toward good, and repentance and seeking God's forgiveness greatly weaken, even destroy, our inclination toward evil and transgression.

Key vocabulary

Transgression: doing something which is forbidden and not allowed.

WHAT DID WE LEARN?

LESSON SUMMARY:

- We hesitate, reason, compare, assess, choose, and then decide to do something
- Without free will, human reason and other faculties have no meaning
- God makes large things out of minute particles, and creates many important results from simple means
- What God writes and what we do are exactly the same; not because God writes it and then forces us to do it, but because we will it and then do it
- Remember that there are not two kinds of Destiny, one for the cause and the other for the effect. Destiny is one.

LESSON REVIEW: INDIVIDUAL ASSESSMENT

1. Name 2 reasons for the existence of human free will from the text.
2. Can a person ever be a victim of destiny? In other words, can something we choose to do ever be destiny's fault? Why or why not?
3. What does Islam proclaim about destiny?
4. Why does destiny not negate or cancel our free will?

ESSAY

"What God writes and what we do are exactly the same; not because God writes it and then forces us to do it, but because we will it and then do it. " What does this mean to you? Explain it in your own words using examples from the text as needed.

LESSON VOCABULARY

- Reconcile
- Assertion
- Transgression

Lesson 4
Conclusion - Belief in Destiny

WHY ARE THERE FORTUNATE AND UNFORTUNATE PEOPLE?

God bestows this world's goods upon whomever He pleases, but gives knowledge only upon those who petition Him for it.

There is good in whatever He bestows.

God bestows material wealth and poverty upon individuals for reasons known only to Him. For example, a poor person might inherit wealth when a rich family member or relative dies. Some people inherit intelligence, shrewdness, and business acumen, while others who could undertake these responsibilities successfully are denied the chance to do so.

"The Prophet is reported to have said that God bestows this world's goods upon whomever He pleases, but gives knowledge only upon those who petition Him for it."

This hadith, although defectively transmitted, is most significant. Clearly, material possessions should not be seen as necessarily good in themselves. God does not always bestow material security and happiness upon those who ask Him for such things.

"There is good in whatever He bestows."

For the faithful individual who does good deeds and gives in charity some of what has been bestowed, wealth is a means of good. If, however, the individual is of weak faith and has strayed from the path of right action and charity, wealth becomes a means of evil. For someone who has deserted the path of right action, poverty might be just the excuse needed to engage in inner or outer (or both) rebellion against God. Those who do not submit totally to God, or who do not try sincerely to act upon the teachings of Islam, will find their wealth a means of distress, a severe and demanding test: *Know that your children and your worldly goods are but a trial and a temptation, and that God's reward is great* (8:28).

This man, the younger brother of Anas, lived a life of complete poverty at the barest level of subsistence, not having enough food or a place to sleep. Although poor and ragged in appearance, such people were the most loved and appreciated for their sincere piety. They were praised, and their actions were esteemed in the Prophet's assurance that they were among those whose promises God Himself keeps.

THINK

We should recall here a saying of the Prophet: "Among you are such people that if they raise their hands and swear by God, He grants them whatever they want and never makes them swear falsely.

Key vocabulary

Shrewdness: having or showing an ability to understand things and to make good judgments

Acumen: the ability to think clearly and make good decisions

Defectively: having a problem or fault that prevents something from working correctly

The Prophet replied: "Don't you agree that they should have this world and we the Hereafter?"

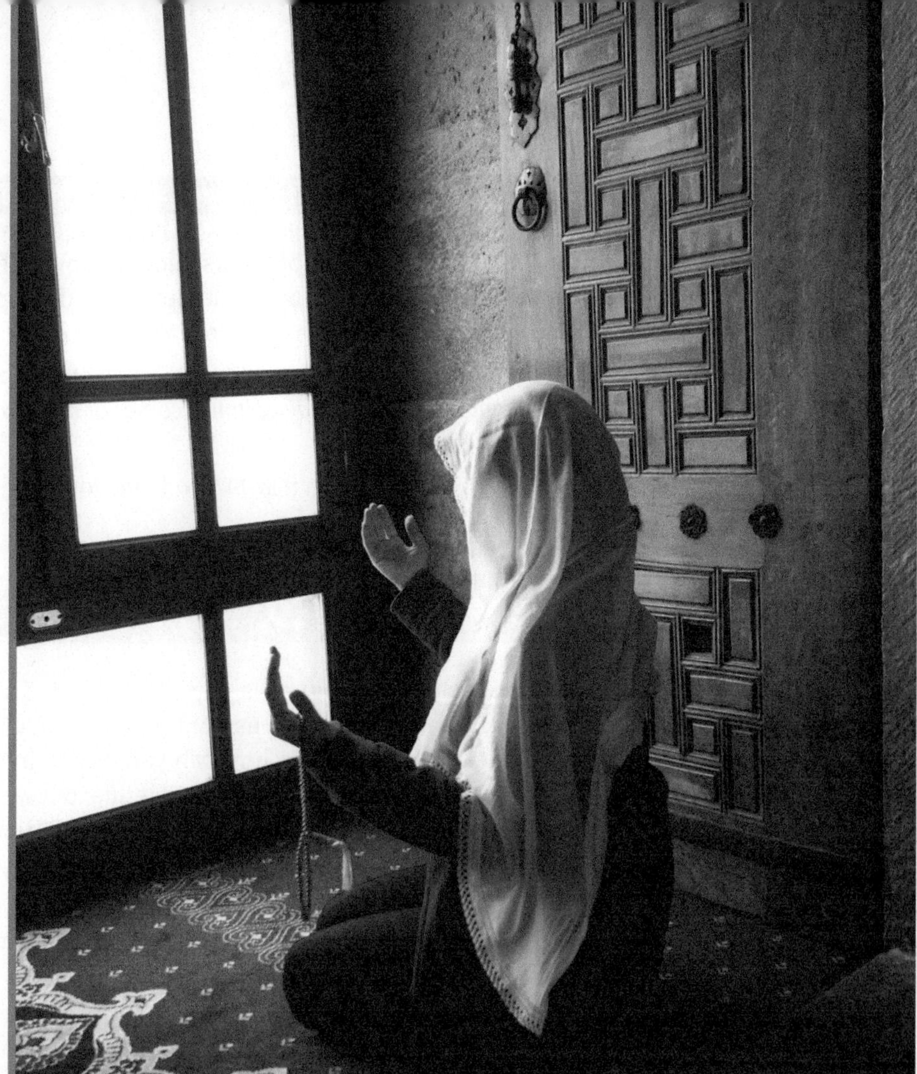

It is recorded that once when 'Umar entered the Prophet's room, he saw upon the Prophet's back the marks of the rough matting upon which he had been sleeping. He began to cry, asking why the Byzantine and Persian emperors lived in such pomp and luxury while the Messenger slept on so rough a bed.

"The Prophet replied: "Don't you agree that they should have this world and we the Hereafter?"

Years later during his caliphate, when the treasuries of these two empires flowed into the Muslim treasury, 'Umar continued to live a life of bare subsistence.

It is not poverty in itself that is good, but rather the state of mind that has disciplined (and triumphed over) the worldly self and set its sight upon eternal life. Poverty may be a means to achieve that state of mind. But in some people it leads to inner distress, rancor, and ingratitude toward God, which is a root of unbelief. Similarly, affluence and material security may delude certain people into pride and self-esteem, causing them to neglect the needs of others and their debt to God. Such arrogance and ingratitude also is a root of unbelief.

Key vocabulary

Rancor: feeling of dislike and hatred towards someone believing treating unfairly

We are not "due" anything, for since we have given Him nothing it is impossible for Him to owe us anything.

The surest way for believers to progress is to understand that whatever God gives is designed to perfect them. Regardless of personal circumstances, believers should strive to improve the welfare of others and trust inwardly and outwardly in the All-Mighty and All-Merciful. The best attitude toward this world, which is only a resting place on the way to our everlasting destination, is expressed in this brief poem:

I accept, my Lord, whatever comes to me from You, For whatever comes to me from You is my good; Whether a robe of honor comes or a shroud, Whether a sharp thorn or a sweet, fresh rose,

If it comes with Your blessing, it is my good that comes.

WHY ARE SOME PEOPLE CREATED "MORE EQUAL" THAN OTHERS?

THINK

Your apparent loss is really a gain. This is comparable to martyrdom, which God rewards with Paradise. Martyrs attain such a rank on the Day of Judgment that even the most righteous and sincere long for it and wish that they had been martyred. What such people receive in eternity is infinitely greater and more valuable than what they lose here.

God created each one of your cells, as well as those of all other animate and inanimate parts of creation, and gave us our human nature. He has given us everything; we have given Him nothing. So how can you complain or accuse Him of being unjust? Injustice comes from not giving what is due. But we are not "due" anything, for since we have given Him nothing it is impossible for Him to owe us anything.

God, the All-Mighty, created each of us out of nothing. Moreover, He created us human, when He could have created us as something else or not at all. If you observe and investigate your surroundings, you can see many creations that are different from you. Whether they are inferior or superior to you is a matter of your own judgment.

Another aspect is the Providence of God. God may deprive individuals of something they value in order to grant them a manifold return in the Hereafter. In this way, God makes people feel their need, impotence, and poverty. This causes them to turn to Him with a greater sincerity and a fuller heart, thereby becoming worthier of His Blessing and Favor. Thus your apparent loss is really a gain.

Although some disadvantaged or disabled people may blame God for their disabilities, and thereby stray from or abandon their faith, many more are strengthened in their faith. It is completely mistaken to use an exaggerated—indeed false—sympathy with the disabled as a pretext for unbelief. It is far better—even essential—that an ardent yearning for eternal life be aroused in such people, for then they can become worthy of an immense reward in the Hereafter.

If the disabilities of some lead others who enjoy good health to recognize that they have much to be thankful for and to improve themselves, their humanity, and their closeness to God, the Wisdom in Divine Providence is confirmed and, to the degree possible, understood.

Key vocabulary

Ardent: having or showing very strong feelings

Providence: governing the universe by God

Deprive: to take something away

ARE THE MANNER AND TIME OF DEATH PREDETERMINED?

Every event, including the manner and time of death, are predestined. Everything occurs within the framework of the Divine Decree, and also within an individual plan for each being. Such plans are always in harmony with one another. This is a system established by God in the past eternity. It never changes, and will continue in the future eternity.

The established and universally acknowledged principles of the positive sciences confirm that everything has been made and runs according to such a design and determination. In the absence such predestination, the universe's order, harmony, and magnificence could not be understood or explained, nor could any scientific advances be made. God's preordained, mathematical, and geometrical design in the universe allows us to conduct laboratory research via reliable principles so that we can explore both humanity and space.

Saying that science is no more than a means to reflect and make known what already exists, to give some names and titles to its governing principles, does not diminish its discoveries or technological inventions. By pointing out science's place and weight, we only recall the significant fact that such order and harmony prevailed long before any scientific discoveries and inventions were made, for the Creator made them the very foundation of the universe.

Key vocabulary

Preordained: decided beforehand to happen

Diminish: lessen the value

Some sociologists attempt to apply to humanity principles that seem to prevail for all other beings. This is extreme fatalism, which deserves to be criticized severely. And yet it may be helpful to the extent that it acknowledges the very predestination on which the universe and its order depend.

Each fact related to faith and creed does not need human support or acceptance, or human acknowledgment of its reasonableness, because it comes from God. However, it helps our cause of calling people back to the right path if we can counter their claims. That is why we engage in such a discourse. Otherwise, it is obvious that everything functions according to a perfect balance, harmony, and order, all of which suffices to prove their predestination by an All-Mighty Sovereign. Since existence began, they have acted in full obedience and submission to His Will, Power, and Preordaining.

Predestination has a different essence for humanity. Although we were created by necessity and at the same time as other creatures, our free will makes us unique. God gave us the moral freedom to think, reason, form opinions, and make choices so that we would have personality, individuality, and character. Indeed, the question only arises because some people consider humanity to be the same as any other member of creation.

We have a real (although limited) free will, power of choice, and inclination. Depending on how we use these, we earn good or evil, reward or punishment.

We have a real (although limited) free will, power of choice, and inclination. Depending on how we use these, we earn good or evil, reward or punishment. As we bring the results of our deeds upon ourselves through our own conscious or unconscious choices, we cannot blame God for what we ourselves set in motion. The ratio of reward or punishment to a particular deed is up to God.

"There is a second aspect: How is human free will reconciled with God's all-encompassing knowledge?"

Fate and predetermination operate according to God's knowledge. To foreknow something does not determine or cause it to be or to happen as it does. Divine Will and Power make things come into existence on the basis of our inclination. Therefore, the things that happened and came into existence did not do so because they were foreknown. On the contrary, they are known as they are. The same is true of predestination. For example, a weather forecaster does not "cause" the weather by "predicting" it accurately. God All-Mighty's Power to foreknow and foresee the outcomes of choices and inclinations, and thus to assure that they will be fulfilled, does not mean that He causes them.

DISCUSS

Some people say that murderers cannot be held accountable for their deed, because they were "predestined" to do it and the victim was "predestined" to die in that manner. Such a claim is ludicrous. The truth is that God takes their inclinations into account, prepares the circumstances according to how they will act, and is perfectly fair in calling them to account for their heinous sin.

ENDNOTE: QUR'ANIC POINT OF VIEW ABOUT HUMAN FREE WILL

Most Western Orientalists accuse Islam of being fatalistic; although only one small Islamic sect (the Jabriya) has ever defended fatalism. On the contrary, almost all Western philosophies of history and, to some extent, Christianity, are fatalistic and based on the supposed irresistibility of historical laws. The outlines of those philosophies of history may be summed up as follows:

- Humanity is steadily progressing toward the final happy end.
- This progress depends on the fatalistic, irresistible laws of history, which are completely independent of humanity. Therefore, we must obey these laws if we do not want to be eliminated.

We cannot criticize the stages through which we must inevitably pass, because we have nothing to do other than to pass through them.

Such views imply the following: Present socioeconomic and even political conditions are inevitable, because they were dictated by nature, which decrees that only the able and the powerful can survive. If these laws favor the West, the communities that choose to survive must concede to the West's dominion.

Key vocabulary

Fatalism: the belief that what will happen has already been decided and cannot be changed

What distinguishes the Qur'anic concept of history from other philosophies is the following:

- While philosophers of history or sociologists build their conceptions on the interpretation of past events and present situations, the Qur'an deals with the matter from the perspective of unchanging principles.
- The Qur'an stresses individual and communal free choice and moral conduct. God tests humanity here so that it should sow the "field" of the world to harvest in the next, eternal life. For this reason, all that happens here are occasions that God causes to follow one another so that good and evil people may be distinguished. Testing requires that the one being tested have free will to choose. Thus, according to the Qur'an, we are the ones who make history, not a compelling Divine Will. God simply uses our choice to bring His universal will into effect. If this point is understood, the Western philosophies of history and their conception of some "inevitable end" are seen to be groundless.

Testing requires that the one being tested have free will to choose. Thus, according to the Qur'an, we are the ones who make history, not a compelling Divine Will.

WHAT DID WE LEARN?

LESSON SUMMARY:

- God bestows material wealth and poverty upon individuals for reasons known only to Him
- It is not poverty in itself that is good, but rather the state of mind that has disciplined (and triumphed over) the worldly self and set its sight upon eternal life.
- The surest way for believers to progress is to understand that whatever God gives is designed to perfect them
- God, the All-Mighty, created each of us out of nothing
- Every event, including the manner and time of death, are predestined
- God may deprive individuals of something they value in order to grant them a manifold return in the Hereafter.

LESSON REVIEW: INDIVIDUAL ASSESSMENT

1. What is the surest way for believers to progress?
2. How was the conversation between Prophet and Umar when Umar saw Prophet with marks of a rough mat on his back?
3. Why are there fortunate and unfortunate people? Is it fair to be wealthy or poor?
4. What distinguishes the Qur'anic concept of history from other philosophies?

ESSAY

Describe your understanding of the Providence of God using details from the text.

LESSON VOCABULARY

- Shrewdness
- Acumen
- Defectively
- Fatalism
- Ardent
- Providence
- Rancor
- Deprive
- Preordained
- Diminish

CHAPTER REVIEW ESSAY

Write a letter to a person of your choice (parent, sibling, friend, etc.) describing to them Divine Decree and destiny. Use at least 5 details from this chapter.

REFERENCES AND FURTHER READING

Bilgen, Osman, Ahmet Ozdemir. 2005. Daily Prayers in Islam, NJ: Tughra Books.

Ezgi, Omer A. 2012. Understanding The Basic Principles of Islam, NJ: Tughra Books.

Gülen, Fethullah. 2005. The Messenger of God: Muhammad, NJ: Tughra Books.

Gülen, Fethullah. 2010. Questions & Answers about Islam Vol 1 & 2, NJ: Tughra Books.

Gülen, Fethullah. 2014. *The Essentials of the Islamic Faith*, NJ: Tughra Books.

Lings, Martin. 1983. *Muhammad: His Life Based on the Earliest Sources*. The Islamic Texts Society.

Mattson, Ingrid. 2013. *The Story of the Qur'an: Its History and Place in Muslim Life*. Wiley-Blackwell.

Merriam-Webster's Learner's Dictionary.

Nursi, Bediuzzaman Said. 2010. The Letters, NJ: Tughra Books.

Nursi, Bediuzzaman Said. 2010. The Rays, NJ: Tughra Books.

Nursi, Bediuzzaman Said. 2013. The Words, NJ: Tughra Books.

Unal, Ali. 2015. *The Qur'an with Annotated Interpretation in Modern English*, NJ: Tughra Books.

Unal, Ali. 2013. An Introduction to Islamic Faith and Thought, NJ: Tughra Books.

The Fountain Magazine - April 2003

NOTES